D0093774

Strangers in Paradise

by th

HIT

STRANGERS IN PARADISE

The Hollywood Émigrés
1933-1950

JOHN RUSSELL TAYLOR

Holt, Rinehart and Winston
New York

First published in the United States in 1983 by Holt, Rinehart and
Winston, 383 Madison Avenue, New York, New York 10017.

Library of Congress Cataloging in Publication Data
Taylor, John Russell.
    Strangers in paradise.
    Bibliography: p.
    Includes index.
    1. Moving-picture industry—United States—Foreign
influences. I. Title.
PN1993.5.U6T33 1983   384'.8'0979494   82-21312

ISBN: 0-03-061944-0

First American Edition
Printed in the United States of America
10 9 8 7 6 5 4 3 2 1

ISBN 0-03-061944-0

For NLC and YYL
because they had to put up with it

Contents

Acknowledgements

Among the many people who have through the years been generous with their time and thoughts and shared with me their first-hand experiences, I would like particularly to mention Michael Balcon, Charles Bennett, Ingrid Bergman, Sidney Bernstein, Charles Boyer, Millie Brook, Luis Buñuel, Charles Chaplin, René Clair, Claudette Colbert, Juliet Benita Colman, Marlene Dietrich, Cary Grant, Joan Harrison, Lilian Harvey, Lillian Hellman, Alfred Hitchcock, John Houseman, Christopher Isherwood, Boris Karloff, Veronica Lake, Fritz Lang, Albert Lewin, Anatole Litvak, Eugène Lourié, Rouben Mamoulian, Sarah Marshall, Otto Preminger, Luise Rainer, David Raksin, Jean Renoir, Leni Riefenstahl, Victor Saville, Robert Siodmak, Susan Sontag, Leonard Stein, Jacques Tourneur, Peter Viertel, Billy Wilder.

The staffs of the Library of the British Film Institute, the Library of the Academy of Motion Picture Arts and Sciences, and the Special Collections of the University of Southern California have been unfailingly helpful.

I would like to thank friends who have answered my questions from their stores of curious knowledge, argued with my too hasty conclusions, or just put up with me: Nicolas Cann, Carlos Clarens, Edgardo Cozarinsky, Eduardo de Gregorio, Peter de Rome, Lotte H. Eisner, Juan Carlos Frugone, John Gillett, John Kobal, Ying Yeung Li, Michael Kutza, Doug and Peggy Robertson, David Robinson, Richard Roud, Kevin Scott, Fred Sill, Anne Wingert.

And I owe a special debt of gratitude to Bill Lewis for time-consuming research in the early stages, to Helen Turk for assisting my faltering German, and to Jean Lane for nobly typing.

Introduction

What first fascinated me, appropriately enough for a study that concerns itself in large measure with the Hollywood dream-factory, was an image. This bizarre image of Central European intellectuals set down with a bump in the sunshine of Santa Monica, having to deal with the day-to-day problems of living in a strange country, speaking a strange language, and integrating themselves (or deciding not to) into a community that was notorious, even within the strange and dangerous United States, for being without culture and without roots.

Some of them at least had the bridge of a shared craft—the film-makers who came, bowing more or less to *force majeure*, to the world capital of film-making. But many had not even that. How did it feel to be Thomas Mann or Bertolt Brecht or Arnold Schoenberg or Theodor Adorno in Los Angeles in the 1940s? How did these German/Austrian exiles relate to one another? How did they relate to other exile communities, such as the British and the French? How far, if at all, did they fit in with their environment? What effect did they have on America and what effect did America have on them?

The first impression one receives from survivors of that era is one of exclusivity. David Raksin, who was a pupil of Schoenberg, told me that Americans on the fringe of that world called the Germans the 'bei-unskis' because they refused to speak anything but German and everything they said was governed by a self-centred *bei uns*. But though it was clearly beguiling to see Los Angeles as a New Weimar, in which it was possible to keep high the flame of liberal German culture while it was all but extinguished in its homeland, the vision must have been easier to live by in theory than in practice.

After all, they had to live somewhere, and on something. They had to deal with local shopkeepers, converse with neighbours, have some sort of social life. And they had to earn a living. Lucky those who, like Feuchtwanger, were bestsellers in many languages of the free world and did not have to worry too much about their specific situation. But even great writers like Thomas Mann were not always so economically fortunate. And there, right nearby, was the colossus of the motion picture industry, which must surely offer some possibilities of employment for writers, musicians, designers, actors. Even if that was not the primary reason for their coming to Los Angeles, at least once they were there it must have been tempting to try to find a place in the industry.

Especially since it was not a hard-and-fast division: American film-makers and foreign outsiders. Most of the founders of Hollywood had been foreign once. Many Europeans had come to Hollywood and the movies in the 1920s and early 1930s for the most obvious economic and professional reasons, and were now well established. Might not these settled inhabitants be stepping-stones? And then there were the natural charms of this southern, mild, still smog-free lotus land to be considered. It was easy to live on very little, easy just to relax and enjoy it.

I had originally planned to study the whole history of foreign participation in Hollywood. But that rapidly proved to be altogether too large and shapeless a subject. For one thing, in the early days it was not a matter of any great urgency how foreign visitors got on in Los Angeles, whether they chose to stay on and acclimatize themselves—as many did—or beat a hasty retreat. The year that Hitler came to power in Germany, matters took on a very different complexion. Then there really were a lot of people, important, talented people, who had to leave their own country at a moment's notice and could not go back for fear of their lives. Most of them settled first in nearby European countries, but then began gradually fanning out to America and eventually to the West Coast. As the Nazis took over more of Europe—Austria in 1938, Czechoslovakia in 1939—and fascist dictatorships flourished elsewhere, more and more people had to think of moving further and further. And with the outbreak of war in Europe at the end of 1939 the trickle became a flood.

So, my subject narrowed itself down naturally to a chapter of world history. Or three chapters, to be precise: from 1933 to 1940, the war years 1940–5, and the immediate post-war era from 1945 to 1950, by which time the hopes and dreams of European liberals were well and truly dashed by the McCarthy hearings and the activities of the House Committee on Un-American Activities, which helped to make many of them yet again exiles and refugees.

I see these years from various points of view. They represent a crucial period in European political and cultural history, and a disruptive interlude in the lives and sometimes the work of many leading intellectuals—not only German, but British and French and by extension American as well. For America it was, or could have been, an opening of doors, an unequalled chance for cultural cross-fertilization. And then in the history of movies and all that bizarre conglomeration we loosely call Hollywood, it was at least a strange interlude, one that perhaps had lasting significance, perhaps not.

It is decidedly odd to consider the degree of cultural isolation implied in the largely escapist entertainments manufactured by Hollywood in the darkest days of the war. It was as though Southern California were somehow an island off the coast of the world. Although many of the newcomers tried to counteract this isolation, few to any noticeable degree succeeded. And some, no doubt, succumbed to the prevailing attitudes: it was, after all, agreeable to be so far away from all that unpleasantness, and easy to insulate oneself from the rest of the world. That has always been a Los Angeles speciality.

Some survived, some did not. Hardly anyone was totally unaffected, or had absolutely no effect. How they came, how they lived, how they went—that is the subject of this book. A page of cultural history, which I hope may enlighten as well as entertain. But first it is necessary to go back to origins and put the emigré presence in Hollywood into its local context in that very curious community, Los Angeles. And for that it is necessary to rehearse a little early history.

BEFORE

1. The People

Los Angeles has always been a city of strangers. Even to this day you hardly ever meet anyone who was actually born there. This may well account for the impersonal friendliness of the place, so intriguing to newcomers, who are amazed at constant exhortations to have a good day and the like. Later they come to feel that perhaps it does not run very deep, that one person is much like another and that the friends you leave with are those you arrived with and have had all along. In a sense, practically everyone in Los Angeles is an émigré from somewhere, and the culture shock may be as acute for someone from Hereford, Texas, or Pocatello, Idaho, as it is for someone from Paris, France. But foreigners, non-Americans, do pose some special problems.

It seems to have been less so in the old, heroic days of early Hollywood. It should be emphasized that Hollywood is not so much a place (west of downtown Los Angeles, north of Wilshire Boulevard, east of Beverly Hills) as an atmosphere. In 1913 Cecil B. De Mille made *The Squaw Man*, the famous 'first film' in Hollywood, around a barn on the corner of Sunset and Vine. Actually, films had been made in Glendale, West Los Angeles and Santa Monica since at least 1906, and in Hollywood proper since 1908, but as so often in the future of the motion picture industry, publicity was more effective than fact, and with De Mille the legend of Hollywood was born. In the 1920s many of the famous film people lived there and a lot of film-making actually went on there. But even then it was more of a generic term that the outside world insisted on attaching to the American cinema at large. Kids ran off to 'Hollywood' to achieve fame and fortune, even if they ended up living (if they were lucky) in Santa Monica or Pasadena and making films in Culver City or Burbank.

And, of course, a relatively small proportion of them ever

managed to do that. Hollywood (i.e. the movies) might be the goal, but Los Angeles often turned out to be the prize. As the film community grew and thrived, more and more service industries were needed, more and more quite irrelevant activities were somehow swept into the growing pattern. The population of the Los Angeles area leapt from some 325,000 in 1910, to 576,673 in 1920, 1,238,048 in 1930, 1,496,792 in 1940, and more than 2 million at mid-century. It was a nice place to live—almost constant sunshine, then unfiltered by smog, a leisurely, Mediterranean way of life that beguiled those from severer northern climes, and an unlimited geographical spread, which enabled almost everyone to live in his own home (perhaps a shack, perhaps a palace) on its own plot of land. It was a city, and eventually a mega-city, which never really felt urban and rarely, except for a small patch of stone- and brick-built office blocks in the downtown financial area, even looked it.

The strangers and sojourners we shall be primarily concerned with came, on the whole, less *to* something than *from* something. They were fleeing from the rise of Nazism in Germany, the expansion of Nazi power over neighbouring states, and finally a large-scale war in Europe. Getting out was the first consideration; where, exactly, one settled in exile was of some importance too, but not paramount. But the foreigners who came to the Los Angeles area during the 1910s and 1920s generally did so for some specific reason, and that reason as often as not had something to do with films. There was not, after all, so much going on in Europe to make flight imperative, and actual political refugees were few and far between— a trickle of White Russians after the Revolution, one or two from the new Eastern European states chipped out of Russia and the Austro-Hungarian Empire who did not find themselves altogether at home with the new regimes.

By the end of the First World War the American film industry in and around Hollywood had established itself as the world leader in cinema. Even though extraordinary things might be happening in the Italian cinema of the 1900s, Swedish cinema in the early 1920s, and French cinema throughout; even though German cinema might rise to unparalleled heights of spectacle and critical acclaim in the 1920s and Russian cinema a little later capture the attention and approval of those seriously interested in the development of film as an art form, Hollywood remained the goal. Film-makers with aspirations to high art might have their difficulties there, but in general it was a fair assumption that whatever you had been doing elsewhere in the world you could do it bigger, better and more conveniently in Southern California.

And so there was a constant stream of immigrants from about 1920 on. Even before that, many of the founding fathers of Hollywood were in a sense foreigners—Louis B. Mayer was of Polish–Jewish origin, born in Minsk in 1885; Samuel Goldwyn (formerly Goldfish) was born in Poland in 1882; Adolph Zukor in Hungary in 1873; William Fox in Hungary in 1879; Carl Laemmle in Germany in 1867. But all of them had come to America (which meant initially New York) in their teens or earlier, and all of them regarded themselves with ferocious determination and a patriotism that only nationals-by-choice can have as 100 per cent Americans, as later comers discovered to their cost whenever they tried to raise a spark of practical sympathy for the misfortunes of their former compatriots back in Europe. In any case, all their professional formation had taken place in the United States, and so there was little or no question (except perhaps purely linguistically, on the level of the famous Goldwynisms) of a cultural cross-fertilization or culture shock on either side. There was little to distinguish these early-acclimatized foreigners or just-Americans, such as the brothers Warner (born shortly after their parents' arrival from Poland), from true-born Americans, such as Cecil B. De Mille or D. W. Griffith or the Gish sisters.

With some other early arrivals it was not exactly so. Charlie Chaplin, a young music-hall comedian who began making films in Los Angeles for Mack Sennett in 1913 (strictly speaking in Edendale, later Glendale, over the Hollywood Hills), persisted in regarding himself as English throughout his long life, sounded English and retained his British nationality. Others, like Erich von Stroheim, whatever their actual origin (it seems he was the son of a Jewish tailor in Austria and held a very humble position in the Austrian army, rather than the aristocratic and military splendours to which he later alluded), recognized early on that a touch of exoticism did not come amiss, and cultivated their foreignness for all it was worth. But who ever remembered that Mary Pickford, for instance, 'America's Sweetheart', was in fact Canadian, or for that matter that the exotic and mysterious Theda Bara was born Theodosia Goodman in Cincinnati? In such a melting-pot most people's origin went unnoticed and unquestioned unless they themselves made an issue of it.

Quite different, though, was the situation of those who came to

Hollywood in increasing numbers in the 1920s, having already grown up and established a reputation in another country. They were, even if they did not will it so, self-consciously foreign, and regarded as such. They were likely to have problems learning English just as a day-to-day means of communication (though for actors in films this was of course still relatively unimportant, until the coming of sound in 1927), and to come with formed ideas about life and work. For them, and for those they encountered in America, the culture shock could be profound.

Strangely enough, there seem to have been few attempts to attract the leading luminaries in the booming Italian spectacular cinema of the 1900s to America. Instead America, in properly competitive spirit, set out to match the splendours of *Cabiria* (1913) with home-grown talent, on the principle that anything Italy could do, America could do better. The first real influx of émigrés taken into the American cinema came around 1911, when the French couple Alice Guy and Herbert Blaché set up production in New York. For several years the other French film-makers who came to join them stayed mostly in the East, but in 1919 the little French film colony centred on Fort Lee transplanted itself lock, stock and barrel to the former Ince-Triangle Studios in Culver City, along with its Louisiana-born French financier-producer Jules Brulatour. In particular, Maurice Tourneur, already regarded as one of the leading artists of the American cinema on the strength of his versions of *The Blue Bird* and *Prunella* (both designed by the French painter-designers Ben Carré and André Ibels), became at once one of the most prominent figures in Hollywood, flourishing his artistic credentials to the culture-starved West as a pupil of Rodin and Puvis de Chavannes.

Nonetheless, this early French colony seems to have kept itself very much to itself, socially and artistically, and had little real impact on Hollywood at large. Though Tourneur left Brulatour in 1920 to become an independent producer associated with Thomas Ince, he never apparently felt very at home in Hollywood, and in 1926, when the breakup of his marriage coincided with major disputes with his new producers, MGM, over his approach to *The Mysterious Island*, starring Lionel Barrymore, he abruptly left after a few days' shooting, returned to Europe and rejoined the French cinema for the rest of his professional career, which ended in 1948. His American period remained the time of his finest works, but he was an exotic transient rather than a real settler.

With the Swedes and Germans who came out to America in the mid-1920s things stood a fair chance of turning out differently. For one thing, most of them came then in a much stronger position than Tourneur and the French, whose films had not been so successful as to get them wooed and cajoled to Hollywood. People like Ernst Lubitsch, F. W. Murnau, Paul Leni, E. A. Dupont, Pola Negri and Emil Jannings from Germany, or Mauritz Stiller, Victor Sjöström and Greta Garbo from Sweden had enjoyed European, indeed world success, and the red carpet was likely to be rolled out for them. Also, they were going of their own volition, because they actually wanted, for whatever reasons, to work in America; they chose America rather than having America thrust upon them.

By this time, for film people, America meant in effect Los Angeles. The film industries of New York and Chicago had died away almost to nothing, and everything was concentrated in Hollywood. The American cinema was still, in almost every respect except technique, in a state of happy naivety. Its leaders were not yet self-conscious about their lack of culture, and it was still early for them, or anyone else, to be concerned as to whether what they were producing was art. Samuel Goldwyn had had some success with films featuring the opera star Geraldine Farrar between 1915 and 1920, and had also done very well distributing such a 'cultural' import as Sarah Bernhardt's *Queen Elizabeth* (sold as a theatrical attraction rather than a movie), so he was not entirely unaware of the purely commercial potential of culture. In 1920 he brought to Hollywood a number of distinguished writers to compose scenarios for films, notably Maurice Maeterlinck and Somerset Maugham. But though most of them wrote diligently to order for a few months, little tangible evidence of their activities appeared on screen, and in general they were content to take the money, be amused or distressed by the rawness of Los Angeles, and run.

Hence, when Hollywood started deliberately wooing European film talent in the 1920s, it was not primarily for cultural advancement, but because this talent represented an effective commercial competition, which it was better to enlist than oppose. The first important figure to arrive in such circumstances was Ernst Lubitsch, who also proved to be the most continuingly successful in his new habitat and remained to become the doyen of the Hollywood–German community.

In later years there was to be a fanciful tendency on the part of many Americans to assume that a European accent automatically means culture, sophistication and quite possibly an aristocratic background; Erich von Stroheim was by no means the only one to capitalize on this. But in the early 1920s the awe was not automatic—not every penniless White Russian émigré was a prince, and while many, who had not been of any importance in their native land, claimed to be (and, like the 'marrying Mdvanis' who bagged a surprising number of film stars and rich society ladies, sometimes did very well out of it), other, genuine aristocrats gained no advantage from their titles if they did not vulgarly insist.

Lubitsch, in contrast, was the son of a Berlin Jewish tailor and not ashamed of it. He had come up the hard way, beginning in his teens as a bit-part stage actor with Max Reinhardt, and then in 1913 initiating a phenomenally successful career on screen as an archetypal Jewish comic character, known as a 'Meyer' or 'Moritz', a little clerk who suffers all kinds of mishaps along the way but always contrives to end up with the boss's daughter—rather similar, in fact, to the kind of role Harold Lloyd would play in the American cinema. Nothing very sophisticated about that. Then, on the strong persuasion of the fiery Polish-born personality (actress would be too strong a term) Pola Negri, he began to direct non-comic films, starting with *Die Augen der Mumie Ma* (1918), a bit of exotic nonsense about obsessive love, which proved an instant sensation for both Lubitsch and Pola Negri. They went on together to make, among others, *Carmen, Madame Dubarry, Sumurun* and *Anna Boleyn*, all of them stunning popular spectacles (Lubitsch had learnt much about handling crowds from Reinhardt) that, while not exactly artistic masterpieces, became box-office sensations in Europe. In 1920 *Madame Dubarry*, retitled *Passion*, repeated its success in America; it was the first important foreign film to be shown on an equal footing in the United States and beat Hollywood at its own game.

The point of all this is that Lubitsch was not brought to America as a European highbrow, but as a commercially hot property. His cultural background was little different from that of many of the American-born film pioneers, and he was in every way a self-made man. His arrival in Hollywood in 1922, under personal contract to Mary Pickford, whom he directed in *Rosita*, was the coming together of like to like. There was the slight problem of his being German, and therefore a recent enemy; could he not, press agents wanted to know, be described as 'Polish-born'? But that was soon overcome. If he could acquire the language, which he rapidly did, there was nothing to prevent him from being perfectly at home in Los Angeles, while his taste for horseplay and his broad, sarcastic sense of humour marked him out as a good fellow, one that his American co-workers could easily approach, enjoy a card-game, beer and cigars with, and not feel out of their element or one down.

Lubitsch rapidly became the model of the émigré who assimilated completely into the Hollywood community. Though for his writers he preferred to work with central-Europeans—first Hans Kräly throughout the silent period, then such as Ernest Vajda and Billy Wilder—usually in collaboration with Americans, in his social life he made no point of seeking out other Germans, but became thoroughly Americanized. Oddly, though, in his professional life he seemed to be more and more a token European. Europeans were popularly supposed to be good at sophisticated and risqué comedy, and though he had never tackled such a thing in Europe, in America he was more than willing to try it. *The Marriage Circle* (1924), based on a German play of amatory intrigue by Lothar Schmidt, set him off in a whole new direction, one which was to dominate the rest of his career. Sex comedy, full of those little visual double entendres and strategic trustings to the audiences' lubricious imagination (for how can a censor pin you down to exactly what is going on behind a closed door?) that became famous as 'the Lubitsch touch', was to be the staple of Lubitsch's film-making right up to his death in 1947.

But this was, it must be stressed, entirely an American phenomenon. Though there were a few European exemplars, such as Stiller's *Erotikon* (1920), the immediate inspiration was Chaplin's single silent film not starring himself, *A Woman of Paris* (1923), a cool and unsentimental account of a fallen woman's doomed attempt to regain respectability. Though it tactfully took place in that city of sin, Paris, it had nothing to do with Chaplin's European experience. Nor had *The Marriage Circle* and its successors really much to do with Lubitsch's European experience, and nothing to do with his European film-making. But Lubitsch caught on immediately as to when and to what extent it was advantageous to appear European and exotic, and when it was not. In his business dealings and private life he was thoroughly American; in his films he profited from living up to the American fantasy of Europe and the Europeans. The European never-never land of princes and princesses, the idle rich and the glamorous adventurers in which most of his films took place was never exactly situated in time or space—it was a sort of waltz-dream cunningly devised for American consumption by an

Americanized European who knew how to recognize and meet a demand.

If Lubitsch was the great survivor among 1920s immigrants, others did not fare as well. He had been imported as 'the greatest director in Europe'. As European success followed European success, other 'greatest directors' arose in their turn, mostly German, and were in their turn tempted to Hollywood. In 1924 the sensation was *Waxworks,* directed by Paul Leni; in 1925 Murnau's film *The Last Laugh* hit America; in 1926 it was Dupont's circus drama *Variety.* All three directors arrived in Hollywood to make films in 1927, joining or soon to be joined by what seemed like the total work-force of Germany's giant UFA film corporation, including the producer Erich Pommer, the director Ludwig Berger, the cameraman Karl Freund, and stars such as Pola Negri, Emil Jannings, Lya de Putti, Conrad Veidt and Camilla Horn. The only really important figure to resist was Fritz Lang, who, despite his moment as the 'greatest director' resulting primarily from *Metropolis* in 1927, firmly turned down all offers to leave Germany, until the advent of Hitler.

None of the new arrivals settled in as long or as well as Lubitsch. Some of them, like Erich Pommer or the Hungarian Alexander Korda, were perennial birds of passage anyway, truly international figures moving from country to country, to wherever, at any given moment, they could work best. Others—the performers in particular—found that the arrival of the talkie created insurmountable problems for them, since they could not sharpen their English to the requisite degree. But much of the difficulty and misunderstanding came from the very marked difference between Hollywood in 1922 and Hollywood in 1927.

When Lubitsch was brought over in 1922 Hollywood was not particularly enamoured of art; it was the hope of crass commercial success that brought him there. By 1926, when Murnau had his turn for the red-carpet treatment, art was the watchword. Not, to be sure, too well understood, but there was a feeling, however hazy, that art was what you ought to have; these Europeans had got it, and it could and should be bought for a price. Especially since the Europeans seemed able, intermittently, to make money from it as well. The ideal was a film combining critical success with comforting box-office returns.

The quest for this desirable combination brought its complications. To import and acclimatize art, you had unfortunately to deal with artists. Lubitsch had no particular pretensions, or if he had, had sense enough to keep them hidden. Murnau was a very different matter. An introverted homosexual, spiky and difficult in society, slow to learn English and mix easily with his Hollywood peers, he paraded his artistic ideals and was intransigent when required to fit in with Hollywood production schedules, closely defined budgets and anything else that might interfere with the perfecting of his next great work. Hollywood was impressed; but it was also somewhat irritated. It was all very well to behave like this—a little show of artistic temperament never did any harm—provided you delivered.

In many respects Murnau's first Hollywood film, *Sunrise*, amazingly expensive as it was, did deliver. Arnold Höllriegel says that what William Fox paid for was something 'infinitely cultured, symbolic, in short completely European', and that was precisely what he got. When the film opened on 29 November 1927 it was greeted with almost unprecedented critical acclaim—Robert Sherwood in *Life,* for instance, called it 'the most important picture in the history of the movies'. But the uncomfortable fact remained that outside the big cities it did not do well at the box-office, and did not recoup its costs.

It was at this point that Murnau's haughty and arrogant manner, his cavalier way of keeping hundreds of extras waiting for days in order to get an effect exactly right, or requiring large and elaborate sets to be built for scenes that occupied only seconds of screen-time, began to rebound on him. The new genius had feet of clay, he was not quite so clever as he thought himself, and who was he anyway to ride roughshod over those around him? Though Murnau still enjoyed the personal support of William Fox, which counted for a lot, on his next film, *Four Devils* (1928), he had to submit to many more limitations of time and money, and a lot more interference from the studio, culminating in the substitution of a new, all-round happy ending in a reworked 'talkie' climax to the film. *Our Daily Bread* suffered even more; a whole poetic documentary aspect of it, presenting the story of wheat, was largely eliminated, and after Murnau had left the studio, it was shortened, reshot and partly synchronized to emerge, belatedly, as *City Girl* (1930).

For what was to be his last film, Murnau took himself off entirely from Hollywood and the studio system to collaborate with the documentarist Robert Flaherty on *Tabu* (1931), a poetic evocation of life in the South Seas. Even here he ran into difficulties. What he had in mind was an abstraction far removed from Flaherty's predominantly realistic approach. They quarrelled and agreed to differ; Flaherty gave way and Murnau completed the film as he thought fit. It was beautiful and thoroughly uncommercial, even had it not been made as a silent film at a time when dialogue was the great craze. Back in California, Murnau, driving up to Monterey, on a caprice confided the wheel of his hired Packard to his beautiful young Filipino valet, who promptly ran the car off the road. Only Murnau was killed, aged just forty-two.

It is difficult to imagine what would have become of him if he had survived. He was a perfect example of the 'difficult' European who was not able to acclimatize himself to Southern California. His family background was (for a time at least) very prosperous, upper-middle-class. He was not Jewish, and though there are stories of his defending Jews against anti-Semitic attack in his youth, he does not seem to have had much interest in politics. There is some argument about the amount of formal education he received, but general agreement about his culture and refinement, his abilities as a writer and designer, and of course his great, if not always very commercial, talent as a film-maker. He might, perhaps, have gone back to Germany, or maybe, like other Germans, found haven in France (his French was apparently excellent). But it is hard to picture him in the Hollywood of the 1930s awaiting perhaps the arrival of those exiled German intellectuals who would again make social life bearable for him.

Murnau's American period was one of singular triumph (*Sunrise* remains by general consent one of the finest films ever made in Hollywood) and equally singular disaster. Paul Leni also died young, at only forty-four (of septicaemia), after making four quite successful films in Hollywood, though he too did not really survive the coming of sound. Dupont made one apparently disastrous film, *Love Me and the World Is Mine* (1927), which was taken to demonstrate that he counted for less in the success of *Variety* than its producer, Erich Pommer, and its leading actor, Emil Jannings, then retired rapidly to England, and returned only in 1933 to make a series of ever smaller, more poverty-stricken productions up to his death in 1956. Korda went to France, then to Britain; Pommer went back to Germany, then to Britain, as did Veidt. Jannings returned to Germany and remained as one of the biggest stars in Nazi cinema; others made what accommodations they could with life and work.

But apart from Lubitsch none of the front-rank figures in the

German invasion of Hollywood during the 1920s remained very long or did very well. And the reasons for their departure, as for their arrival, remained purely professional. There was a good prospect of work: they came. The work proved temporary (till the coming of sound) or illusory: they left. Hardly anybody was actually forced to do anything. The same is true of most other foreigners in Hollywood at the time (except for the British, who obviously found themselves more at an advantage than a disadvantage in the talkies). The careers of the two great Swedish directors, Mauritz Stiller and Victor Sjöström, took very different paths. Stiller, the discoverer of Greta Garbo, followed a rather similar pattern to Murnau, a year or two earlier. Also homosexual, also of lofty artistic temperament and uncertain temper, he got fired from his first Hollywood film, Garbo's *The Temptress* (1926), after disagreements with the leading man. He then completed a couple of films with Pola Negri and Erich Pommer with fair success, but was fired from a third film at Paramount after refusing to reshoot to studio requirements. He left for Sweden in 1928 and died shortly afterwards.

Sjöström was more obviously a survivor, directing in all eight major Hollywood films between 1923 and 1928, though some of his finest works, like *The Wind* (1928), with Lillian Gish, were virtually shelved by the studio. He found directing sound films a problem and returned to Sweden in 1928; one more Hollywood film in 1930 did not make him change his mind, and for the rest of his long life he concentrated almost entirely on acting in his native language. A third notable Scandinavian director, the Dane Benjamin Christensen, after a large and slightly scandalous success with *Witchcraft Through the Ages*, made in Sweden in 1922, went to Germany, then on to Hollywood, where he directed three horror films and three comedy mysteries in 1926-9. Then, like Sjöström, he returned to Europe with the ascendancy of sound.

Of all the important Scandinavians in the American silent cinema, only one, Greta Garbo, survived the transition to talkies. She, after all, needing to demonstrate that she could master the English language, was in the most risky position of all, and her talkie debut was delayed as long as possible. But, finally, in *Anna Christie* (1930) Garbo talked, and a new legend was born, one that was to keep her on top in Hollywood throughout the 1930s.

Evidently the slow upsurge of the talkies between 1927 and 1929 was decisive for most of the first generation of Hollywood émigrés,

25

Lubitsch and Garbo always excepted. But already there was a new generation coming in, one geared to the sound cinema from the outset and sought out or encouraged to come just because of this special expertise. Not so many came all at once from Europe (except a few English actors and directors trained in stage diction), since the language barrier was a problem. But then there was a rapid, if temporary, revival when it was realized that one way of tackling the sudden reduction of foreign markets for American films caused by exclusive use of the English language, was to make films in alternative language versions with sometimes different directors and different casts. For a while, at least, Germans and French and the generally polyglot were in demand again.

It was just on the brink of this development that two important members of the Hollywood émigré set in the 1930s and 1940s arrived: the director Berthold Viertel and his actress-wife Salka. In 1927 Murnau summoned Berthold (who was also, coincidentally, a distinguished poet) to Hollywood to work on the script of *Four Devils*. Once he got there, he was offered a three-year contract by Fox to write and direct, so he called Salka out and they set up house in Hollywood. As it happened, his first directing job was the last silent film Fox made, *Seven Faces* (1929). From then on Viertel was involved entirely with the new sound medium, where his extensive theatrical experience came in particularly useful, while on the technical end he had the assistance of a young Austrian cameraman, later to become a notable director in his own right, Fred Zinnemann.

Viertel himself seems to have been a curious mixture of shrewdness and impracticality. Hopelessly forgetful of the little everyday details of life, helpless with anything mechanical, constitutionally incapable of arriving on time for any appointment, he yet rapidly made himself useful around the studio, doctoring story-lines and salvaging films in trouble, and seems to have fitted in as a tolerated eccentric. He was a competent director, if endowed with no special cinematic talent, and his films hardly survive even in the history books. But his poetry has lived after him, and his personality is lovingly recalled, under a transparent disguise, in Christopher Isherwood's novel *Prater Violet*, which fictionalizes Isherwood's collaboration with him on a later film, *Little Friend*, made in England in 1934.

Berthold Viertel was in and out of Hollywood for the rest of his life, but latterly more out than in. Salka, however, after initial misgivings, settled in very firmly, and stayed there until 1953, all through the days of Nazism in Germany, the war in Europe, and the post-war trials of the Hollywood Ten. Unable to find work as an actress, she took up script-writing as her new profession, and became one of Hollywood's leading script-writers in the 1930s, working primarily on Garbo films.

Almost at once the Viertels were thrown into the midst of the German community in Los Angeles, most of whom were then preparing to leave. One of their first social engagements in Hollywood was a party given for them by Emil Jannings and his wife in the palatial house they rented on Hollywood Boulevard. Also present that night were Conrad Veidt and his wife; Lubitsch and his; Ludwig Berger, recently arrived under contract to Paramount and kicking his heels because they did not know what to do with him; and Max Reinhardt, just then passing through. Reinhardt said he loved Southern California. Jannings said he hated it and could not wait to get away. The others were not so sure, and Lubitsch kept his own counsel.

Some of these people had known one another before, back in Germany. But in Hollywood they were thrown together as though beleaguered. Faced with the enemy of crass American commercialism they tended to cling together for reassurance and protection. At least that was the way they saw it. If, to the Americans around them, they seemed snobbish and stand-offish, that was merely another way of looking at it. Salka Viertel did not, apparently, altogether share this view. Even if most of the people she would know in Hollywood through the years were Europeans of one kind and another, at least she kept her mind open to the place and the people. She and Berthold rented an inexpensive house in West Hollywood on Fairfax Avenue, the most intensely Jewish area of Los Angeles, brought over their two sons, and settled in. Salka really wanted to live by the sea in Santa Monica, but everyone insisted the climate was impossible, and anyway it was half an hour further away from the studio. Eventually she got her own way, and in 1928 the Viertels moved into 165 Mabery Road, just up from the beach. For émigrés, if for no one else, it was to become the most famous address in Los Angeles.

Within a year or two most of the Germans had gone. But other Europeans came to replace them. Late in 1928 the French director Jacques Feyder and his actress wife Françoise Rosay arrived. He was never quite sure why he had been put under contract by MGM, but suspected it was because they had some glimmering already that the talkie would require a more incisively international approach, and imported him to help supply it. His first job at the studio was to direct another last, in this case the last silent film made in Hollywood (Chaplin apart), Garbo's *The Kiss* (1929).

The film was a success, to such an extent that Feyder's next job was to direct Garbo again, not in the English version of her first talkie, *Anna Christie* (that job was given to Clarence Brown) nor in a French version, since none was ever made, but in German and Swedish versions. Feyder spoke neither German nor Swedish, but he was Continental, wasn't he? So it was presumed all of Europe was his province. The Feyders and the Viertels were close friends: Salka's only acting job in Hollywood was in the German version of *Anna Christie*, and she claims that Françoise Rosay played a veiled Arab woman in Berthold's first American film, though it seems unlikely and she was perhaps thinking of a later film of his, *The Magnificent Lie* (1931), which certainly featured Rosay, along with Charles Boyer.

Feyder went on to make French-language versions of several other MGM films, including *Le Spectre Vert* (*The Unholy Night*), advertised as 'the first 100% French-speaking film made in America', and *Si l'Empereur savait ça* (*His Glorious Night*). Françoise Rosay played in various French versions also, including, improbably, Buster Keaton's *Parlor, Bedroom and Bath*, directed by another short-term visitor, Claude Autant-Lara. Then, in 1931, when the habit of making multiple-language versions proved disproportionately expensive and was gradually abandoned, the Feyders left their large house in Santa Monica and went back to further triumphs in France.

During the time that the Feyders were at Metro, one of the more bizarre and unlikely episodes in Hollywood immigration took place at another studio, which might as well have been in a different world. In June 1930 there arrived at Paramount, under rather vaguely defined contract to Jesse Lasky, a trio of three Soviet Russians: Sergei Eisenstein, his assistant Alexandrov, and his cameraman Tissé, along with a left-wing British go-between, Ivor Montagu. Eisenstein came with a reputation that was in certain ways enviable, in certain ways not. He was said to be a genius—it was recorded that when Douglas Fairbanks and Mary Pickford saw *Battleship Potemkin* on their much-publicized visit to Moscow, Fairbanks' immediate comment to Eisenstein was: 'How long does it take you to pack your bags?' On the other hand his films were revolutionary, obscure, and the delight of the highbrows—qualities that might impress the Hollywood moguls but also filled them with distrust. Eisenstein had been let out of Russia for a year with his associates on the general understanding that he was going to Hollywood, home of the talkie, to learn all about how it was done. The party line on the arts was under radical revision at home, and it was a tactful time to be away. Paramount did not seem to be risking very much to put the new genius under short-term contract just to see how he worked out, or, indeed, if he worked out at all, since all they were paying were expenses of $900 a month for his whole five-person group for six months, pending agreement on a subject he would develop for the studio. So, after a few months roaming Western Europe, there he was.

The group established themselves in a comfortable, isolated house at the top of Coldwater Canyon. Needing to move fast, while Eisenstein was still the new kid in town, they delayed instead, took their time, explored the Russian enclave of Los Angeles, were lionized by would-be intellectuals, drank in the atmosphere and worked, desultorily at first, on a possible subject, *Sutter's Gold*, based remotely on a novel by Blaise Cendrars about the Californian gold rush. They went to the endless round of Hollywood parties, then, after becoming, like most foreigners in town, friendly with the Viertels, began to avoid the party round, though they followed Garbo's sensible advice: 'Never refuse. Accept and then don't go. Nobody ever misses anybody.' They were seeing a lot of the most powerful and independent people in Hollywood, like Chaplin, who at a moment's notice took them all on a three-day trip on his yacht to Catalina Island. When questioned about the havoc this would surely cause back at the studio, Chaplin simply remarked that there was no point in his working if he was not feeling creative.

Meanwhile Eisenstein worked on script ideas. For a few weeks it was an original notion about a lot of people living literally in a glass-house, then back to the first thought, *Sutter's Gold*. The script developed into a film poem, which did not fire Paramount's enthusiasm. Then Jesse Lasky suggested a new project, an adaptation of Theodore Dreiser's novel *An American Tragedy*, which, because of its left-wing political implications, was at once a logical and a very dangerous subject for the Russians and their socialist British associate, Ivor Montagu, to tackle. Since they did not have much alternative, however, they decided to follow through and produce as best they could an adaptation that would respect what they saw in the original. The scenario was, however, ecstatically received. Then, almost at once, the contract with Paramount was cancelled—political pressures had been brought to bear by right-wingers in Hollywood and in the House of Representatives, and Paramount had bowed to them, perhaps not without a certain sense of relief, for how, finally, did you manage a genius?

Other possibilities were offered in Hollywood—including a surrealistic encounter with Goldwyn, in the course of which he said 'Please tell Mr Eisenstein that I have seen his film *Potemkin* and admire it very much. What we should like would be for him to do something of the same kind, but rather cheaper, for Ronald Colman.' Eventually, like Murnau, Eisenstein found what seemed to be a solution by leaving Hollywood patterns of film-making altogether and going off to make a semi-documentary somewhere exotic—in his case Mexico—at the behest of the left-wing American novelist Upton Sinclair. The story of the making and unmaking of his Mexican film, *Que Viva Mexico*, is one of entirely predictable disaster arising from clash of personality, money problems and the total unfamiliarity of the Russians with American ways of doing things. Eisenstein left Hollywood decisively in December 1930, after scarcely six months there, worked on *Que Viva Mexico* throughout 1931, and left for Russia again, the film still unfinished (and destined never to be finished according to his plans), in April 1932. His fate could stand as a horrible warning on incompatibility of European intellectuals and the whole Hollywood way of life. But in all fairness one would have to add that much of what he went back to in Russia was, in its own way, at least as damaging and frustrating—the émigré's dilemma in a nutshell.

Only one more significant figure from Europe settled in Hollywood in the early sound period, by way of the brief vogue for films made in alternative language versions. Marlene Dietrich, though not exactly, as she now likes to claim, an unknown at the time she was 'discovered' for *The Blue Angel* (1930), achieved international stardom in this one film. Her discoverer and Svengali, Josef von Sternberg, was not, as he allowed it to be supposed, some scion of a noble Austrian house, but humbly born in Vienna and raised (before he had ever thought of the 'von') in New York with occasional trips back. All of his professional formation was in America, and he certainly could not be regarded as an émigré. He had impressed Hollywood with his independently made *The*

Salvation Hunters in 1925, and subsequently directed several successful films in Hollywood, most famous among them being *The Last Command* (1928), with Emil Jannings.

In 1930, at the invitation of Erich Pommer, who was now back in Germany, he went there to direct, in German and English, his own adaptation of Heinrich Mann's novel *Professor Unrat*. Jannings again was to play the lead, a schoolteacher totally debased and ruined by his fatal attraction to a vicious cabaret singer, Lola-Lola. And for that role, after a long search, he came up with Marlene Dietrich. The rest is history. The film was enormously successful, but the reputation of the new screen siren flew ahead of it, and she had already come to Hollywood with her mentor and made her first American film before it was even released in the United States. *Morocco* (1930) was followed by five more collaborations between Sternberg and Dietrich, finally reaching their apogee in totally uncommercial abstraction with *The Devil Is a Woman* (1935).

They are something absolutely on their own, the unique product of some kind of artistic *folie à deux*, standing outside the mainstream of American (or any other) cinema. They chronicle, or seem to chronicle, a complex and ever-changing relationship between puppet and puppeteer (for which finally is which?), the details of which, in any case largely a subject for speculation, have little to do with our main line of study. But more to the point is the fact of Dietrich's successful importation at this time, when fashion and common sense seemed to be set against exotic non-American stars. Garbo was, as usual, the exception that proved the rule. But it was Dietrich alone who, in the early 1930s, set producers combing Europe again for strange new beauties. The search did not meet with much success—the nearest were perhaps Goldwyn's Russian discovery Anna Sten, Paramount's briefly glimpsed Italian import Isa Miranda and, later still, MGM's Austrian Hedy Lamarr, on the strength of a flash of nudity in a 1933 Czech film. But Dietrich herself remained impregnable, an inescapable part of the Hollywood scene as long as she chose to stay.

By the time Dietrich left Germany, life there was already beginning to get uncomfortable. But, despite the prescience of some intellectuals, liberals in general tended to believe it couldn't happen there. Till, of course, it did. Some packed their bags and left the day of the Reichstag fire. Others took a little longer, felt a little less urgency. But the time of the real émigrés, those who were forced to leave their countries and head for freedom abroad, was approaching fast. The difference it was to make to America at large was incalculable. To Hollywood? Ah, well that is a different matter, and one on which it is not easy or desirable to make snap judgements. Best that we take things as they come, and try to piece together the picture slowly and surely. But before we do we had better take a more detailed look at the place itself—on the eve, as it were.

2. The Place

Most of the legends about Los Angeles are true—even when they are mutually contradictory. The least arguable of all is its tremendous physical spread. Of course, this depends to some extent on what one means by Los Angeles. Dozens of administratively independent cities have now been carved out of the continuously built-up area covering hundreds of square miles, to leave Los Angeles proper a strange tentacular structure, but for all practical purposes 'Los Angeles' is the whole conurbation. Even in the 1920s, when the built-up area was much smaller, this was already so. Los Angeles County then comprised 4,083 square miles, more than the state of Connecticut, and whatever the city one nominally lived in—Beverly Hills, Santa Monica, Pasadena, even Long Beach—the feeling was that one lived in Los Angeles.

But this 'Los Angeles' was a strangely elusive, amorphous entity. Nineteen suburbs in search of a city, someone called it. Like London, it had developed on a sort of web system, gradually taking in more and more originally independent, self-sufficient townships. But unlike London, it never had an original centre powerful enough to dominate the community as a whole. The essence of the place was that it was spread out and, as they say today, laid back. For many years, indeed, concentration was positively resisted. In 1906 municipal ordinances limited building to a height of 150 feet or 13 storeys. This was partly to cut down fire and earthquake hazards, but almost as much to preserve a non-urban (or at least suburban) atmosphere, in contrast to the soaring cities of the East Coast. With very few exceptions, such as the 32-storey City Hall, the restriction was adhered to until the mid-1960s, and the downtown area of Los Angeles, which was anyway only about eight blocks square, was the only part that even consistently built up towards the limit.

It was therefore a very strange-looking place that the first arrivals in Hollywood came to. And it only got stranger. In the early 1920s it was already beginning to look like one vast residential suburb, with every few miles a little centre of shops and facilities that might well be, for many locals, the usual limits of their horizon. For New Yorkers or immigrants from the major cities of Europe, this gave it a very curious, though not necessarily unpleasant, atmosphere—especially when taken in conjunction with the pleasantly mild, relaxing Mediterranean climate. Many of the new arrivals did not have even this problem of adjustment. They came out from a small town somewhere in the Midwest or the South, like W. C. Fields and his family in *It's a Gift*, to sit in the Californian sun and grow oranges (an increasingly optimistic image as the century progressed) or work in the oil wells of Long Beach, the aeroplane factories of Inglewood, the docks of San Pedro and Wilmington or in one of the varied industries of East Los Angeles—or even to work somehow in the movies. These newcomers felt themselves immediately at home in the largest small town in the world.

Gradually, as the decade progressed, strips of building joined the suburban centres closer and closer. The one- or two-storey residences spread further and further over the level plain of the Los Angeles basin and the adjoining San Fernando Valley, and snaked up through the canyons in the Hollywood Hills. Northeast were the palaces of the very rich in Pasadena. Westwards their homes expanded past Culver City, an early independent centre of movie-making, to engulf Westwood Village at the gates of UCLA and meet Santa Monica at the sea, then on up the coast to Malibu. Southwards, industries sprawled all the way to Long Beach, and beyond that refined seaside resorts lined the coast further and further towards San Diego.

More or less in the middle of all this, was Hollywood itself. Oddly, Hollywood is not a city, though it had city status for seven years between 1903 and 1910, but is merely a district of Los Angeles. It was founded and named in 1887 by prohibitionists from Kansas, and, ironically, considered itself far more respectable than its riotous eastern neighbour, Los Angeles. Then the movies came along. During the years between 1911 and 1920 the population of Hollywood jumped from under 5,000 to more than 80,000 almost entirely as a result of the movies and ancillary industries.

In the early 1920s the quiet streets between bustling, garish Hollywood Boulevard and the foot of the Hollywood Hills were a logical place for important film people to live, close to the studios—Columbia, Goldwyn, Paramount—that were actually located in

Hollywood. But even then the more expensive residential areas had begun to spring up south and west of Hollywood proper, and Tudor mansions, Mexican haciendas and Arabian Nights' dreams arose in extravagant rivalry among the palms and eucalyptus trees.

Soon the richest and most independent stars, directors and producers started to live even further afield. A weekend beach-house (sometimes of gigantic proportions) in Santa Monica or Malibu became fashionable. Beverly Hills was prosperous and refined, and kept one away from the more obviously industrial aspects of the movie business, so that by the late 1920s it had become, more than any other area, *the* home of the stars. But in a part of the world where public transport was minimal and virtually everyone who was anyone had a car, distances were no great problem and the whole Los Angeles area was open to occupation. People, especially those who did not have to commute daily, thought nothing of living in Pasadena or Santa Monica, ten or fifteen miles away from their places of work.

Even though the road system did its best to keep pace with these scattered developments, they nevertheless left their mark on the social patterns of Los Angeles life—a mark that is still visible today. People often complain about the impersonality of New York because everyone is pressed so tightly together that the preservation of privacy and sanity requires an embattled attitude. People complain about the impersonality of Los Angeles for the opposite reason, because residents are usually so far apart. Lack of any one centre where the most frequented theatres, cinemas, concert halls, restaurants, nightclubs and bars are to be found means that there is little chance of just bumping into friends and acquaintances, as there is in New York or any major European city. Work brings people together, but it also carries them apart, and the movie studios in particular were, in their heyday, like so many separate worlds; luminaries of similar stature who happened to be under contract to different studios might very easily never meet.

Los Angeles was and is the easiest place in the world to disappear in. Where social contacts of any kind have to be consciously, consistently kept up, it is very easy to let things slide or to contract out. A former power down on his luck could, without any difficulty at all, be avoided, even if he did not deliberately choose to stay out of the way. Though there were meeting-places like the Brown Derby Cafés or the famous Coconut Grove, most social life actually went on in private homes. Party-giving was a frequent activity often, in the grander circumstances, arranged around or including a private screening of a new film. But even the humblest tended to see one another mostly at home, and generally by previous, though not necessarily formal, arrangement, since the distances involved inhibited casual dropping-in.

The automobile and the telephone: without either you were in difficulties; without both you were lost. But then by no means everybody who came to the area had any desire at all to be part of the film community. A lot of the wealthy and retired came because of the climate, and chose to live in splendid isolation in their palatial residences in Pasadena (Henry Huntington's San Marino is only the grandest of many), or, more modestly, by the seashore. Others came to work in industries that had little or nothing to do with Hollywood and the movies. Consequently, quite distinct social circles developed, circumscribed by class, location, or special interests. When the political refugees began to arrive, they often proved to fit in more readily with these groups than with the movie-orientated, and lived in happy innocence of the whole movie-making way of life, encountering it occasionally very much as they would life on another planet.

In Los Angeles this was perfectly possible; almost anything was possible. But what kind of place was it for those not totally involved in movies? In particular, considering the backgrounds and intellectual interests of many who were about to arrive, how far did it deserve its reputation of being a cultural desert? It is certainly true that the arts were slow to develop in Los Angeles—no familiar profusion of opera, ballet, classical theatre and satirical cabaret greeted the wandering European. But, on the other hand, the cultural deficiencies of the city are easy to overstate.

Live theatre, for instance, never flourished mightily as an independent native tradition, but it was far from lacking. Supplied largely by touring companies at first, from the 1880s on, it brought many of the major theatrical figures out from New York on a regular week of a national tour. Soon local stock or repertory companies, and by the beginning of the movies there were a dozen theatres in the area. A further change came with the foundation of the Pasadena Community Playhouse in 1917, one of the leaders of the 'little theatre' movement and a great attraction for important players from all over the country, who appeared there in new plays by dramatists famous and obscure. This lent, for the first time, a little tone to theatre in the Los Angeles area.

After something of a post-war slump, the years 1924–7 saw the biggest boom Los Angeles theatre had ever known, with no fewer than eight new theatres built and opened, some of which were to gain new distinction from the work of such illustrious émigrés as Leopold Jessner and Bertolt Brecht. Even with the onset of the Depression the boom continued, and it was not until 1932 that commercial theatre was really badly hit. The field was then left clear for the little theatres and amateur groups—some of them amateur in name only, in that they benefited from the participation of movie actors who were out of work or who looked for more of a challenge than movies usually gave them.

Music was something else again. Chamber music flourished from the 1880s on, and the first successful symphony orchestra, the Woman's Symphony, was founded in 1895. The Los Angeles Symphony Orchestra of 1897 survived until it was replaced in 1919 by the even more successful Los Angeles Philharmonic. The summer home of the orchestra, and one of the centres of local cultural life, was the Hollywood Bowl, a natural open-air amphitheatre in the Hollywood Hills that was inaugurated in 1916. Its uses were mainly musical, occasionally dramatic and sometimes, though rarely, operatic and balletic. At this time, as often since, the main cause for cultural complaint in Los Angeles was the absence of any permanent opera or ballet company, and the paucity of visits by touring companies. Virtually the only more or less home-grown effort in this direction was the work of the Japanese dancer-choreographer Michio Ito, who settled in Los Angeles in 1929, ran a dancing school there until repatriated to Japan in 1942, and staged from time to time spectacular dance evenings in locations like the Hollywood Bowl and the Pasadena Rose Bowl. Though his 'symphonic dance compositions' to works as varied as *The Blue Danube* and *Prince Igor* were received with enthusiasm by locals, they were too infrequent to be regarded as a regular part of Los Angeles cultural life. Here at least many Europeans would not find themselves at home.

On the other hand, the coming of sound films meant that enormous supplies of professional musicians were always on hand, and local recording facilities were among the best in the world. The writing of music for films—other than the scores for musicals—tended, however, to remain a specialized craft and few of the distinguished composers who, from time to time, visited or even lived in Los Angeles for long periods left much mark on the movies, or indeed the movies on them.

Painting and sculpture remained the most backward of all the arts in Los Angeles, though paradoxically architecture and the decorative arts were among the most advanced and innovative. Southern California had its share of conservative landscape painters in the 1900s; the Los Angeles School of Art opened in 1890, the Pasadena Academy of Fine Arts in 1897, and by the end of the 1890s arts-and-crafts activities were thriving, particularly in Pasadena, where the architects and furniture designers Charles and Henry Greene settled in 1893, to be surrounded eventually by other craftsmen, the most famous of whom, Ernest Allen Batchelder, set up his kilns for the making of decorative tiles in Pasadena in 1909. Though distinguished artists all, enthusiastically rediscovered in the last few years, they were at the time rather conservative and provincial, and that remained the tenor of the visual arts in the area till after the First World War.

A first taste of the avant-garde came in 1919, when Stanton Macdonald-Wright, a painter who had been raised in Los Angeles, but had studied in France from 1907, embraced Cubism and invented his own prismatic offshoot Synchronism, returned to the area to paint abstractions, write, teach and dabble in colour photography and experimental film-making. He settled in Santa Monica, and in 1922 staged the first real show of the modern movement at the Los Angeles County Museum (opened as an all-purpose exhibition centre of 'art, science and industry' in 1913). A year later the first serious art dealer, Alexander Cowie, set up his gallery stocked with Western painters, such as Frederic Remington and Charles Russell; in 1925 Dalzell Hatfield started the first gallery in the area to show and sell Impressionists. Some moderately distinguished artists, belonging more or less to the modern movement, settled in Los Angeles in the 1920s—Boris Deutsch from Lithuania in 1920, Knud Merrild from Denmark in 1923, Hans Hofmann from Germany in 1930—but on the whole they did not have much local impact.

In fact, the only area in which the modern movement did really work for Los Angeles was architecture. In 1920–2 Frank Lloyd Wright designed a number of buildings for the Los Angeles area, but as he was largely occupied with building the Imperial Hotel in Tokyo he sent a young Viennese architect, Rudolph Schindler, from his office to supervise the works and design some houses on his own. Schindler stayed in Los Angeles for the rest of his life and became the Los Angeles architect *par excellence*. Almost at once he benefited from the open-mindedness (or ignorance, some would call it) and lack of preconception in Southern Californians, and began designing and building strikingly simple, geometrical houses that made their effect by subtle massing and a minimum of ornament. In 1921 the German architect and designer Kem Weber, marooned in San Francisco by the First World War, moved down to Los Angeles and set up as a commercial designer; by the mid-1920s he, too, was dedicated to the modern style. In 1929 a third Middle European adherent of the modern movement, Richard Neutra, settled permanently since 1925, built the Lovell house in the Hollywood Hills, one of the monuments of twentieth-century architecture. Los Angeles was in the forefront of modern architecture, wherever it might stand in any of the other arts, and for that it had to thank an early contingent of émigrés.

In sum, by the end of the 1920s Los Angeles had a pretty fair representation of cultural organizations and artistic activities, such as one might expect to find in a new and fast-growing community. Still little compared with New York or Chicago, let alone some lesser European capital like, say, Budapest. But these things could not be expected to happen all at once, however much material prosperity there might be around. What Los Angeles did still signally lack, though, was an intelligentsia—any loose, informal grouping of movers and shapers, any sense of that intellectual ferment from which movements might be born. The constituents of Los Angeles society were varied enough, ranging from some of the richest people in the country to some of the poorest. But two things were missing: any significant intellectual element and any sense of overall cohesion.

The cohesion would never come. In fact the incoherence of Los Angeles social life was to remain one of its most individual characteristics and for many one of its greatest advantages. With no clear pecking order and no too detailed inquiry into where you came from and what you had done before, it offered extraordinary opportunities for rapid advancement (as well as for instant eclipse). As for intellectual life: while the early movie people in Hollywood, as anywhere else in the world, began as vulgar showmen, with no pretensions to be artists or thinkers, self-consciousness rapidly developed. Making and spending so much money on what was rapidly coming to be recognized, willy-nilly, as an art, they suddenly began to feel a dreadful sense of inferiority and insecurity. Screen sirens also, world famous with no more training or education than they would have needed to be waitresses back home, wanted to become ladies, to learn how to behave as such, to acquire class. The brighter screen executives, *nouveau riche*, discovered the pleasures and advantages of fine cuisine, haute couture, art patronage; many a boy from the slums began to comport himself *en grand seigneur*.

They needed help, and were willing to pay for it. But where was the help to come from? Why, from those roving bands of Europeans, who often had nothing but their education and breeding to sell, and here found the perfect market for it. Dukes and princes, cut adrift and often impoverished by the Russian Revolution and the dissolution of the German and Austro–Hungarian Empires, could run grand restaurants and tutor *arriviste* Americans in the ways of the great world. They could even, sometimes, marry film stars or heiresses, trading their name for money and glamour. Out-of-work English actors could teach the Americans how to speak; Elinor Glyn, least intellectual and most commercially successful of the European writers imported by Hollywood in 1920, could promulgate the etiquette of English society and teach Rudolph Valentino European refinements of romance (kiss the palm of the hand, not the back). Europeans of all kinds fitted in naturally as all-purpose experts on art and decoration, music, painting, fashion and all those other areas where Americans—especially West Coast Americans—felt themselves lacking.

During the 1920s a whole peripheral society of such people grew up around Hollywood. Usually their credentials were not of the best—it was to their advantage that people did not check too deeply and a little European accent went a long way, or perhaps they would not have stayed. Certainly most of the bona fide intellectuals and aristocrats who visited kept their visits brief. But at least they gave an international flavour to the place, and opened new vistas. Virtually whatever nationality you were, you could rely on finding a group of compatriots somewhere in Los Angeles. And even if you did not have much in common with them, at least, strangers in a strange land, you would tend to huddle together for comfort and protection. As we have seen, Germans tended to see Germans, French to mix with the French, and the English colony, though more given to social mixing, also retained its autonomy and individual flavour. When the émigrés really began to arrive in considerable numbers, they found the way already somewhat prepared for them—if they wanted to follow it.

THE THIRTIES

3. The Gathering Storm

It is always surprising how thoroughly human beings can ignore whatever does not suit them and they do not want to believe. On 20 January 1933, Thomas Mann, presumably one of the most perceptive observers around, wrote to a friend: 'Yes, things look bad in Germany, but, once again, they are surely not so bad as they look,' and backed up his observation with the statement that 'Germany is big and a love of freedom and rationality are basically more widespread and more powerful than the screaming of the ruffians and the know-nothings allows one to think.' On 30 January Adolf Hitler assumed the office of Chancellor. Nearly a month later, on 27 February, the Reichstag went up in flames; the Nazis took advantage of the alarmism that followed to promulgate the Enabling Act of 23 March, which meant the effective end of even a vestige of democratic rule in Germany.

By the time that came about Mann was out of the country; as it happened the Nobel Prize-winning author had a lecture tour arranged, in Holland, Belgium and France, to be followed by a holiday in Switzerland. He was able to pause, take stock and decide that all things considered it would not be advisable for him to go back. True enough, for ever since Hitler's days of obscurity in the early 1920s Mann had been one of his more vocal opponents and therefore high on the list of enemies to be taken care of should the Nazis ever come to power. At least he was not Jewish, coming of solid Protestant stock from Lübeck, but he had accumulated just about every other mark against him in the eyes of the Nazis. Indeed, only very recently, he had become more of a political figure than ever before with a rousing speech to a group of socialist workers in Vienna, expressing solidarity with them and denouncing the rising tide of right-wing nationalist feeling.

Mann's older brother Heinrich, also a distinguished literary figure and author of much more than *Professor Unrat*, the novel *The Blue*

Angel is based on, had done worse: throughout the 1920s he had recognized the frailty of the Weimar Republic and was one of the most vocal critics of totalitarianism in all its forms, but particularly National Socialism. He saw the writing on the wall even more distinctly than Thomas, and had already begun late in 1932 to plan against the inevitable time of exile by arranging to have his royalties transferred to Paris and checking out the possibilities of Nice as a home abroad. After Hitler's assumption of power he left at once, crossing the border to France with only the clothes he stood up in and the notes for his next book. He was the first, but would be by no means the last.

Naturally, most of those who left aimed first of all at just getting across the border—to France, or maybe to Switzerland or Austria, where at least they could hope to be among people who spoke their own language. For the more determinedly left-wing, Czechoslovakia was a favoured haven; the Social Democratic party, completely outlawed like all other dissident political parties in Hitler's one-party state, set up its headquarters in Prague. And the long-argued-over German-speaking fringe of Bohemia, the Sudetenland, became the most active centre of anti-Nazi agitation and propaganda just outside Germany's national boundaries. Bertolt Brecht, for example, left with his wife Helene Weigel and their son the day following the Reichstag fire. They went first to Prague, then made the rounds of the German borders, more or less—Austria in March 1933, Switzerland in April, France in May, Denmark in June. At each stop Brecht ran into other early exiles— Hanns Eisler and Peter Suhrkamp in Vienna, Alfred Doeblin and Anna Seghers in Zurich, Lion Feuchtwanger in Lugano, Kurt Weill and Lotte Lenya in Paris. There, in collaboration with Weill and Lenya, Brecht wrote and staged *The Seven Deadly Sins*. Finally he joined up again with his family in Denmark, and decided to buy a house and settle there before the summer was out.

For the time being this was a common pattern: the first wave of refugees got out as soon as they could, settled themselves wherever they could, kept in touch with one another (even if they had not been particularly friendly at home), took stock and considered what to do next. They were mostly in fairly straitened financial circumstances, even the most formerly prosperous of them, since for the majority of writers in German, Germany was naturally the first and principal market for their works, and one of the first things the Nazi regime did was to confiscate their property and ban their publications.

Thomas Mann remained for a while an exception to this rule. Though his property and bank accounts were instantly taken from him, at least his books were still published in Germany, even if such works as the first volume of *Joseph and His Brothers*, an obvious provocation for anti-Semites, were greeted with open hostility in the press. The Nazi government had immediately deprived Heinrich Mann of his German nationality; in December 1936 they did the same to Thomas, and brought the farce of his 'line of communication' with Germany to an end. By that time both Heinrich and Thomas had become Czech citizens, though that was to be only a temporary solution.

It does not seem, initially, to have occurred to many of the refugees to travel further afield than the territories bordering on Germany. Perhaps many of them shared Thomas Mann's rather unreasonable optimism about the possibility of a quick downfall for the Nazis and the re-establishment of law and order in at least part of Germany—hope springing eternal, Thomas was still pretending, to himself possibly as well as to others, that he believed this in December 1933. And of course, one might ask, what else were they to do? It was not easy for those of them who depended for their livelihood principally on words to adapt themselves to another language, though all would naturally be done, by themselves and their well-wishers, to build up their audiences and sales in translation. There were also brave little émigré reviews and presses in places like Karlsbad, now Karlovy Vary, in Czechoslovakia, and Amsterdam, where Thomas Mann's son Klaus edited, from September 1933, a refugee magazine *Die Sammlung*. This was going to be a source of dissension in the émigré camp when, in October, Thomas Mann, Alfred Doeblin and René Schickele were persuaded, for the sake of the lines of communication being kept shakily open for German exile authors not yet blacklisted, to disown all connection with *Die Sammlung*. But then, unity of spirit and purpose had never been very characteristic of German liberal intellectuals during the 1920s, when they might have done more to save the Weimar republic, and now Schickele predicted to Thomas Mann that within a year the German émigrés would all have gone their separate ways and all trace of the ideal of a 'new Weimar' abroad would have vanished. Strangely enough, his gloomy prediction was not totally borne out, though it took a world war and eventual reassembly on the shores of the Pacific to prove him wrong.

If the major writers were somewhat circumscribed in their movements (unless like Feuchtwanger they had the benefit of being established international bestsellers), people connected with the performing arts were not—or not so much. Though things were not always easy for Brecht, he could continue to function as a practical theatre artist in other places—his first work outside Germany, *The Seven Deadly Sins*, was rapidly staged in Paris, London and Copenhagen, if without spectacular success in any of them. But at least he was able to take an active role in the working-out of his own destiny. Musicians obviously had the advantage of not being exclusively tied to one language; likewise painters and sculptors. The case of actors and film-makers was not so clearcut; for them, after all, language could be a real barrier, and for some of them, as the advent of the talkies showed, an almost insurmountable one. All the same, during the 1920s film people—and some theatre people—in Germany had got into the habit of thinking internationally. If Hollywood had been eager to buy up international talent before, and still from time to time showed an interest in what was going on in Europe, it might well be worth while looking so far afield again, when necessity was driving one away from home anyway.

Be that as it may, the first shock of exile was such that most of the film people, like the writers, stayed for the time being as close as they could to home, while they took stock. Few of them, as it happened, had been all that politically active in Germany, so unless they were Jewish they did not always seem to have much reason to move out right away, until they found out for sure how things were going to go with the new regime. Even if they were Jewish the situation was not immediately as clear as might have been expected. Robert Siodmak, for instance, a pioneer of bourgeois realism with his *Menschen am Sonntag*, made on a shoestring with a non-professional cast in 1928, had since been making a minor mark for himself directing for Erich Pommer such German-French co-productions as *Stürme der Leidenschaft*, with Emil Jannings and Anna Sten, and *Quick*, with Lilian Harvey and Hans Albers. He had just made his first film as producer/director, *Brennendes Geheimnis* (based on a story by Stefan Zweig), when Hitler came to power; it had the misfortune to open the day after the Reichstag fire. It was remarkable, seeing that it was directed by a Jew from a story by a Jewish writer, that it was permitted to open at all—it seems in fact to have been the last Jewish-made movie to open in Nazi Germany—but considering that it did, Siodmak and his writer-brother Curt waited around to see what would happen. After a month on release, however, it was the subject of a denunciation by no less a personage than Goebbels in the *Völkischer Beobachter*; Siodmak was accused of being a 'corrupter of the German family' through his preoccupation with the theme of unhappy marriages and disoriented children. The Siodmak brothers got on the next train for Paris.

Fritz Lang was another film-maker who was not so precipitate in his flight. Austrian by birth, he had studied painting in Paris, drifted into writing for films, and then had become a director, rising by the mid-1920s to be the most expensive, influential and sought-after film-maker in Germany. A brief visit to America in 1924 had apparently not impressed him unduly—he found that Germans were still being treated there as enemy aliens—and later, after the international success of *Metropolis* (1927), he refused all offers to go to Hollywood. In effect, he did not need Hollywood: for his films he had resources in Germany rivalling anything Hollywood could offer, and he suspected the kind of studio interference one might run into there. In any case, he felt himself very much a German, took German nationality, and made quite self-consciously German films: his two-part *Die Nibelungen* (1924) was a deliberately conceived national epic; even his thrillers about crazed super-criminals, like *Doctor Mabuse* (1922) and *Spione* (1928), were closely tied to the German scene and his observations on the German character.

He had had one of his biggest successes in 1931 with his first sound film, *M*, starring Peter Lorre as a child murderer. This had already aroused the mistrust of the Nazis because they took its provisional title, *Mörder Unter Uns (Murderer Among Us)*, to refer to them. And with his next film, *Das Testament des Dr Mabuse*, a sequel to his master-criminal thriller, he took the opportunity to refer unfavourably to the Nazis by putting what everyone would recognize as Nazi slogans into the mouth of the psychopathic Dr Mabuse's ghost. The film, made like many in the latter days of pre-Hitler Germany as a Franco-German co-production, was ready for showing in 1932. Lang was informed by Nazi officials that they objected to the film; imperiously he told them that if they thought they could ban a Lang film in Germany they should go ahead and try. On 29 March the new censorship, not surprisingly, turned it down flat.

What was surprising, though, was the conciliatory attitude adopted by Goebbels when he summoned Lang to his office in the

Ministry of Propaganda. Feeling somewhat chastened, Lang went along in his most formal clothes, to be kept kicking his heels for a while moving through a whole series of guards before he reached the inner sanctum. At that stage, however, Goebbels was totally charming; in the mildest terms he explained to Lang that the only thing they objected to was the ending, since they felt that the mad professor who takes on Mabuse's character should be destroyed by the fury of the people instead of going mad. (Actually, apart from the unmistakable anti-Nazi references in the film, Goebbels seems to have felt that the film's dissection of terrorism was so detailed and explicit as to inspire members of the audience to do likewise against the newly constituted state.) However, though the film had to be confiscated, it was only a small slip that could be forgiven and forgotten. Hitler had admired the spectacle of *Metropolis* (and no doubt its final message about the reconciliation of hand and head, the forces of labour and an elite rule) more than any other film, and so Goebbels offered Lang the leadership of the new National German film industry. Lang listened to all that he said, agreed to his suggestions, and left the same evening for Paris.

There he found already ensconced a number of former colleagues, mostly of Jewish extraction and therefore with every reason to get out early. Lang himself, as it happened, was half-Jewish, but it seemed that little details like that could be forgotten, for the moment at least, if Hitler was personally enthusiastic about an artist and his work (later Franz Lehár's wife Sophie, though Jewish, was made an 'honorary Aryan' by Hitler because he was so devoted to *The Merry Widow*). Among the new Paris colony were the producers Erich Pommer, long expert in international productions and recently particularly involved with Franco-German co-productions, so he already had a foothold in France, and Seymour Nebenzal, who had produced *M* and *Menschen am Sonntag* as well as his quota of Franco-German co-productions, such as G. W. Pabst's recent version of the famous old fantasy warhorse *L'Atlantide*. Pabst too was in Paris, since his talkies either took, like *Westfront 1918* and *Kameradschaft*, a pacifist, liberal line not at all to the Nazis' liking, or, like his version of Brecht's *Die Dreigroschenoper* (also a Franco-German co-production, soon to be banned in Germany), were based on the work of known militants of the left.

Other recent arrivals included Robert and Curt Siodmak and Billy Wilder, one of the several collaborators on *Menschen am Sonntag* who were later to become famous in their own right. With exceptional prescience, Wilder had set off westward a few days after the Reichstag fire, taking with him $1,000 in hundred-dollar bills, which he had laid by for such an emergency, and equipped with the names and addresses of a dozen cheap places to stay—not to mention a rich girlfriend who very soon headed back to Germany.

It was not only film people and writers who gathered in Paris. On 17 May another distinguished refugee arrived, supposedly on his annual holiday from the Prussian Academy of Arts in Berlin. Arnold Schoenberg had been teaching in Berlin since 1926, had never taken any very active part in politics, and had left the Jewish religious community in 1898, when he was twenty-three years old. However, though almost as thoroughly German in his music as Lang was in his films, he was still Jewish by birth and, in his music at least, revolutionary. He had been worried years earlier by the rising tide of anti-Semitism in Germany, and when, on 1 March 1933, the president of the Academy stated publicly that Jewish influence in it and in national life at large must be suppressed, Schoenberg decided to offer his resignation, asking only for an equitable settlement of his contract, which had two more years to run, and permission to take money out of the country to Vienna. No decisive answer being forthcoming, he hung around until 17 May, then in response to warnings of all kinds from friends and relatives, took flight for Paris with his wife and one-year-old daughter and just such belongings as they might be expected to need for a brief business trip-cum-holiday.

For form's sake, Schoenberg wrote to the Academy from Paris that he was planning a holiday, probably in Spain, for his health. (He suffered badly from asthma.) But obviously his mind was made up to exile, and in July he took the step of formally returning to the Jewish faith. Not much prospect of work offered in Western Europe, and as he was in need of money to live on he jumped at a chance to teach at a small (he did not realize quite how small) private music school in Boston. His teaching job in Berlin was formally terminated at the end of October, but by then he had already taken ship, on 25 October, for America, never to return.

Schoenberg's two most important contemporaries in the advanced musical circles of Germany, Alban Berg and Anton Webern, were both living in Austria and continued to do so, but not without becoming, at moments, targets of Schoenberg's suspicion, for in émigré circles there was naturally a lot of gossip circulating and a feeling that those who are not with us (physically) are against us. At the end of 1933 Berg had to assure Schoenberg, humorously, that he had not yet written any variations on the Horst Wessel song, and Webern found that he had been accused by gossip of Nazi sympathies. Berg died of blood-poisoning in 1935, before the annexation of Austria made the position of 'cultural bolsheviks' like himself difficult. Webern lived on, his music banned from performance, until he was accidentally shot during the American occupation of Austria in 1945.

Apart from the Jews, who were obviously affected at once, there was no immediate exodus of visual artists from Nazi Germany either. They seem anyway to have been in many cases more international in their attitudes than the rest, more likely to be travelling, painting or teaching in countries outside their own for reasons quite removed from politics. The famous Bauhaus School, most dynamic and influential centre of modern design in Germany in the 1920s, was closed down in Dessau in October 1932 by the newly elected provincial government, already Nazi-dominated, and many of its teachers and students did not move with its then director, Mies van der Rohe, to Berlin, but drifted off to do other work. Political pressures had indeed already mounted to such a point that several of the most important members, among them Walter Gropius and Laszlo Moholy-Nagy, had resigned in 1928.

Some of these early leavers were already living abroad, or at least working a lot there and easily able to make the transition to exile if they wished. The same was true of many of the other modernists, survivors of such earlier revolutionary groups in the German arts as the Expressionists, Dada and the savagely satirical group Die Neue Sachlichkeit. The old Dadaists, Max Ernst and Kurt Schwitters, for example, were already living in France before the Nazis came to power. Oskar Kokoschka was in Austria, and moved to Prague for primarily non-political reasons in 1934. Moholy-Nagy found congenial work in Amsterdam in 1933, able to pursue his experiments in photography and colour film with a large printing company. George Grosz, most biting of satirical draughtsmen, was a guest lecturer at the Arts Students League in New York in 1932 and prudently decided to settle there permanently. Almost the only notable artist to leave directly as a result of the Nazis' rise to power was Vassily Kandinsky, erstwhile Expressionist and early abstractionist, and for a while instructor at the Bauhaus. Russian by origin, he had become a German national in 1928, but left early in the Nazi ascendancy and settled instead just outside Paris, at Neuilly-sur-Seine.

Many others, even those most closely associated with institutions and groups that were deeply suspect to the Nazis, stayed on in Germany for the time being, perhaps hoping for the best. Expressionists like Emile Nolde and Karl Schmidt-Rottluff, social commentators like Otto Dix and Käthe Kollwitz, abstractionists like Willi Baumeister, stayed throughout the whole Nazi period, though dismissed from their teaching posts, held up in the propaganda shows as terrible examples of 'decadent art' and forbidden otherwise to exhibit or have any kind of public presence. More curious still, leaders of the Bauhaus, like Gropius, Mies van der Rohe and the German-American Lyonel Feininger, stayed on hoping to find work and a way to go on living in Germany. Gropius was one of the few artists involved with the Werkbund association of craftsmen and designers to resist its annexation by the Nazi party, and as late as February 1934 he was still fighting anti-Semitism in the German state to an extent that his colleagues found embarrassing. He left for England later that year, and finally arrived in America as head of the Harvard School of Architecture in 1937. Mies did not cease trying to practise architecture in Germany till 1937, when he also went to teach in America, at the Armour Institute, later the Illinois Institute of Technology. Feininger continued to live in Berlin until 1936, when he returned to America for the summer as an instructor at Mills College, Oakland, California; a year later he moved back for good to New York. Gradually, throughout the 1930s, Aryan German architects and artists of avant-garde tendencies left in response to some particular profes-sional opportunity, and spread out all over the world: Martin Wagner to Turkey, Ernst May to East Africa, Bruno Taut as far as Japan.

But in Paris, in spring 1933, most of this was still some way ahead. The urgent and immediate problem was, how were all these penniless émigrés going to make a living? For most of them, the first necessity was to learn French. The second was to see what help their reputations, their fellow-émigrés and any contacts they already had abroad might be to them in this crisis. As so often in the history of the German cinema, Pommer was unstoppable. Though naturally the German end of his co-production deals, UFA, was now out of the question, he still had all his French connections, and was soon able to set up a deal with Fox to make one quite ambitious film in France, before himself proceeding to America to produce for Fox there. The French film was a version of Molnár's play *Liliom*, later best known to the English-speaking world as the basis of the Rodgers and Hammerstein musical *Carousel*.

Pommer's unlikely choice to direct this lightweight fantasy, about a fairground worker given one chance on earth to redeem himself after death, was Fritz Lang; comedy, after all, had never been his strong point. Shooting did not get under way until December 1933, and the film was finally released in May 1934, to a mixed response. Lang's own view of the reason for this was that the first part of the film, showing Liliom's earthly life, was too realistic, so that when the tone switched to comic, even at times farcical fantasy in the heavenly sequences, audiences could not accept the change of pace. All the same, the film, which starred Charles Boyer, a young French actor with some inconclusive Hollywood experience (including a couple of films directed by Berthold Viertel), served its purpose. It kept a number of German refugees in work—writers Robert Liebmann and Bernard Zimmer and composer Franz Waxman as well as Pommer and Lang—and it eased the way of both Pommer and Lang to Hollywood. Pommer went off almost immediately to produce *Music in the Air* for Fox with more wandering Germans (Joe May, Billy Wilder). Lang met David O. Selznick on one of the talent-buying tours that were a feature of Hollywood practice at the time, and on 1 June 1934 in London he signed a contract with Selznick to direct movies in Hollywood.

The rest of the film people managed as best as they could. At one point Billy Wilder was living in the same cheap boarding house, the Hotel Ansonia, as the actors Peter Lorre and Paul Lukas, and the composers Friedrich Hollaender and Franz Waxman. Lorre got a job first, playing a small role in a film being directed by Pabst called *Du Haut en Bas* (photographed by Eugen Schüfftan and designed by Ernö Metzner, both émigrés). Wilder, whose French happened to be excellent, spent nine months in Paris trying to get work in film, and eventually managed to set up a film based on an original story of his, *Mauvaise Graine*, about a gang of young car thieves. It was made entirely on location, in Paris and Marseilles, the budget being scraped together from eight individual investors and the whole thing co-directed by Wilder and a Hungarian called Alexander Esway. The film is notable today mainly for being one of the very early performances of Danielle Darrieux, but had no particular success at the time. Finally, late in 1933, Wilder managed through the agency of the director Joe May to sell a script of his, *Pam-Pam*, to Columbia in Hollywood, where May was a producer at the time; the

sale brought with it a one-way ticket and a six-month contract.
Many stayed where they were, in Paris. Siodmak made quite a
successful career for himself in French cinema, cut short only when
the Germans invaded France in 1940; he arrived in Hollywood as
part of the second big wave of immigration. His brother Curt moved
to England, and then to Hollywood before him in 1938, to write, of
all unlikely things, the Dorothy Lamour vehicle *Her Jungle Love*.
Lorre also decided to try his luck in England, and had sufficient
success in his first English-language picture, Hitchcock's *The Man
Who Knew Too Much* (1934), to be offered a Hollywood contract.
Pabst stayed in France, apart from a brief Hollywood adventure in
1934, until he returned to Germany just before the outbreak of war
in Europe, there to make three major films for the Nazi cinema,
swallowing, we may suppose, his earlier socialist principles.

For the literary figures even more than for the film people, France
provided the most comfortable haven. Once the immediate drama of
exile was over, they had to decide how to lead their lives, where to
live and what to do. Heinrich Mann was the only one who
immediately regarded this as a permanent exile, taking a pessimistic
view of even the ultimate victory of reason. Thomas Mann was still
hoping some time later that the reign of terror would quieten down a
bit so that he could go home to Germany. It was a little easier for
him to think this way, since his books had not been included in the
first of the Nazi book-burnings on 10 May 1933 and his latest books,
the first two volumes of *Joseph and His Brothers*, were still
published in Germany, by a surviving Jewish publisher, Fischer-
Verlag. Admittedly, this was only at the cost of a certain ambiguity
in his apparent attitude to Nazi rule.

All the same, he did not for the moment actually plan on going
back, even briefly. Heinrich had headed immediately on his
departure from Germany for Nice, where he temporarily settled and
took up work on his sequence of novels about Henry IV of France,
as well as writing in French a series of fighting articles on Nazi rule
for the *Dépêche de Toulouse*. His friend, and Thomas's, René
Schickele, was already living just along the French Riviera in a little
town called Sanary-sur-Mer, and in June 1933, when Thomas was
looking for somewhere comfortable to spend the summer after his
first months in Switzerland, Schickele suggested he move there.
Heinrich moved to Bandol to be nearby, and the German colony at
Sanary was soon supplemented by other visitors, such as Alfred
Doeblin, Ludwig Marcuse, Ernst Toller and Bertolt Brecht.

Sanary, in fact, had some history of intellectual and artistic residence. In the 1900s many painters had visited, and before the First World War Katherine Mansfield regularly wintered in Sanary. Through her, D. H. Lawrence had found it, and eventually through him Aldous Huxley and his wife, who bought a villa in 1930 and regularly spent time there till early 1937. And because of them, other English writers like Cyril Connolly and Brian Howard also came. The distinguished German art critic Julius Meier-Graefe was already living there when the Nazis came to power. But it became and remained the most important meeting-place for German exiles, largely owing to the influence of the most important new permanent resident it acquired in 1933, Lion Feuchtwanger, the internationally popular novelist. Feuchtwanger had, as it happened, been in America on a lecture tour when the Nazis came to power. He was advised not to return to Germany; his wife was in Austria, so they met in St Anton, went on to Switzerland, and from there to a new home in Sanary. In February his house in Berlin was ransacked, all his property in Germany was confiscated, and he figured in the first list of Germans deprived of their nationality on 23 August.

Very soon Feuchtwanger assumed the role of leader in the exiled German community—partly, no doubt, because of them all he had the greatest financial independence from the tremendous sales of his books in translation, and so wherever he lived became a focal point of émigré social contact and intellectual activity. It was largely because he had chosen to live in Sanary that so many others gathered around, some of them initially just for the summer or for brief visits, others, like Franz Werfel after the invasion of Austria in 1938, with the intention of making it their permanent home.

Not that the émigrés in Sanary, even though they had a certain common cause in their hostility to the Nazis, and/or the Nazis' hostility to them, were ever as unified a group as one might suppose. Sybille Bedford observes in her biography of Aldous Huxley that:

They were roughly divided into two main clans. One, the haute culture, revolved round Thomas Mann—the Magician as his children called him—and his friends and peers; the other clan dominated by Lion Feuchtwanger, and the bond between him and his satellites oddly enough was communistic leanings and/or financial success; each clan patronised the other. Both ... looked down upon the Anglo-Saxons—Aldous Huxley and his friends.

Social gatherings that were not clearly centred on one or other of the local luminaries tended to be uncomfortable, though there were evenings of culture and entertainment when they suffered one another more or less gladly and kept the flag of liberal Germany flying. It was all rather like a rehearsal for what was to come. For at least Sanary was a Mediterranean haven, with its seaside villas, its palm trees and blue sea. And if one should be forced to move further afield, to America, say, where could be more like it than the seaward side of Los Angeles....

4. Music in the Air

It sounds like a suitably ironic introduction to the Hollywood dream-factory that the first film on which the refugees worked should be called *Music in the Air*. Even more, that it should have been an adaptation of the Jerome Kern/Oscar Hammerstein operetta about the amorous intrigues of a tempestuous German musical star, set in a never-never version of Munich and designed, of all things, as a comeback vehicle for that quintessential Hollywood star, Gloria Swanson. But *Music in the Air* had already been successful in the theatre (as the film was not to be) and Erich Pommer as producer already had to his credit such charming trifles as *Congress Dances*. Therefore it seemed a logical choice for his first film as a producer with Fox.

For their first months in Hollywood, Pommer and Joe May, who directed the film, lived like kings, or at least like visiting celebrities, with the regulation mansions complete with pools, the regulation round of extravagant parties—for one of Pommer's, it is recorded, the penniless Billy Wilder got paid $80 to jump into the pool fully clothed, though why this was thought to be a good idea does not seem to be recorded. As soon as the film opened in December 1934 and proved to be a failure, matters were rather different. True to the old Hollywood adage that you are only as good as your last picture, they suddenly found offers of work few and far between. Pommer kicked his heels around Hollywood for a year or so without managing to get anything more on to the screen, then went back to Europe to produce a couple of films for Korda and form an independent production company in England with Charles Laughton; May did not make another film till 1937, and from then on was consigned to B features for various studios.

But the point is, neither their early affluence nor their later reverses had anything really to do with their being political émigrés. It is doubtful, even, if many people in Hollywood clearly understood the political aspect. It was, after all, still the era of what Fritz Lang described as trophy-hunting in Europe by Hollywood producers. They would go off on a holiday-cum-talent scouting expedition, and try to come back with at least one big-name: actor, director, writer or whatever. And of course everyone else in Hollywood had to be convinced that the result was a great catch—hence all the initial display. So it was merely fitting in with Hollywood convention that Pommer and May, coming over to make a big, important film, should live like big, important people. Obviously, no one must realize that they were down on their luck in Europe, or they would not be taken so seriously, paid so much, treated so well. It may be wondered how anyone could not realize that the implications of the Nazi takeover in Germany put people like them very much at a disadvantage. But Southern California was far away indeed from the problems of Central Europe, and tended to make no clear division, for instance, between German Jews and liberals, who were in difficulties, and Austrians, whose troubles were yet to come. In the same year, 1934, one of the biggest names in German theatre, Max Reinhardt, breezed through Los Angeles to stage one of his most spectacular productions ever, his vast *Midsummer Night's Dream* at the Hollywood Bowl. Clearly, he was not there out of painful necessity; he always had his directorship of the Salzburg Festival in Austria to go back to—at least until 1938.

And Pommer and May had been—were—big names in Europe. Pommer, as head of the giant UFA combine, had been until very recently one of the most powerful producers in Europe. May, though his biggest successes, including serials and a two-part spectacular, *The Indian Tomb* (1921) scripted by Lang, were some way back, had acquired a new reputation as a realist with *Asphalt* (1929) and had recently been directing light comedies and musicals in France successfully enough. Anyway, the publicity machine in Hollywood conspired to build up the talents of unknown qualities, and political consciousness in Hollywood early in the 1930s was hazy enough to be neither an asset nor a liability to the émigrés: their plight, if it was mentioned at all, was likely to be at most the subject of a few moments' polite party conversation, and that was that.

Of course, you had to have something to build on in the first place. Billy Wilder, whose first real job in Hollywood was working on the script of *Music in the Air*, arrived—one of the earliest of the political refugees to do so—in January 1934 as a complete unknown.

Even the fact that a Hollywood company had remade one of the films he had helped to script in Germany (*Ihre Hoheit Befiehlt*, written with Robert Liebmann, who also worked on *Music in the Air*, had become Universal's *Adorable* in 1933) did nothing for him. He was, after all, only one of hundreds of hopefuls arriving in Hollywood, and he was there primarily for the traditional reason of wanting to try his luck in the movie capital of the world. That he was unwelcome in Germany was unfortunate for him, of course, but if he had wanted, he could have continued in France or, being Austrian, gone back to Austria to work. If he chose Hollywood instead, he had to take his chances like everybody else.

It was, consequently, the rough underside of Los Angeles that Wilder first encountered. He could speak almost no English, so he set about improving it by listening endlessly to the radio—mainly soap operas and baseball commentaries. He lived in a tiny room in the Chateau Marmont in Hollywood, and scraped what sort of a living he could from doing odd jobs like walking on the wing of a plane flying over the coast and selling gags and bits of business to people in the industry, notably Ernst Lubitsch, whom he managed to get to know at this time. His initial contract paid him a princely $125 a week. He was given no work to do, though, and the contract ended after the specified six months. In any case, to get a proper immigration permit he had to leave the country and wait in Mexico until he received it. On his return, he got the job on *Music in the Air* and went on from there to *Lottery Lover*, another failure directed for Fox by another German émigré, William Thiele. Thiele had made his name in Germany primarily with musicals like *Drei von der Tankstelle* and *Liebeswalzer*, both starring Lilian Harvey, who was now also in Hollywood, but for entirely non-political reasons.

Thiele did not work for a couple of years, then, like Joe May, found himself stuck mainly in B features. Lilian Harvey, who made several films for Fox, quite successfully, went back by way of her native Britain to Nazi Germany and several more frothy comedies and musicals. Wilder starved, sharing for a while a room with Peter Lorre and living on a can of soup a day. Then he sold a couple of scripts to a short-lived company and visited Paris and Vienna on the proceeds. Finally in 1937 a story of his was bought by Paramount, he was put under contract, and his career really took off. But it had been four hard years.

Naturally, in the rigid class structure of the Hollywood studios, he would have had little to do with anyone grander and more established than himself. Lubitsch seems to have been the only one of his acquaintances to remain in the upper echelons—which finally came in handy when Wilder's first notable writing assignment for Paramount was a Lubitsch film, *Bluebeard's Eighth Wife* (1938). In any case, Lubitsch was Wilder's kind of person, or Wilder Lubitsch's. With his abrasive, iconoclastic sense of humour, Wilder can hardly be imagined altogether at home in the rather grand, reverential circles in which Salka Viertel was moving, under the aegis of Garbo and MGM, though apparently he did make friends more to his own taste, especially people he could play tennis with, at Salka Viertel's salons. But the mere fact of being central-European and an émigré did little to break down social and temperamental barriers that would have existed anyway, back in Europe as much as in Hollywood.

Fritz Lang, the next important arrival, was in a rather different category. He had come over under personal contract to a real American producer, David O. Selznick, who was at that time working for the most prestigious and luxurious of studios, MGM. Lang was also, as he never hesitated to tell people, 'the most famous director in Europe', and if studios had not been exactly fighting over his services, as they would have been a few years earlier, after *Metropolis*, there was at least no denying that he was a catch. Even at MGM his work was held up as a model: Irving Thalberg, the revered boy-genius of the place, screened *M* for a group of writers to study and learn from. But the pay-off was also relevant: when one of the writers asked Thalberg how he would have reacted if brought the self-same script, Thalberg admitted, 'I would probably have said, "Go to Hell".' In other words, Lang might, like so many European intellectuals imported through the years, be admired in principle, but that did not mean that Hollywood was in practice ready for his ideas, or even ready to give them a try.

The consequence was that for the whole year of his contract Lang was given nothing to do. He was well paid for doing nothing. He was able to work on his English—for his first few years out of Germany he refused to speak or write a word of German. He was even able to take time off and live for two months among the Navajo of Arizona, studying their way of life and photographing their sand-paintings. He also saw a lot of American films, talked to a lot of everyday Americans in streets and bars, read a lot of comic strips. He accepted with, it seems, reasonable equanimity the news that his wife and regular script collaborator, Thea von Harbou, who had elected to stay on in Germany, had joined the Nazi party and was suing for divorce. The only thing he could not manage to do was to make a film—ostensibly the reason for which he was there.

He had begun well enough. Shortly after his arrival in America there was the notorious fire on board the *Morro Castle,* in which 125 people were killed. With Oliver Garrett he wrote a script called *Hell Afloat,* based on the disaster. It was shown to Selznick on Christmas Eve and, curiously for such a black subject on such a day, Selznick was enthusiastic about it. But after Christmas with the family he had changed his mind, thought it was unmakable, and promptly washed his hands of Lang. For the next six months the studio continued to announce his name in connection with various projects, but nothing concrete came of any of them. To fill his time, Lang worked on another original script, a psychological thriller called *The Man Behind You,* which combined ideas from *Doctor Jekyll and Mr Hyde* and *The Testament of Doctor Mabuse.* But no one was interested, and nothing came of that project either.

All the same, Lang was determined to stay on in America. In February 1935 he got his first American citizenship papers. In June, at the same time that Selznick had announced his intention to leave MGM, the studio tactfully informed Lang that his option would not be picked up. Appealing to the sporting instincts of Eddie Mannix, the right-hand man of Louis B. Mayer, he pointed out that he had not been given a chance to work, and his reputation would suffer grave damage if he was dismissed without even the opportunity. Mannix, a fair man and a friend of Lang's, agreed. According to one version of the story (Lang told several), Mannix handed him a four-page outline of a story by Norman Krasna about a lynching and told him to go ahead with it; according to another, Lang himself had found it and told Mannix this was what he wanted to do, make or break. Whichever is true, the fact remains that this was the genesis of Lang's first American film, *Fury.*

The more likely explanation seems to be that Lang had somewhere found the subject himself, for anything less like the kind of thing usually done at MGM in those days would be hard to find. Of all the studios in Hollywood, only Warner Brothers had any kind of established interest in making films about current social issues, and they tended towards tough gangster melodramas such as would provide suitable vehicles for stars like Edward G. Robinson and James Cagney. Even at Warners, really hard-hitting films like *I Am a Fugitive from a Chain Gang* (1932), the story of an innocent man unjustly convicted and turned into a hardened criminal, figured far less frequently. Lang's powerful study of mob hysteria was not permitted to be made exactly as he intended it. The black victim had to be changed to white, and Lang's original concept of the hero as a lawyer and a person of superior intellect and articulacy was changed, in deference to the studio's tastes in such matters, to a man-in-the-street, John Doe sort of character who could be played by Spencer Tracy and who could command a universal sympathy that an American audience was likely to withhold from an obvious leader-figure. But the wonder was that in MGM, home of the glossy star vehicle, he was allowed to make it at all.

Especially since he had caused trouble because of his unfamiliarity with American ways. He had, for instance, snubbed Louis B. Mayer—because, he claimed rather improbably, he was shy and self-conscious about his bad English—and that was something no one on the Metro lot did with impunity. In any case, with his monocle, his habit of command and his clipped 'Prussian' military manner, which many found offensively arrogant, he was the last person in the world to hit it off with the sentimental, Jewish, semi-literate Mayer, who was quick to take offence and merciless in his campaigns against those who had offended. Once he began shooting the film Lang made further trouble by getting absorbed in what he was doing and presuming that, as in Germany, he could just continue till he was ready to break, without regard to the fixed working hours laid down by union regulations. Another source of trouble was his political insistence on more respect for the rights of the creator in films, exemplified initially by his involvement in the setting-up of a 'union' for directors, the Screen Directors' Guild (January 1936), which was for some time regarded by the studios as no better than a subversive, communist organization and was particular anathema to Mayer, who had been the most vocal opponent of the Screen Actors Guild and the Screen Writers' Guild a couple of years earlier.

Nonetheless, *Fury* was made much as Lang wanted it, weathered a series of previews—part of the normal procedure in Hollywood at that time—and was subjected to no crucial cuts: a couple of little scenes involving blacks were excised, since in Mayer's view they could only be shown on screen as shoeshine boys or railroad porters; a few too liberal lines of dialogue were taken out of the script, and a kiss forced on Lang as a fadeout. The problem then was, what was the studio going to do with it? It seems to have been saved from being shelved or slipped very obscurely into release by the intervention of Billy Wilkerson, editor of *The Hollywood Reporter*, who insisted on seeing the film even though people at the studio told him: 'It's a lousy one from this lousy German son-of-a-bitch, not worth looking at,' and then wrote about it so enthusiastically that the studio was forced to show it to the rest of the press. When, to their genuine amazement, it was received with equal enthusiasm, the studio finally premiered it on 5 June 1936, more than two years after the appearance of Lang's previous film, *Liliom*. Lang went to the premiere with Marlene Dietrich and left to thunderous applause.

The film was a big hit, and at last firmly established Lang in America—indeed, for some years afterwards he was always tagged as the director of *Fury*. MGM did not learn, however, and never made a film remotely like it again; nor did Lang work for MGM again until 1953, long after Louis B. Mayer had left. Fortunately there were other producers in Hollywood more receptive to his ideas and his talent—notably Walter Wanger, a liberally inclined independent for whom he made his next film, *You Only Live Once* (1937). Lang, too, had learnt some lessons from the experience: first and foremost, perhaps, always to keep his independence and be contractually tied down to only one picture at a time rather than being, as most directors then were, under long-term contract and at the beck and call of a studio that had total rights over what, if anything, they should or shouldn't do.

Beyond this, *Fury* is a significant film in the history of Hollywood and in the relations of the émigrés with it. For one thing, it was the first really successful film made by an émigré director in Hollywood during the sound era, which at the same time brought something unfamiliar, something of the way they did it back in Europe, to the American scene. There were, of course, Middle-European film-makers who had continued working successfully since silent days. Lubitsch, Michael Curtiz (formerly Mihaly Kertész), who had made a transition from foreign-language versions to films in English, and William, formerly Wilhelm, Dieterle, a Reinhardt actor and Murnau's Faust, were the most successful. But they had succeeded by dint of submerging their foreignness in a typically American style of film-making or, like Lubitsch, inventing their own fantasy of foreignness specifically for the American market.

Lang was different. In acclimatizing to the American cinema he had the advantage over most of the other, earlier German imports in that his films in Europe, for all their frequent elaborations of costume and set, their powerful atmospherics, had been firmly based on narrative. American cinema was, and has remained, primarily a place for telling stories—the significance of the film is articulated through the plot and the pacing of the story. And *Fury*, whatever else it may be, is a relentless piece of story-telling. The first part builds inexorably to the climax of the attempted lynching, as the innocent man is gradually encircled by circumstantial evidence that he carried out a kidnapping, and the mob gradually becomes inflamed against him. The second part, in which, after a miraculous escape, he sets out to get his revenge on the people responsible, builds more steadily by logic and the marshalling of courtroom evidence in the shape of a newsreel film which clearly demonstrates that the people who claimed to have been miles away were actually present at the burning of the jail.

It is as punchy and direct as any American could desire. And yet, integrated with this, are clear indications of Lang's European background: the use of visual symbolism, sometimes rather heavy, as when gossiping women are intercut with cackling hens, sometimes much subtler, as in the night scene immediately after Joe's escape, when the darkness he requires without (for safety's sake and to save his sore eyes) reflects the darkness within. There is also virtuoso play with cross-cutting between related actions, to produce suspense or ironic contrast, and many moments when lighting and composition take us straight back to silent German cinema, or at least to *M* or *The Testament of Doctor Mabuse*. The final effect of the film is a fusion of these two elements—American narrative drive, European subtlety of suggestion—which makes it quite unlike anything else up to then in the American cinema and points clearly in a direction that many more were subsequently to follow; towards, especially, the *film noir* of the 1940s, which was almost entirely Germanic in its origins and very frequently so in its leading creators.

While Lang had been waiting around for what proved to be his big chance, other political émigrés had begun to trickle in. Dupont was back in 1933, after a flying visit in 1932 making exteriors for his German film *Der Laeuffer von Marathon*, in which the drama took place against a background of the 1932 Los Angeles Olympic Games. He had left Hollywood in 1927, praising the technical efficiency of American studios and the flair, vivacity and *joie de vivre* of the average American film as compared with the slowness, heaviness and sombreness prevailing in Europe. But he insisted that European cinema was finally more creative and artistically innovative, particularly in its visual qualities. Now, after an interval making progressively less impressive films in England and Germany, he returned with little surviving fame to make a series of low-budget films. He was a director of the old school, hard-drinking, womanizing, given to large-scale tantrums on set and known to strike his leading actors if he did not get what he wanted (also, in the wake of his off-set revels, to forget to film vital scenes). He could be a pampered genius or nothing, and in the new, streamlined Hollywood of the thirties nothing was what he rather rapidly became. In 1938 he was removed from directing a film (a little drink problem, it seems) and became an agent and publicist before reappearing in the 1950s, directing a collection of exploitation quickies with titles like *Problem Girls* and *The Neanderthal Man*.

At least, after a fashion, he lasted in Hollywood. The other big name to arrive at this time, G. W. Pabst, did not. He was apparently well established in France, but his big film of 1933, *Du Haut en Bas*, did not do well and when Warners, who had had a hand in the backing of his film, *Die Dreigroschenoper* (*The Threepenny Opera*), renewed their invitation to him to direct a film in Hollywood he accepted, though hesitantly because he was unfamiliar with the ways of Hollywood studios. He did not have any subject to hand, and for some months examined and turned down everything the studios offered him. Finally he chose Louis Bromfield's bestseller *A Modern Hero*, which seemed to him to have the makings of a powerful social statement. It is about a circus artiste who makes his way unscrupulously in the world until he becomes a rich car manufacturer. But then he loses his money in a crooked stock deal and his illegitimate son in a car accident, and returns to his origins to try to build his life again.

However, Pabst knew nothing of the American life he was trying to depict, had no control over the editing and, with his halting English, very little over the actors, and, finally, when the film was cut down to a seventy-minute programme-filler he washed his hands of it. Subsequently he would not talk about the film and did not wish it to be included in his filmography. In 1937 he wrote a rather bitter essay for a French publication denouncing Hollywood for censoring anything of real seriousness and social significance in films while leaving the kind of wish-fulfilment fantasy that was ultimately much more dangerous.

Certainly his next project, an original subject called *War Is Declared*, fell afoul of official sensibilities in the US. It was for Paramount, and was to star their new contract player Peter Lorre as a demented radio operator on board an international liner, who announces that war has been declared and so sets off personal and national rivalries in passengers to such an extent that a real battle starts, and the ship sinks. It is only after the survivors are picked up that they learn the whole thing was the operator's delusion, and resolve, rather belatedly, to mend their ways. In an America trying steadfastly to turn its back on international problems this seemed tactless, to say the least, and was shelved after representations from Washington. Pabst then went to New York to make a film version of Gounod's opera *Faust*, with Lawrence Tibbett, but that too, presumably for purely commercial reasons, fell through, and Pabst returned to France.

While in Hollywood Pabst mixed almost exclusively with fellow Germans and Austrians, and avoided as far as possible becoming involved in any way with Americans and the American way of life (in contrast to Lang, with whom for a while he became close). The reasons for this stand-offishness (as it was generally interpreted) no doubt had something to do with the conflicts of self-imposed exile, but probably more to do with Pabst's general psychological state, in transition between his overtly socialist, pacifist work of the early sound era and the exotic aestheticism hinted at in *L'Atlantide* and *Don Quichotte*, which was to become his dominant mode in the series of relatively trashy thrillers and romances he made on his return to France. Among all the great directors of the German silent cinema, the personality of Pabst remains the most mysterious and elusive; his brief encounter with Hollywood is just one more element in the mystery.

Max Reinhardt's practical contact with Hollywood film-making was scarcely less brief. In the early 1930s he was famous in America as the showman of giant spectacles, such as *The Miracle* and *Everyman*, which had created a sensation wherever they were shown, not least in New York. The other sides of his talent, demonstrated in Germany and Austria by his subtle and stylish opera productions and his minutely realistic dramatic productions in the tiny Berlin Kammerspiele theatre and elsewhere, were unknown in the US. In 1934 he staged another giant spectacle, this time based on one of his favourite and most frequently directed plays, *A Midsummer Night's Dream*. It played in three places on the West

Coast, for the California Festival Association: the Hollywood Bowl, the War Memorial Opera House in San Francisco and the University of California Greek Theatre in Berkeley. But it was designed first for the Hollywood Bowl, and there by general consent achieved its maximum effect.

This was enough for Warner Brothers, who were at this time looking for a little culture to add to their lists. Reinhardt was commissioned to make a lavish film of the play, no expenses spared. Though the idea of overwhelming spectacle was to be held over from the stage production, initially everything else was rethought in film terms—even the casting, which was almost entirely from the Warners' stable of contract players, such as James Cagney as Bottom, Dick Powell as Lysander, Anita Louise as Titania and Victor Jory as Oberon, with only Olivia de Havilland (Hermia) and Mickey Rooney (Puck) kept from the stage original. Reinhardt had, in fact, directed two silent films himself, not very successfully, back in 1913–14, but to provide the cinematic know-how this time he was given William Dieterle, a Warners contract director who had formerly been a leading man with the Reinhardt troupe back in Germany.

Just about everything that could go wrong did. Enormous forest sets were built in the studio, so that every element of the fantasy could be controlled. Then it transpired that wonderfully detailed though they were, rivalling the famous sets built in Germany for Lang's *Siegfried*, they could not be lit to get the right other-worldly effect. The production was going to be closed down after eight weeks' shooting, but a new photographer, Hal Mohr, was called in and given a free hand. This resulted in an overnight orgy of aluminium spray-painting (so that the areas of light and shadow were actually painted in, as in a German expressionist film), plus a plentiful application of spangles and sparkled filters in front of the camera, so that the final effect came somewhat closer to Reinhardt's and Dieterle's hazy concept.

Even so, as might have been predicted, the film, though often magical and astonishingly well acted by its unlikely cast, turned out to be very long (132 minutes), very expensive and not, despite a big publicity campaign trying to sell Shakespeare as fun and culture, very popular with the mass public required to return a $1,300,000 investment. Reinhardt had a seven-picture contract, and was already planning to follow *A Midsummer Night's Dream* with *The Gambler*, after Dostoevsky, *Die Fledermaus* and *The Tales of*

Hoffmann. Naturally, none of these was made and his contract lapsed.

But Reinhardt had acquired the taste for Southern California, and from then on divided his time between Los Angeles and Europe, particularly his annual stint at the Salzburg Festival. In 1936 an American version of his Hofmannsthal spectacle *Everyman* was staged by one of his former assistants in Los Angeles. But Reinhardt played no direct part in the production. In 1938 Austria in its turn was annexed to the German Reich and there was no room in it for 'the Jew Goldmann', as the Nazis derisively called Reinhardt. He settled again in Los Angeles, this time until after the war; staged an elaborate production of *Faust* at the Pilgrimage Play Theatre in 1938, ran a drama school, and made occasional, not too successful forays in the direction of the New York stage. Though old friends and colleagues like Lubitsch, Dieterle and Dietrich did their best to involve him with the cinema again, he never made another film.

Otto Preminger was another victim—or beneficiary—of a Hollywood producer's scalp-hunting trip to Europe. An ex-actor, he was in spring 1935 managing Reinhardt's Viennese theatre, the Josefstadt, when Joseph M. Schenck, head of Twentieth Century-Fox, came to Vienna collecting new talent for the company. He told Preminger: 'I hear you are a very good director. Any time you want to come to America, just write to me.' Once Preminger was persuaded that Schenck meant what he said, he gave Reinhardt six months' notice, started learning English seriously, and on 16 October 1935 left Vienna for America. It was purely a career move, and the fulfilment of a romantic dream; there were no political considerations involved, though Preminger was Jewish and later, after the invasion of Austria and his parents' hazardous escape, he showed himself a very articulate anti-Nazi. Preminger's first stop, on his way to Hollywood, was in New York to direct for Gilbert Miller *Libel*, a play he had already directed in German. He developed an abiding love of New York, a love that he never came to feel for Los Angeles, even though he was given a suite at the Beverly Hills Hotel and full star treatment on his arrival early in January 1936.

Preminger recalls that at the time, he met half of Hollywood, including many of the great names he had revered from afar, like Mary Pickford and Chaplin, but did not find the atmosphere particularly conducive to making close friends. He saw something of his old boss, Reinhardt, but otherwise did not seek out the German community, concentrating rather on perfecting his English and learning his job as a film-maker by observation. Fox, like MGM, did not rush its new acquisitions into work before they were ready. Since Preminger had made only one film in Europe, a comedy starring Paula Wessely, he was given nearly eight months, living on expenses and without any further contract, to haunt the sound-stages and observe, and see movies, before Darryl Zanuck, the production-chief of the company, asked him if he was ready to make a movie himself. The project was *Under Your Spell* (1936), a quickie to work off the unwanted half of a year's contract with the opera star Lawrence Tibbett, whose last film had flopped disastrously.

The film went well, and so did his next, a comedy, *Danger—Love at Work* (1937), starring Ann Sothern as a last-minute replacement for Simone Simon, a French discovery of Zanuck's whose English was not up to the challenge. Zanuck was now enchanted with Preminger, whose contract had ten months to run before its next option. Zanuck showed his favour by assigning him to the studio's biggest upcoming project, an expensive screen version of Robert Louis Stevenson's *Kidnapped*. Since Preminger knew nothing about Scotland and his English was still not good enough to read the book, he wanted to refuse, but everyone warned him against this—it would constitute a terrible snub to Zanuck and he would never be forgiven. Reluctantly, he began to work on the film while Zanuck was away. When Zanuck came back he was (rightly, Preminger thinks) very displeased with what had been shot, and after a violent argument with Preminger (no easy man to get on with either) fired him from the film.

Now the other side of Hollywood became apparent. Suddenly close friends like Joe Schenck, who had declared himself a second father to Preminger, would not speak to him because he had displeased the almighty Zanuck. No one else in town would employ him, and pressures were brought to bear on him to terminate his contract. This only put Preminger's back up, so he determined to sit out the next ten months, idle if necessary, collect his pay and improve his English. To this end he enrolled for an acting class at UCLA, only to be asked to leave when his true identity was discovered because they thought he was a studio spy. As soon as the contract with Fox ran out, at the end of 1937, Preminger and his wife set out for New York with their small savings and a determination never to come back to Hollywood. Instead, he was going to return to his first love, the stage—which he did with great success.

Eventually he came back to Hollywood on his own terms (though still pursued by the enmity of Zanuck), but that was not until well into the war, and a new era in the history of the Hollywood émigrés.

Another import of 1936, who received the red-carpet treatment and somehow survived it, was Anatole Litvak. Details of his early life are mysterious, though it seems that he was born in Russia in 1902, was directing short features in Leningrad when he was twenty, and contrived to join the group of White Russian émigrés in Paris headed by the rich producer/director Nicholas Volkoff, by the time he was twenty-three. Whatever the truth of the matter, he became a director in his own right on talkies in 1930, aided in this era of multiple-language versions by his fluency in a great variety of languages. Some of his films were purely French, but several of them were Franco-German co-productions, made in Germany at the UFA studios. Since he had the reputation (oddly, considering the rich and aristocratic circles in which he had moved) for being rather leftish, he found it politic not to work in Germany after 1933, but continued working comfortably in France until the tremendous international success of *Mayerling* (1936) made him and its two stars, Charles Boyer and Danielle Darrieux, seem like desirable properties to Hollywood.

Boyer had made two previous trips to Hollywood, in 1930–2 and 1934–5, and appeared in a number of films there, but had never quite caught on. This time would bring him his period of major stardom in the American cinema—of which more later. Darrieux made a couple of films in Hollywood, but never overcame her problems with English and her reputation for being difficult; she went back to France and major stardom there instead. Litvak had the luck, or good sense, to get his arrival in Hollywood stage-managed by the great press-agent Charles Feldman, who built up such a mystique around this European genius that no one dared interfere with him in any way while he was busy directing his first two Hollywood films, an American version of his French success *L'Equipage* and an adaptation of Jacques Deval's comedy *Tovarich*, set among the Russian émigrés in Paris he knew so well at first hand. As neither of these films did spectacularly well, the reverence vanished overnight. But meanwhile Litvak had proved himself to be a capable and versatile contract director, handling Warner stars like Bette Davis and Edward G. Robinson with discretion, so he happily stayed on. His main subsequent claim to fame, as far as we are concerned, is that he directed Hollywood's first overtly anti-Nazi film, *Confessions of a Nazi Spy*, in 1938.

Of course, as we are reminded by mention of Charles Boyer and Danielle Darrieux, as well as Simone Simon, not all of the foreign talents brought back hopefully by Hollywood producers were directors. There was a constant stream of stars and would-be stars, who came mostly for obvious professional reasons and only some of them, incidentally, for political reasons as well. Here ability to handle the English language was of paramount importance. Germans and Scandinavians seem in general to have done best; French, Italians and miscellaneous Eastern Europeans have usually had trouble. It is difficult to pin down exactly what 'ability to handle English' means. Some whose English is technically near perfect still seem to find it a barrier, something that perhaps produces a certain kind of self-consciousness, and obscures the expression of a personality, that may be vivid when they are performing in their native language. (Discomfort is something the camera always mercilessly picks up.)

A few managed to turn the obvious flaws in their command of English into an asset. Maurice Chevalier, for example, who was one of the biggest stars in Hollywood from 1929 to 1935, always spoke charmingly broken English. Since so many of his Hollywood successes were in Lubitsch films, it is tempting to suggest that he provided the same kind of American-oriented fantasy view of European charm and sophistication that they did. Certainly there were those who suggested unkindly that he must have to take refresher courses to keep up his accent as his greatest professional asset. And, it should be noted, Chevalier went back to France for entirely practical reasons: when fashion turned against the kind of film he had always been associated with, and the American cinema became more solemn and puritanical, he went where the work was, and did not return for more than twenty years, until the times had changed again.

In a different way, suited to a different era, Charles Boyer managed to exploit his foreignness. As so often in the career of major stars, it was one happy chance that did it. After appearing in more than a dozen American films playing second fiddle to such impressive leading ladies as Dietrich (*The Garden of Allah*) and Garbo (*Conquest*, alias *Marie Walewska*), it was a relatively low-budget film, *Algiers* (1938), a remake of a successful French vehicle for Jean Gabin, which planted forever in the American mind the image of the handsome, elegant, fated gangster Pépé le Moko sacrificing his life for love. From then on anyone could recognize an impersonator of Boyer saying, 'Come with me to the Casbah'—though in fact he never says it in the film. *Algiers* also made an American star out of a beautiful Austrian import, Hedy Kiesler, renamed Lamarr. The differences between their subsequent careers hinged possibly on the fact that Boyer was gifted; Lamarr was not.

But by and large, with a few obvious exceptions like Garbo, Dietrich and later Ingrid Bergman, brought over from Sweden by David O. Selznick in 1938, foreign stars did not adjust all that well to Hollywood. What frequently happened was that an actor who could play a wide variety of roles in his own language was type-cast in English to one nationality or one type of role (more often the latter, since to most people in Hollywood European accents were interchangeable). Thus Bela Lugosi, who had been a famous (though one cannot help wondering if he was a very good) Hamlet in Hungary, never in Hollywood managed to break out of the mould his success as Dracula created for him. Much the same happened, less obviously perhaps, to many more distinguished émigrés. French women had to be kittenish (that, of course, was before they had to be 'mature'). Italians had to be tempestuous. And Germans, or any old Middle-Europeans for that matter, found themselves as the 1930s advanced inevitably cast as a variety of sneering Nazis: it happened to Paul Lukas in *Confessions of a Nazi Spy* (though he also played a 'good German' in Lillian Hellman's *Watch on the Rhine* on stage and in its film version), but before long it was happening to Conrad Veidt, Walter Slezak, Otto Preminger and many more.

Peter Lorre, who made his first Hollywood film in 1935, after the regulation period starring in Germany and France, might at first seem to be an example of Hollywood's limiting the potential of a European actor to a narrow range of conventionally foreign types. But his first big success, as the child murderer in Lang's *M*, was after all a freak role and his diminutive stature and strange, round, baby face would hardly seem to fit him for most principal roles in America or anywhere else. By a curious coincidence, his first two American pictures were both subjects that had been filmed before in Germany by Robert Wiene, the director of *Caligari*, *The Hands of Orlac* (called in its Hollywood version *Mad Love*) and *Crime and Punishment*. Both were directed by directors with Europeanized ideas about film-making, the cameraman Karl Freund for *Mad Love* and Josef von Sternberg for *Crime and Punishment,* and in both Lorre played obsessed, haunted characters not so far removed from the role in *M* that had made him famous. It took Hitchcock in England to see in Lorre the potentialities of unsmiling villainy (*The Man Who Knew Too Much*) or comical eccentricity (*Secret Agent*).

Back in Hollywood, he became immediately sidetracked, quite profitably, into a series of B features in which he played Mr Moto, a Japanese detective. A different sort of type-casting again took hold of his career in the 1940s, when his playing of a picturesque villain in *The Maltese Falcon* (1941) in which Sidney Greenstreet played a contrastingly picturesque villain, suggested to Warner Brothers the possibility of their similarly decorating corners of many films, separately or together. It is easy to say that Lorre's career would have been very different, and perhaps more uniformly distinguished, if he had been able to stay on in Germany. But he was such an obviously special case as an actor that it is hard to be sure.

5. Hollywood by the Back Door

In thinking of the Hollywood film industry and its possibilities for the émigré, we tend naturally to think primarily of the big studios and the feature film. But there were those who came to Hollywood and never had anything to do with Hollywood society and seldom if ever entered the gates of a big studio: some, like Dupont, gradually declined to Poverty Row, but many never managed to find work anywhere else. Edgar Ulmer, who had first come over as an assistant to Murnau on *Sunrise* and *Four Devils*, never rose higher in the scale of things than *The Black Cat*, a low-budget horror film for Universal starring Boris Karloff and Bela Lugosi: most of his forty-odd films as a director were the cheapest quickies, or made in New York in Yiddish or Ukrainian. Frank Wysbar (or Wisbar in the States) made a couple of the best German films of the Nazi period, *Anna und Elisabeth* (1933) and *Fährmann Maria* (1936) both strange supernatural subjects, before emigrating to the US in 1938. In Hollywood he worked almost exclusively for the poorest of all the Poverty Row outfits, PRC (Producers Releasing Corporation), making at least one supernatural classic, *The Strangler of the Swamp* (1945), and ran and presented an early television programme, *Fireside Theatre*.

Gustav Machaty, a Czech director who worked mainly in Germany and is remembered, if at all, for discovering Hedy Lamarr and directing her in *Extase*, with its notorious nude scene, followed much the same path to America with much the same results: one cult quickie called *Jealousy* (1945). Later still the Czech actor/director Hugo Haas, who escaped from Czechoslovakia in 1939 and France in 1940, made a bizarre corner for himself. Though he acted in the original Los Angeles production of Brecht's *Galileo*, he became best known for writing, starring in and directing during the 1950s a number of sensational B features, such as *Pickup* (1951), *One Girl's Confession* (1953) and *Bait* (1954), each co-starring some big-busted, usually blonde, 'discovery'.

All of these, no doubt, were the ones who lost out in their transition from fame in Europe to virtual nonentity in America. But not all aimed in any way at Hollywood success, even if they came to Hollywood to work and did have some functional connection with the movies. Two such were the Danish artist Kay Nielsen and the German Oskar Fischinger. The two could not be further apart in their artistic tastes or histories. Virtually all they had in common was that both arrived in Los Angeles in 1936 and both worked for Disney on sections of *Fantasia* (1940). Kay Nielsen had known his greatest fame in the 1920s as an illustrator, in a manner somewhat akin to Rackham and Dulac, of elaborate coloured gift-books, mostly fantastic or exotic in subject matter. He had also been, in Copenhagen, an important and influential stage designer, and it was with this in view that he was summoned to Los Angeles in 1936 to design a spectacular version of Hofmannsthal's *Everyman*, directed by a Reinhardt pupil, Johannes Poulson of the Royal Opera, Copenhagen, and offered at the Hollywood Bowl by the California Festival Association as a follow-up to Reinhardt's own *Midsummer Night's Dream* of two years before. That done, he was signed on by Disney, whose animation work at this period was much influenced by European fantasy illustrators (he tried, in vain, to tempt Arthur Rackham over to design for him).

N elsen seems to have worked away happily enough to Disney, turning out many of the visual ideas that the Disney Studios found so useful, alongside other artists of similar backgrounds and talents like the Swiss Albert Hurter. It seems that Nielsen was not always happy about the way his drawings were inevitably developed and distorted in the processes of animation, and he could at times be haughty as well as impractical. The major segment of a Disney film for which he received credit is the 'Night on Bald Mountain/Ave Maria' sequence of *Fantasia*, which was in preparation from 1938 to 1940. After it was finished Nielsen got a leave of absence before continuing with his next Disney project, one close to his heart, a film of Hans Christian Andersen's *The Little Mermaid*. But then the film was cancelled, and the rest of Nielsen's life in Los Angeles (where he died in 1957) was mostly a tale of neglect and poverty, his later illustrations unpublished, his great mural for a Los Angeles high school (1942) stripped from the wall and largely destroyed within a year owing to local politics.

Fischinger was a younger man than Nielsen (thirty-six when he came to Los Angeles, while Nielsen was fifty) and had a very different formation as an artist. His closest connections, personally and stylistically, were with the Bauhaus, and since he had started working on animated films in the early 1920s his work had always been, by preference, abstract. He had been able to turn his skills to commercial uses, however, notably in creating and animating the special effects for Lang's science fiction fantasy *Frau im Mond* (1928) and in making advertising films using various animation techniques. At the time the Nazis took over he had his own successful studio. But naturally he was somewhat suspect, since abstract art was declared degenerate and un-German. In 1935 he not only made a purely abstract film, *Composition in Blue*, but unwisely entered it unofficially in the Venice Festival, where it won the Grand Prix for a short. This made Fischinger more than ever *persona non grata* with the Nazis.

However, a copy of the film was taken to America by an agent, along with a commercial for Muratti cigarettes showing them marching along, and previewed to enthusiastic response. Someone from Paramount saw the preview and offered Fischinger a contract, which he instantly accepted, leaving Germany in February 1936. Like so many other artists used to working more or less by themselves, without outside interference, in Europe, Fischinger had terrible difficulties accommodating to the Hollywood factory system, complicated by the fact that Paramount, having once put him under contract to snatch him from the grasp of rival studios, really had no particular idea what to do with him. In any case, they were more taken with the cuteness and novelty of the marching cigarettes than the playful abstractions of *Composition in Blue*, and when they finally, after three months of idleness, assigned him to produce a novelty sequence for the low-budget revue film *Big Broadcast of 1938*, they soon made it clear that they did not want anything too abstract and, moreover, the film's budget did not allow for it to be in colour.

Fischinger did complete the sequence, belatedly and in colour, devised to a musical score by the Paramount staff composer, Ralph Rainger. But Paramount hated it; it was eliminated from the feature and shelved, and Fischinger's contract was politely but firmly not taken up. He had, for the moment, no other prospect of work, but he took his agent's advice that in Hollywood one must never seem to be in need of a job, as that was the one sure way of not getting one. He had a few friends in Los Angeles, including William Dieterle, and other contacts in the art world from back in Germany, among them the painter Lyonel Feininger, who had come back from Berlin (where he, equally, was being harassed by the Nazis as a decadent artist) in the summer of 1936 to teach at Mills College in Oakland. It was partly on the advice of Feininger that Fischinger began, for the first time, painting in oils.

Eventually, mainly through the good offices of Dieterle, Fischinger was offered a contract to make a novelty animated short for MGM. This time he was to be paid a flat fee and left completely to his own devices, making the film just as he wanted in his own studio and handing over the finished product to MGM for release in theatres; if it was successful more films might be commissioned on the same basis. The result was *An Optical Poem*, a seven-minute abstract made to Liszt's Second Hungarian Rhapsody (specially recorded by the MGM studio orchestra), which was well received by Metro and quite widely shown, achieving more success, naturally, with sophisticated urban audiences. Unfortunately, Fischinger's temper did not help his situation at this point: he got into a fight with an agent over the contractual arrangements for the film, and was jailed on charges of assault and battery, thereby confirming his not altogether undeserved reputation for being trouble. And when the animation department of MGM had a change of policy, favouring a more frankly popular approach to the cartoon film, Fischinger's option was not picked up.

In 1938 he went to New York and had a couple of successful shows of his paintings there, but came back to California in response to an offer from Disney that he should devise for the forthcoming 'concert film' *Fantasia* a sequence based on Stokowski's orchestral arrangement of Bach's Toccata and Fugue in D minor. Though Fischinger hoped that he would again be given a free hand, he found that, like Kay Nielsen, he was only contributing ideas to the general pool. The Disney studios might seem to be more artistically orientated than other Hollywood concerns, but their success was built on the same application of factory methods, and the individual artist had to be very much part of a team, his work subject to criticism and modification by the rest, in order to produce a consistent product that would meet the expectations summoned up in audiences by the Disney brand-name. Many of Fischinger's ideas did come through in the final film, though always drastically simplified (in accord with Disney's 'rules' about what audiences would and would not accept) and somewhat sentimentalized by the introduction of representational elements (outlines of musical instruments, clouds, shafts of sunlight) to give audiences something to hang on to. Fischinger's name does not appear on the credits of *Fantasia* (Nielsen's does), and he is not credited either for odd ideas that he contributed to *Pinocchio* and other Disney films of the time; now, it seems, Disney studios do not even have any record of his ever having worked for them.

This was not even quite the end of Fischinger's attempts to work through the channels of normal Hollywood film production. In 1941–2 he was employed by Orson Welles's Mercury Productions and then, when America entered the war and it became for a time illegal for 'enemy aliens' to be employed in the studios, by Welles personally, to work in some nebulous capacity on Welles's Pan-American episode film *It's All True*. But first the episode abstractly evoking the life and music of Louis Armstrong was dropped, then the whole film was scrapped and Mercury Productions disbanded. Fischinger continued to live in San Fernando Valley and work in Los Angeles for the rest of his life, in little studios on Sunset Strip and later in Westwood, near UCLA. He made more completely non-representational shorts on grants from the Guggenheim Foundation, did a number of commercials and worked on a dream sequence (not finally used) for Fritz Lang's *The Secret Beyond the Door* (1948); he even returned to science fiction special effects for the television series *Captain Midnight*.

And most of all, he became a sort of resident guru for the young avant-garde cinema that grew up on the West Coast in the 1940s. Though he had little to do with conventional Hollywood circles, he was a central figure in the artistic life of the community. Particularly productive were his friendship with the art dealer Galka Scheyer, the great proselyte of twentieth-century German painting in California, and his meetings through her with avant-garde composers, such as Edgar Varèse and John Cage. He also became involved in the study of various kinds of oriental mysticism then fashionable in Los Angeles, and gathered round him a group of student film-makers, among them Curtis Harrington, Kenneth Anger, Maya Deren and John and James Whitney (the only abstractionists of the group) who found in his detachment from Hollywood commerce an inspiration, and regarded him as their great living contact with the classic European avant-garde of the 1920s. By Hollywood standards his history was one of neglect and failure; but in terms of cultural interchange, receiving and transmitting influences and ideas, he probably had as much effect as any émigré on Los Angeles at large.

Most of the European figures who came to work in Hollywood in the 1930s had to cope, somehow, with being regarded, just because they were European, as a kind of special case. Some managed to play on this, assuming the airs of a visiting genius and seeing whether or not the gamble came off (if you raised expectations of that sort you had, sooner or later, to deliver something spectacular, as Lang most notably did). Others, like Litvak or Lorre, took the first opportunity of fading into the landscape and becoming accepted as a regular, workmanlike part of the Hollywood scene. But there were also those who came over with that intention from the outset. The producer Joe Pasternak, for instance. Though Hungarian-Jewish in origin, he had lived and worked for many years in America, and become an American citizen, before being sent back to run Universal's Berlin offices. With the arrival of the Nazis he moved the operation to Budapest, but determined that it was politic to keep the way back to Hollywood open. Early in 1936, in the last days of the veteran Carl Laemmle's rule at Universal, with its special friendliness towards Germans and Middle-Europeans, he took up a producer's contract in Hollywood and arrived with his favourite director, Henry Kosterlitz (soon shortened to Koster), whose complete ignorance of English he had carefully disguised.

Once there, with a new regime in charge, they soon found themselves in the same sort of position as Preminger at Fox, with some months to run on their contracts, but everything being done to force or ease them out. Not that either of them had any ambitions to make arty, European-styled films, or do anything other than what was popular and commercial—but all the same they were looked on with mistrust. Finally they managed to come up with a project, a lightweight musical comedy called *Three Smart Girls* (1936), and a new star, a thirteen-year-old singer called Deanna Durbin. The fact that she sang light classical music confirmed the studio's suspicions, but the film was inexpensively made and proved to be a big hit, thereby bearing out Pasternak's and Koster's assumptions that when it came to popular entertainment American taste was not so different from European after all. The follow-up, *100 Men and a Girl* (1937), was even bolder, in that it co-starred Deanna Durbin with Leopold Stokowski and featured (the '100 men' in question) a symphony orchestra put together from unemployed musicians, thus sneaking in some social comment about the Depression.

If this popularization of 'serious' music was found at the time more impressive than perhaps it really deserved, it was at least a straw in the wind. Pasternak himself went on to other things, proving along the way to be a good friend to many European residents and new arrivals, ranging from the writer Felix Joachimson (soon Jackson), who wrote several films for him and eventually married Deanna Durbin, to Marlene Dietrich, whose flagging career he revived by casting her against type as a brawling saloon-girl in *Destry Rides Again* (1939; script by Jackson, music by another émigré, Frederick Hollander; formerly Friedrich Hollaender). *100 Men and a Girl* spawned in its turn a whole series of films in which Hollywood, slightly self-conscious about its cultural deficiencies and very definitely aware of extensions in the tastes of its popular audience, began to flirt with classical music—though usually, it is true, forcing visiting classical musicians to end up playing or singing boogie-woogie in order to show that they were regular guys like the rest of us. Even so, culture, it seemed, was catching on.

Not that this alarming development made much difference to the lives of most of the important musicians who settled in Los Angeles during these first years of the exile. Arnold Schoenberg, for example, was never roped in to play boogie-woogie, and it is doubtful whether, for much of his time in Los Angeles, most of Hollywood knew he was there or would have been any the wiser had they been told. He had arrived in Los Angeles in September 1934, mainly because his health demanded a dry, warm climate. He and his wife were still on a visitor's visa, which strictly limited the length of their stay in America. But in the meanwhile he settled in a furnished house in Hollywood and began to take in private pupils, some of them already professional musicians in the Hollywood studios (including Hugo Fredhofer, David Raksin and Alfred Newman), and give lectures at the University of Southern California.

Schoenberg resumed his on-off friendship with Otto Klemperer, now conductor of the Los Angeles Philharmonic Orchestra (even though he reproached Klemperer for not playing his music often enough) and conducted a concert with the Philharmonic, which included his *Verklärte Nacht* and some of his Bach arrangements as well as a Brahms Symphony to sweeten the pill. Shortly after, in May 1935, Klemperer conducted the first performance of his new Suite for String Orchestra, a relatively unrevolutionary, tonal work that went down well. And he was beginning to be sought after by cultivated Los Angeles, which was becoming aware of his presence and invited him to broadcast and give public lectures, one of which, about the situation of émigrés, was significantly entitled 'Driven into Paradise'.

If Los Angeles was not unequivocally a paradise for Schoenberg, at least it was a very comfortable and agreeable place to live. His visa was renewed shortly before it would have expired, and in July 1935 he was offered a professorship of music at UCLA, for two years in the first instance, which paid him a living, if not princely, wage—$4,800 a year. He also began to get to know people in Los Angeles, mainly in two distinct but overlapping groups—the Germans and the musicians. Among the former his closest friends were the director William Dieterle and his wife Charlotte, for whom in 1935 he wrote a birthday canon based on the text 'One can think what one likes about Schoenberg.' Among the musicians he became (at first glance improbably) friendly with was George Gershwin, with whom he shared a passion for playing tennis.

Gershwin was in Hollywood in the summer of 1936 writing the score for the Fred Astaire/Ginger Rogers film *Shall We Dance?* Wanting to improve his grasp of musical technique, he asked a friend what he should do. The friend suggested he could not do better than take lessons with Schoenberg in the four-part fugue. It seems that he never actually did so, but out of his friendship with Schoenberg came his purchase of a private recording of Schoenberg's string quartets, as well as his sponsoring of a series of photographs of Schoenberg by the celebrated American photographer, Edward Weston. When Gershwin died unexpectedly of a brain tumour in 1937, Schoenberg was deeply grieved and spoke an obituary of him on radio as well as contributing to a memorial volume, in both of which he expressed his belief that Gershwin was a great musician.

It was through another Los Angeles friendship that Schoenberg had his only real taste of the very special world of Hollywood film-making. At the end of 1935 Irving Thalberg was preparing at MGM a film version of *The Good Earth*, Pearl Buck's novel about the life of Chinese peasants, to be cast, characteristically, with Paul Muni, originally an actor in the New York Yiddish theatre, and Luise Rainer, a recent import from Vienna, in the leads. One evening Thalberg, who was, as Hollywood producers went, a surprisingly cultivated and open-minded man, heard a radio performance of *Verklärte Nacht*, which Schoenberg had written nearly forty years earlier, while still in his tonal phase. The idea struck him that Schoenberg might be the man to write the score for his movie. He got his 'lieutenant', Albert Lewin, to mention it to the ubiquitous

Salka Viertel, who was then working at MGM on a script for Garbo about Marie Walewska. She pointed out tactfully that Schoenberg's recent music was very different, and no doubt far from what Thalberg might want, but at any rate she arranged a meeting.

Thalberg, exceptionally, was on time, in deference to the distinction of his visitor. Schoenberg, unexceptionally, was late; it transpired that by mistake he had been taken on a studio tour. Thalberg and Schoenberg got on very well, despite some little hitches, such as (according to Salka Viertel's very circumstantial and perhaps embellished account of the meeting) Schoenberg's insistence on having complete control of the soundtrack and that the dialogue should be delivered in a highly stylized *sprechstimme*, as in his earlier classic *Pierrot Lunaire* (duly reproduced by Mrs Viertel for Thalberg's dubious attention). However, negotiations were not instantly broken off, and Schoenberg did go so far as to sketch a few themes (tonal, approachable and probably quite acceptable to Thalberg's taste, for Schoenberg was by no means so much of an impractical idealist as he has been painted), but finally the project foundered on Schoenberg's requested fee, $50,000, which was about twice what the studio was willing to pay. With some relief Schoenberg returned to his teaching and composing, and a few months later Thalberg was dead, aged only 37.

This was not quite Schoenberg's only prospect of working in Hollywood movies. William Dieterle, for some years a successful jack of all trades as director at Warners, was now planning to do something of his own—a screen biography. Among various subjects proposed, his choice fell on Beethoven, and he immediately concluded that Schoenberg would be the ideal musical adviser and arranger. Schoenberg thought about it for a month or so, but finally decided that he could not undertake the job all by himself: he suggested Klemperer instead, and offered himself to advise Klemperer on details of style and composition. In the event the film was never made, but Dieterle was to establish himself in the next few years as a master of screen biography with such popular films as *The Life of Emile Zola* (1937) and *Juarez* (1939). He even, eventually, made a musical biography, of Wagner (called *Magic Fire*), but that was not until 1956, five years after Schoenberg's death.

In 1936 Schoenberg felt sufficiently at home in Los Angeles to consider building himself a house. What he would really like, he decided, was something in the style (rather fin-de-siècle, with lots of marble) of his Viennese friend, the architect Adolf Loos.

However, he did discuss the possibility with Richard Neutra, who at least had the right sort of training and background. 'He also appears to be of Loos' circle,' Schoenberg wrote to Alma Mahler-Werfel, 'and does very nice houses, even if a bit more doctrinaire than Loos, more studied, and not uninfluenced by Bauhaus principles. Still, anyway, he has Viennese taste and knows what a scribe needs.' Before the idea could come to anything, he changed his mind when he and his wife found a suitable, vaguely Spanish-Colonial house in the western suburb of Brentwood Park, a refined, still rather countrified area, which was not too expensive, and not far from his teaching at UCLA.

At the beginning of 1937 there was a series of chamber concerts at UCLA, financed by Schoenberg's principal American patron, Mrs Elisabeth Sprague-Coolidge, at which all his string quartets were performed, climaxing with the world premiere of the fourth. And as if to prove that Hollywood was not all bad, Schoenberg's pupil Alfred Newman, who was musical director for United Artists at the Goldwyn Studio, took the opportunity to make private-issue recordings of all four quartets at the studio: using all the company's recording facilities, with the blessing of Sam Goldwyn himself. In February Schoenberg's early orchestral tone poem *Pelléas and Mélisande* was performed in Los Angeles, himself conducting, by the Federal Music Project Symphony Orchestra, a body formed of out-of-work musicians—a curious indication that Joe Pasternak's contemporary *100 Men and a Girl* was no wild fantasy (though it would be a bit much to expect an orchestra conducted by Stokowski in a Deanna Durbin film to play Schoenberg, even early Schoenberg).

Schoenberg's workload at UCLA was getting heavier and heavier, his classes bigger and bigger, so that he found he was getting insufficient time for composition. Also he retained his poor opinion of culture in Los Angeles, feeling that the standards were, by European criteria at least, painfully low, though he made exception of a few of his friends, such as the Dieterles. And after the invasion of Austria he felt compelled to advise his son-in-law Felix Greissle, who had just arrived in New York, not to come to Los Angeles as the prospects of work for musicians were very grim. But for all his troubles, in a curious way Schoenberg had become part of the life of Los Angeles—that part of it, or one of those parts of it, which had little or nothing to do with Hollywood except as a geographical location. In this, up to 1940, he was rather a solitary and exceptional figure. But with the war in Europe all that soon changed.

Though Schoenberg was far and away the most important composer to settle in Los Angeles in the 1930s, he was by no means the only one. Most of the others were attracted at least in part by the possibilities of making a living somehow in connection with the movies, and some surprising people did dabble. Few of them, of course, wrote in a style as inaccessible as Schoenberg's to the average Hollywood producer. Ernst Toch, for example, who was to spend many years as a professor at the University of Southern California, his prestige in academic circles little less than Schoenberg's own, was stylistically very approachable.

Toch had left Germany in 1933, and stopped off first in England, where he made immediate contact with the émigré community and contrived to do his first film scores for Korda, on *Catherine the Great* (1934) (starring one émigré, Elisabeth Bergner, and directed by another, her husband Paul Czinner) and *The Private Life of Don Juan* (1934). He also wrote the music for Berthold Viertel's film *Little Friend* (1934), scripted by Christopher Isherwood. His first work on his arrival in America, to teach in New York, was an orchestral fantasy based on the chimes of *Big Ben*, which was, perhaps not coincidentally, the trademark of Korda's London Films. It was a popular introduction to his music for American audiences, and was followed by an overture suggested by *Pinocchio*, the first performance of which, by the Los Angeles Philharmonic under Klemperer, conveniently coincided with his arrival in Los Angeles in December 1936. As a film composer he worked for Paramount from 1936 to 1940, then for Columbia till 1944. Paramount in particular seems to have been proud of its catch: he was generally credited, grandly, as 'Dr Ernst Toch', which makes it the more ironical that he usually worked on such improbable films as the Bob Hope vehicles *The Cat and the Canary* and *The Ghost Breakers*.

At least Toch managed to find a more comfortable niche in Hollywood than Ernst Krenek, another distinguished German composer eventually to make his home in Los Angeles. Krenek, though unimpeachably Aryan, had come under attack from the Nazis as 'decadent', partly for his toying with a 'jazz' idiom in his widely successful opera *Jonny Spielt Auf* (1927), partly for his later adherence to the school of Schoenberg and strict twelve-tone composition. In 1938 he left Germany to settle permanently in America. One of the first places he went to, to get the lie of the land, was Los Angeles. The modernist American composer George

Antheil, who knew him from Europe, was at that time working for Paramount in Hollywood, and determined to try and get Krenek work, so he and Ben Hecht went to see Goldwyn. As Antheil tells it in his autobiography, Goldwyn had never heard of *Jonny Spielt Auf* or Krenek, but began to respond a bit when Hecht added optimistically that of course Krenek's *Rosenkavalier* was a big hit. Antheil, taking his cue, claimed that really *Faust* was bigger. Hecht then unfortunately topped it by saying that *La Traviata* was his biggest. Goldwyn responded: 'So he wrote *La Traviata* did he! Just bring that guy around here so's I can get my hands on him. Why, his publishers almost ruined me with a suit just because we used a few bars of that lousy opera. We had to retake half of the picture for a few lousy bars.' Whether or not the story is apocryphal, Krenek retreated to teach at Vassar on the East Coast; he never worked for a Hollywood company, and did not return to Los Angeles to live until 1947.

But to set against these stories of those who never did fit into Hollywood there is at least one spectacular story of émigré success. Erich Wolfgang Korngold was, in fact, a spectacular success from amazingly early in his life. He was a famous child prodigy; son of one of Vienna's leading music critics, he began composing at the age of seven, was pronounced a genius by Mahler at the age of ten, and by the time he was eleven his first major work, a ballet mime-drama called *Der Schneemann*, was staged at the Vienna Court Opera and in dozens of theatres elsewhere. When he was sixteen he composed two one-act operas, one comic, *The Ring of Polycrates*, and the other, *Violanta*, a romantic drama. They were both performed all over Europe, and *Violanta* was even produced at the New York Metropolitan Opera House in 1927. His most famous works, the incidental music to *Much Ado About Nothing*, later turned into an orchestral suite, and the opera *Die Tote Stadt* (*The Dead City*) followed in 1919–20, when he was in his early twenties. *Die Tote Stadt* was also staged at the Metropolitan, and in opera houses all over the world.

In 1927 Korngold was called in by Max Reinhardt to rearrange the music of the Johann Strauss operetta *Die Fledermaus* for Reinhardt's substantially reworked new staging. In 1929 he selected and arranged the music for a fictionalized life story of the Strausses called originally *Waltzes from Vienna* (under which title it was filmed by Hitchcock in 1933) and later, in a revised version for the New York stage, *The Great Waltz*. As a composer, arranger, conductor and teacher (at the Academy of Music, Vienna) he was one of the most prominent figures in Viennese musical life, all by his early thirties. Then in 1934 his old collaborator Reinhardt invited him to America to arrange and supervise the Mendelssohn incidental music for his lavish film version of *A Midsummer Night's Dream*. This was in fact a larger job than it might seem; it involved providing from Mendelssohn material an almost continuous score, which Korngold, with Reinhardt's encouragement, set out to treat operatically.

It was Korngold's first visit to America; he came with his wife and two sons, settled in Hollywood for six months, and enjoyed it thoroughly. He came as a European celebrity in a way that no other composer for films managed to do, and Reinhardt saw to it that he had responsibilities in the film more far-reaching than any composer had before. As he later described the process:

> For this production I had to make preliminary recordings, the so-called playbacks, of Mendelssohn's Scherzo and Nocturne [used in balletic interludes choreographed by Nijinska] which were relayed over huge loudspeakers during the actual filming. Further, I conducted an orchestra on stage for complicated, simultaneous 'takes', and lastly, after the film was cut, I conducted a number of music pieces which were inserted into the completed picture as background music. In addition, I had to invent a new method, which was a combination of all three techniques, for the music that accompanied the spoken word. I wrote the music in advance, conducted—without orchestra—the actor on the stage in order to make him speak his lines in the required rhythm, and then, sometimes weeks later, guided by earphones, I recorded the orchestral part.

The film, of course, was not much of a success for Warner Brothers, but they seem to have been very impressed with Korngold—presumably because he was so thoroughly professional in his working methods, was personally very approachable and, though an internationally famous composer, still wrote in a tonal, lushly romantic style, with melodies any layman could appreciate. And, always a useful way of impressing Hollywood producers, he very evidently did not need them. After his special assignment in Hollywood he went straight back to Vienna to take up his teaching again and complete a new opera, *Die Kathrin*. There was no reason he should ever come back, unless he was specially tempted. In fact, within four months Paramount came up with a temptation. They were looking for a vehicle for their two newly acquired opera stars,

Gladys Swarthout and Jan Kiepura (this was at much the same time that Fox had Lawrence Tibbett, RKO had Lily Pons and for a few months Hollywood thought that any or all of them might become movie stars), and asked Korngold to collaborate with Oscar Hammerstein on an original screen operetta, *Give Us This Night* (1936).

Though the musical part of this was well served, the film otherwise had little to recommend it. Korngold was somewhat disillusioned by the changes (for the worse) the script underwent in the course of production, and felt that he had not been able to exercise as much control as he would wish over the film as a whole. But it was no doubt a salutary experience, since it gave him warning of how to deal with Warner Brothers' offer of a contract to write film music exclusively for them. He began by refusing completely and avoiding their phone calls. Then he agreed at least to see the film they wanted him immediately to score, a costume picture starring Errol Flynn, called *Captain Blood*. This was, in fact, exactly the kind of full-blooded romantic subject that appealed to him. So he agreed to write the score for that film only, and see how it went. He then discovered that he had to write the whole thing in three weeks, and so had to use an orchestrator for the first time and use some Liszt for one action scene that he did not have time to compose himself. All the same, he managed to write a score considerably more complex and elaborate than any written for Hollywood films up to that time, with a thoroughgoing use of Wagnerian leitmotif and a fund of late Romantic melody such as could only be matched by Puccini.

The film was enormously popular and began a whole series of swashbuckling epics with Errol Flynn at Warners, who were now moving away from their early-1930s image of gritty realism and anti-romantic toughness (not to mention penny-pinching on everything but Busby Berkeley). It was the ideal sort of situation for the deployment of Korngold's expensive, conservative talents. But he still fought shy of a long-term contract, and continued working from film to film. He did a bit on the black musical folk-play *Green Pastures*, which taught him a lesson about racial prejudice in Hollywood when he discovered that even the stars of the film could not eat at the Warners commissary, but had to go to the cafeteria instead. Then he was shown *Anthony Adverse* (1936), another epic costume romance, and was excited by its 'operatic' possibilities in the same way as he had been with *Captain Blood*. Given more time with this one, he composed one of the screen's most copious scores—rather too copious by modern tastes, in that there is an almost continuous wash of sound on the track, underpinning all the dialogue, and surging to the forefront in a succession of mini-climaxes whenever there is no speech. It is, in fact, exactly as though this is a screen opera with the words spoken instead of sung, but all intimately related to the music, which was carefully written just below the pitch of the actors' voices and taking into detailed account the rhythms and timing of the dialogue.

Anthony Adverse won Korngold an Oscar (though for some time he did not get it, as Oscars then went to the music department, not to the actual composer) and confirmed him as Hollywood's great composer-in-residence. Except that he still refused to regard himself as a resident, contracted only for one film (of his choice) at a time, and continued to heed his father's warnings from Vienna about the danger and indignity of being regarded as (let alone being) primarily a film composer.

Towards the end of 1937, after nearly two years in Los Angeles and taking the first steps to become an American citizen, Korngold went back to Vienna to prepare the premiere of his opera *Die Kathrin*. But delay followed delay—the star, Richard Tauber, and the conductor, Bruno Walter, would not be available until October—and finally, after the Anschluss in March 1938, the Nazis banned its performance altogether. Korngold meanwhile had headed gratefully back to California, partly using as an excuse the need of his younger son for a warm climate, and finally resolved to settle in Los Angeles and take up the contract Warners had so long and eagerly pressed him to.

But it was a contract unlike any other ever given to a composer in Hollywood. He insisted that in exchange for his large salary he should have an absolutely free choice of what films he would compose (not more than two a year in any event) and could refuse anything he considered unsuitable. He would also have a generous allotment of time to write his scores, would have complete control over the musical side of the films, and would retain copyright in his own music (which usually went automatically to the studio) so that he could re-use it in any way he wished. Many of his later concert works, such as his Violin Concerto and his Symphony, were in fact based on material from his film scores. And, he got billing no other composer had ever had, including a complete frame of the credits to himself—at that time most uncommon—and mention on every poster on which the director of the film was mentioned.

Satisfied with these terms, he bought a house, in the hills near Toluca Lake a short walk from Warners' Studios, and settled down to await an assignment he deemed suitable.

The first film he was offered was another swashbuckler, *The Adventures of Robin Hood*, which like *Captain Blood* starred Errol Flynn and was directed by Michael Curtiz. It sounded ideal, but Korngold turned it down because he felt it had too much action and too little dialogue for him to be able to compose a fitting score in the seven weeks allotted. However, the head of the music department talked him into it, by agreeing he could work week-to-week, and if at any point he wanted to withdraw someone else would complete it. This conversation took place on 12 February 1938, the day the Austrian Chancellor Schuschnigg had the meeting with Hitler that paved the way for the Nazi invasion of Austria. By the time Korngold had completed the score the Anschluss had taken place, and his property in Vienna had been confiscated; fortunately he had followed the advice of friends in Austria (for he himself seems to have had little political awareness) and had already got his parents and brother out and to America.

Despite Korngold's misgivings, *Robin Hood* (1938) turned out to be one of his best scores, an indication that he had found his ideal niche in the world in Hollywood, which musically was about fifty years behind the times and dramatically was still capable of cultivating the Edwardian world of Anthony Hope and the Baroness Orczy. This was very much Korngold's own imaginative world: oddly, for a man just forty at this time, he was composing in such an old-fashioned style that he might have been Schoenberg's father, when chronologically he could have been Schoenberg's son. This is not to dismiss Korngold's talents, which were in their way considerable. But he did belong to an almost extinct species, and it is hard to imagine his flourishing equally anywhere else in the musical world at that time—certainly as composer. Even in Hollywood there were signs of changing ways, of sparer, less lush scores and a discreet use of silence and natural sound in films. But for the moment, as long as Warners were doing big historical subjects like *Juarez* (directed by William Dieterle, incidentally), *The Private Lives of Elizabeth and Essex* and *The Sea Hawk*, he was the obvious person to add a musical dimension.

And he was treated very well; at this period he wrote of Warners:

I feel very happy as an artist here. No one tells me what to do. I do not feel part of a factory. I take part in story conferences, suggest changes in the editing when it is dramatically necessary to coincide with the musical structure. It is entirely up to me to decide where in the picture to put music. But I always consult thoroughly with the music chief... I also keep the producer well informed and always secure his consent for my musical intentions first. But in none of my pictures have I ever 'played' my music first to either the music chief, the director, or the producer. And the studio heads never make the acquaintance of my music until the day of the sneak preview...

One can hardly imagine any other of Hollywood's resident composers being given quite so much freedom, or fitting in so well. No doubt the secret, as so often in Hollywood, was in the image: Korngold was exactly Hollywood's idea of what a great composer ought to be, as though he had been sent round to fill the role from Central Casting. But a great composer who was human, humorous and eminently workmanlike; who intimidated the philistine studio bosses just enough, but not too much. Only natural then that among the émigré musicians, in Hollywood's own terms Korngold reigned supreme.

6. Out in the Midday Sun

Now the English in Hollywood were something else again. Most seem to have succumbed at least to the physical attractions of the place. Thus, for instance, John Galsworthy described staying at San Ysidro, later to be Ronald Colman's ranch, near Santa Barbara:

> How beautiful! when the wood smoke goes up straight and the pepper trees stand unstirring, and behind the screen of tall Eucalyptus trees, the fallen sun glows, a long slow fire over the sea, and the lavender colour mist rises between. How beautiful the mountains, behind us, remote in the late light, a little unearthly! The loveliness of these evenings moves the heart; and of the mornings, shining, cool, fragrant. There is something in it all of that dream as of Paradise...

On the other hand, Hugh Walpole, on his second trip to Los Angeles in 1935, saw another side too. After describing his impressions of the big new MGM musical *Broadway Melody*, previewed the previous evening, he confided to his journal:

> In Hollywood itself...nothing else is talked about, morning and night, but this and similar efforts. No wars, no politics, no deaths, make any effect here. We are all on a raft together in the middle of the cinema sea! The unreality is partly from this, but also from America itself. America (where I am always very happy) has a hollow inside itself. Go a little way down and you find nothing. Death itself is quite unreal. On Friday as reported in the paper there were, in Los Angeles alone, three suicides, six deaths from motor crashes, two murders. Nobody cares. The nice Chief of Police at M.G.M of last year, Ellinger, was murdered just outside M.G.M. gates last December by a jealous lover of his girl. No one cares. Will Rogers's death roused a tempest of sentiment, fine speeches, regrets, all genuine. In a week he will be completely forgotten. Nothing is real here but salaries.

Admittedly, Walpole was writing at a very tense time, with Mussolini invading Abyssinia and things getting worse in Central Europe, which presumably meant more to Walpole than to most inhabitants of Southern California. But that, in a way, was the point. Los Angeles was a place in the sun, away from it all. But did not one feel, perhaps, a little guilty about enjoying it so much? And could one not, all too easily, see through it? Constance Collier, an English actress who, after a distinguished stage career on both sides of the Atlantic, was then on the threshold of a profitable new career as a character actress in Hollywood, remarked to Walpole shortly afterwards:

Hugh, this place is just like Donington Hall. When the German prisoners first went there they were amazed by its splendour and beauty. 'Aren't the English fools!' they said. 'Why, it's better to be prisoner than free.' Then after walking in the grounds for a few days they discovered the barbed wire. A month later all they did was to walk on the same track up to the barbed wire and back again.

Walpole admitted freely to enjoying the splendour and the beauty—not to mention the luxury and the sheer silliness—but at the same time felt that he had discovered the barbed wire. When he left he told a friend:

This place is making me lazier and lazier. It isn't a good sort of laziness in which you recuperate, but a bad sort in which your character becomes weaker and weaker and you care less and less whether you do anything properly or not. I've just been telling John Collier that he'll be completely and utterly damned, body and soul, if he stays here much longer, but he tells me that he wants to be damned and is longing to know what it's like.

Not all Los Angeles lotus-eaters were so aware of the situation or so disturbed by it. If, indeed, it was true for everybody. Some, like Galsworthy or H. G. Wells, who just came for a visit in the process of seeing the world, seem to have found the Los Angeles experience idyllic. But among those who actually settled and lived for some years in Los Angeles, the British seem in general to have been about the most readily acclimatized. Naturally, the language situation helped. And then there was the peculiar nature of British acclimatization. For though the British mixed very freely with the rest of Hollywood society, they seemed also able to retain a certain separateness from it. Everybody was always conscious they were

English, even if they did not necessarily cling together in a coherent national group. Their bearing often seems, from contemporary accounts, to have been—without any offence meant or on the whole any taken—that of colonialists in some far-flung part of the empire, retaining from the old country their interests, their sports, their normal patterns of life, however inappropriate they may have been to the new circumstances.

Arrogance or insecurity? A little of both, perhaps. And also, maybe, a businesslike appreciation of the advantages of their own exoticism. The accent, for instance, was a readily saleable commodity, and therefore something to be kept up. Artur Rubinstein noted of Ronald Colman, a friend for many years: 'I admired his beautiful English speech, his beautiful accent. It became better and more marked with time instead of becoming Americanized, which was rather characteristic in some other Englishmen in Hollywood.' Much the same was true of many English actors, whether there was any obvious professional reason for it or not. Chaplin's accent never became Americanized (and of course he never became an American citizen), even though he remained silent on screen longer than anyone else. And an English accent did not seem necessarily to confine an actor to specifically English roles, though some, like C. Aubrey Smith, founder of the Hollywood cricket club, made a special corner in odd Englishness (in his case crusty English colonel characters). But neither Ronald Colman nor David Niven (at one time groomed by Goldwyn as a replacement for Colman) was ever exactly strangled by the old school tie professionally, even though they never shed their English accents to the extent that, say, Cary Grant or Ray Milland did. And how often did anyone remember that Boris Karloff (real name: William Henry Pratt) was unmistakably, even absurdly English till the day he died?

Of course, the accent was frequently an important part of the reason that the British were there in the first place. Hardly in the case of, say, Charles Chaplin or Stan Laurel, and it is always surprising to realize that two of the most famous English gentlemen of the screen, Ronald Colman and Clive Brook, were very well established silent stars long before cinemagoers had learnt that they sounded as gentlemanly as they looked. But the coming of sound was certainly the signal for a major influx of stage-trained English actors, and around 1934, when well-upholstered versions of English classics became the vogue, there were even more, some quickly in and out,

some to stay. Obviously the production of a film like the Cukor/
Selznick *David Copperfield* (1935) provided a field day for British
actors. In that specific instance one need only look down the cast list
to see Freddie Bartholomew, Maureen O'Sullivan, Frank Lawton,
Elizabeth Allan, Roland Young, Basil Rathbone, Elsa Lanchester,
Hugh Williams, Jean Cadell—not to mention Charles Laughton,
first cast as Micawber then replaced by W. C. Fields, and the
scriptwriter Hugh Walpole, roped in to play the small part of the
vicar. And there were many other films in the 1930s that drew, if not
quite so heavily, on the reserves of English actors in Hollywood.

It might be wondered how much of a separate identity the English
colony really kept. In some circles they appear to have remained
very much apart. Not only the relatively eccentric areas of
Hollywood cricket teams, or the annual public school dinner,
chaired by C. Aubrey Smith (Winchester) and featuring such others
as John Loder (the only Etonian, he grandly notes in his
autobiography), Herbert Marshall and H. B. Warner. But
friendships from the old country naturally tended to continue and be
augmented by others along the same lines. There was Ronald
Colman's famous tennis set, which was about half British, half
American, including such as Clive Brook, Percy Marmont and
Ernest Torrence, along with William Powell, Richard Barthelmess
and Tim McCoy—all of them brought together by a shared passion
for tennis and poker, and later, at the urging of William Powell and
Richard Barthelmess, water-skiing as well.

The tastes of most of the British film colony seem indeed, as one
might expect, to have been pretty hearty, extrovert and even
philistine—much the same as their American fellows. At any rate,
British observers would expect this; Americans perhaps not so
much. The accent and the European background tended to do
strange things to American expectations. Maurice Chevalier recalled
his first night on board ship on his way to a Hollywood contract like
this:

> I put on a dinner-jacket, for I was to dine in magnificence at the
> Captain's table, there to meet the most distinguished of his
> passengers and, presumably, to enjoy sophisticated conversation.
> 'Sophisticated' and 'sophistication' were words which were to
> haunt me from now on. We were sophisticates to a man, it
> seemed, we Latin types from Paris. Actually, the term was double
> Dutch to me and I had to have it explained, but you couldn't let
> the public down and for the future, to prevent disappointment, I

should certainly have to dispense sophistication by the ton. To do so was foreign to my nature, but by this time much else was going on that was foreign to my nature and I saw no likelihood of ever being able to halt the glamorous, perilous enterprise of it all.

Of course, a large part of the sophistication of a 'Latin type from Paris' was expected to be sexual, and there the English did not have to compete (unless they actually wanted to). The English were expected to be sophisticated in a different way—elegant, epigrammatic, a bit eccentric, very correct, impeccably educated. Useless to point out that only a few of them qualified for admission to the public school dinner, and their backgrounds were as varied as those of the Americans around them. The stereotype was always going to be more potent than the exception immediately within Hollywood's field of observation.

True, Ronald Colman had one of the most extensive libraries in Hollywood as well as his abiding passion for sports—and true also that at certain times in his life, before his second marriage, to another British émigré, Benita Hume, in 1938, he was quite a ladies' man. But the dreamy idealist stereotype (embodied definitively in his role as Robert Conway, the man selected to preserve civilization for posterity in *Lost Horizon*) always seems to have taken precedence, even for those who knew him well. Much the same was true, if anything even more so, for a regular visitor to Hollywood throughout the 1930s—Leslie Howard. In life he was a strange combination of the mean and the feckless, passionately fascinated by horses and, though very articulate, nothing at all of an intellectual or a scholar; he was also so orthodox in his Jewish faith that he would never work on the sabbath, something virtually unheard of in the Hollywood Jewish colony. And yet on screen and stage he always projected—and was required to project—the perfect image of the WASP thinker and scholar.

Moreover, he loved Hollywood because of its climate, being as passionate a sun-worshipper as anyone there. This was a common English taste, at a time when it was only just becoming fashionable for native Americans, so the English were always likely to be foremost in any open-air activity, even if it was only drinking by one of the innumerable Hollywood pools. Few of them seem to have stopped, as Hugh Walpole did, to consider whether, agreeable as this might be, it was not also perhaps debilitating. Few of them indeed, one is tempted to say, ever seem to have had much thought in their heads at all. Clive Brook, who had arrived a week before Ronald

Colman in 1923, and had a rather similar career playing a succession of handsome leading men, appears to have shared some of Colman's initial doubts. In 1926, in a *Photoplay* interview, Colman said:

> Hollywood is the most physical city in the world. I don't mean sex alone. Take athletics. They all go in for them. Fine things, of course, but entirely physical. And they all have motor cars and extreme luxury. Their homes are burdened down with it. I love California, its beauty, and its warmth, its color, but it is almost impossible not to lose perspective out there. There is something of the tropics about it, I suppose. When I finish a picture or whenever I can get a vacation, I go away. Down to the sea, usually, but at any rate to some wild spot where I can be alone.

Brook, to judge by an interview he gave in 1933, seems to have felt this even more strongly:

> Hollywood is a chain gang, and we movie actors never escape. We never became fugitives from the chain gang. It isn't because we can't be. We lose the will to escape. The links of our chains are forged not of cruelties, but of our luxuries. The chain gang of Hollywood knows satiety, not starvation. We are pelted with orchids and roses, not nails and lashes. We are underworked, not overworked. We are overpaid, not underpaid.

But then he really was the ideal strait-laced British family man (even in Hollywood, scandal town *par excellence*, there was never any breath of scandal about him), and in 1934, suiting his action to his words, he went back to England for good.

Few others felt so strongly or were so determined. Unless they were willing to see things strictly in terms of 'take the money and run', they tended—the actors at least—to be seduced by the place and stay on and on. As a rule there were perfectly valid professional reasons for this. What would the C. Aubrey Smiths or the Nigel Bruces, with their carefully preserved collection of *echt*-English mannerisms ready to be paraded for American tastes in such things, have found to do so often or so lucratively in Britain, where they would have been anachronisms at best? And as long as less exotic actors found plenty of work in Hollywood, why should they go anywhere else? Not to mention those, like Cary Grant (arrived 1932) or Ray Milland (arrived 1931) whose Englishness was neither here nor there, since they so rapidly adapted to playing American roles, and if anything gained in popularity (and certainly general usefulness) thereby.

The degree of residual Britishness beneath the manner was to be tested in 1939, when Britain entered the war. Until then, though, things were fairly plain sailing for the British in Los Angeles. They could, if they wished, join the British clique. Cedric Hardwicke, arriving in 1934, noted that, 'As a recruit to the English colony, whose members kept the flag flying and poured tea each afternoon at four, I paid my due respects to C. Aubrey Smith, the senior member of the colony, whose craggy manner suggested that he had just completed a ceremonial tour of all four corners of Queen Victoria's empire.' But though obviously the British would be as likely to know one another as to know anybody else, it is hard to resist the conclusion that the British colony as something coherent, consistent and close-knit was largely a Hollywood fantasy, an image it was amusing to project, that made good copy.

I myself recall in 1977 being contacted by a British journalist in Los Angeles for a few days who wanted to write a story about the British colony of cricket-players and afternoon tea-drinkers. I told him that if it ever existed I thought by then it had literally died, since one could hardly imagine the new generation of ex-Beatles and Stones and other tax-exiles of the Rock scene keeping it all up. I pointed him towards a couple of Swinging London shops and strictly-for-tourists English pubs in Santa Monica, and gave him introductions to one or two aged British survivors, and left him to his own devices. All the same, in due course the expected story about the colonialist English on whom the sun never sets appeared, culled, as far as I could tell, from files of 1930s fan magazines rather than from any actual experience.

One often feels that those stories themselves owed more to vivid journalistic imagination than to life. The *Christian Science Monitor* came up in June 1936 with a classic statement of the stereotype:

British customs notoriously prevail among the British colony. Speaking a language which at least approximates that of the Americans, they maintain a stricter aloofness than do most other nationalities, are harder to absorb, even after years. Several English cake shops exist and cater almost exclusively to English trade. Once a year, on New Year's Eve, the principal members of the British colony gather at a Hollywood café to hear the bells of Big Ben ring out over the radio...

Which all sounds very neat and tidy. But look a little closer and you find odd contradictions. The famous Hollywood Cricket Club certainly did exist, and C. Aubrey Smith and Boris Karloff (close friends anyway) were certainly its stalwarts (Karloff even had the tyre cover of his Ford emblazoned with its insignia). But beyond that it is curiously difficult to find out who actually belonged: Ronald Colman and Clive Brook, people say automatically, and yet Karloff told me he scarcely knew Colman and never to his knowledge met Brook at all. And though in certain respects he led a very 'English' sort of life during his Hollywood years (in a Mexican-style hacienda in Coldwater Canyon), surrounded by dogs, eating mostly English food and lovingly tending his garden, he pooh-poohed the idea that the English stuck together in any noticeable way. Most of his friends and day-to-day contacts were in fact American, and except for the Sunday cricket matches he had little to do with the other English.

The English writer R. J. Minney, in Hollywood briefly in 1934, to script *Clive of India* (a Ronald Colman vehicle, of course), describes an evening that he implies was fairly typical:

> We found at Sydney Howard's a whirr of English voices, dominated by Sydney's own insinuating Yorkshire accent which sweeps along the scales like a scenic railway. The English colony is so large that the Americans have been provoked into reviving their forgotten War of Independence sentiment in a song entitled 'The British are Coming. Bang! Bang!'
> Heather Angel arrived with Ralph Forbes. They had eloped over the week-end and got married at Yuma. Frank Lawton came with Evelyn Laye. She had arrived that very morning from England. He was in side-whiskers, freshly grown for his part in *David Copperfield*. Actors here go about with all the face fungus they need for their screen roles. Elsa Lanchester was without her husband, Charles Laughton: he was ill in hospital, and when I saw him some weeks later, looked like a filleted edition of Mr. Barrett of Wimpole Street. Boris Karloff came and talked to me. Anyone more unlike a monster it would be difficult to conceive. He isn't even Russian. His name is Pratt; he's an Englishman. One of his brothers, Sir John Pratt, is in the Foreign office. Another brother was a magistrate in Bombay and had Gandhi sent up for trial. His niece Gillian Lind played the role of Lady Clive in London...

And so on, all fulfilling the conventional image. Except that elsewhere in his book, *Hollywood by Starlight*, Minney seems to see little or nothing of this English colony, though he does see quite a bit of Ronald Colman in connection with the movie and does from time to time run into Hugh Walpole.

Nor did Walpole himself stick at all closely to the English when he was out in Hollywood. One gets the impression that as a novelist, even a popular novelist, he counted as enough of an intellectual to be suspect in the eyes of most of the British, while for his part, being more interested in buying books and pictures than in horse-racing, he just did not naturally make accidental contact with them so often. Edgar Wallace, now, had been a different kettle of fish. Even if he wrote books, he was the sort of chap Hollywood could get on with: mad about horse-racing and gambling, no arty-tarty European pretensions (he told a Hollywood interviewer on his arrival: 'A highbrow is a man who has found something more interesting than a woman'), and an amazingly fast worker. As he remarked in an early letter home, 'I believe if I get past with my quick work I shall make a lot of money, always providing they don't get scared by the very rapidity of the work and spend six months talking it over before they shoot.' Since his screen stories ('I never do more than one story a week') included *The Beast*, which became *King Kong*, and the original outline script for *Tarzan the Ape Man*, evidently he more than got by. Unfortunately, he died unexpectedly from diabetic complications within ten weeks of his arrival in Hollywood, already the most successfully assimilated of all visiting English authors.

But if this whirlwind career was in marked contrast to the Hollywood months of Hugh Walpole, the underlying principle was the same: making an impression, projecting an image, demonstrating early on that you can do the work. Naturally the image Wallace projected—a man very much at home in the world of sports, in the theatre, in journalism—was very different from that projected by Walpole—rather prim and old-maidish, or at any rate donnish, a relatively highbrow author, the last person anyone might expect to enjoy Hollywood or be able to function in it. Of course, Walpole had another stereotypical British characteristic—of being a lot tougher and more practical than he looked: his Hollywood career was a sort of *Destry Rides Again* scenario, and Hollywood loved it.

Although he and Wallace were both there largely at the behest of Selznick, perhaps it was fortunate that Walpole did not have to deal with one of the smaller, cheaper studios like RKO, where Selznick was at the time Wallace worked for him. (Selznick was then so relatively unimportant that Wallace never manages in the whole of his *Hollywood Diary* to spell the name right.) By Walpole's time, in

1934, Selznick was playing an important part in the affairs of a top studio, MGM, and Walpole, imported to give a literary flavour to the script of one of their big prestige productions, *David Copperfield*, was given plush treatment. He was expected to behave like an eminent man of letters, and he did. He found the studio way of working irksome; writing and rewriting and re-rewriting, with no time or energy for anything else ('Everyone asks me out— Charles Laughton, Katharine Hepburn, Wallace Beery, Charlie Chaplin—but you have little time to make real friends with anyone...').

But at least Walpole was grateful to be in foreign parts and away from the British intrigues: 'I think why I am really happy is that here I am free for the first time from all the English jealousy that I've suffered from for years. No one here cares a hang about the relative merits of English writers!' No wonder he does not seem to have sought out the British colony in Hollywood—though it does not sound as though they, individually or collectively, would have given much of a hang either.

His principal friends in Los Angeles were nonetheless European— the Danish actor and book collector Jean Hersholt, and the Russian director Richard Boleslawski, a colourful figure who had been in the Polish Lancers and escaped from Russia after the Revolution, had made some reputation in the theatre and proved an indifferent film-maker (*Clive of India*, *The Garden of Allah*) if a man of great personal charm and culture. Walpole also got on well with his producer, Selznick, and his director, George Cukor. When he was prevailed upon to play the small role of the platitudinous Vicar of Blunderstone in *David Copperfield* he undertook to improvise the sermon. Cukor and Selznick cooked up a little plot to require retake after retake for various specious technical reasons just to see if they could dry him up. But on each of the eight takes he preached a different sermon with the same pompous fluency. They might have known their man better: his father had been Bishop of Edinburgh.

The rest of the six-month trip was spent, equally busy, working on a screen version of his own book *Vanessa*. As soon as his ex-policeman companion Harold Cheevers arrived he settled down to a thoroughly domestic life, playing chess a lot with Harold and—his major regular outing—accompanying him to the fights every Friday, an interest of Harold's much more than his. Before leaving he signed a contract to return for another six months the following year. In the event, he remained more than nine: he spent the first few days staying with George Cukor in his elegant home in the hills above Sunset Boulevard, then moved into a small Spanish-style house he had rented in Benedict Canyon, Beverly Hills—rather nearer to MGM studios. There he felt an increasing sense of unreality ('There is more actual positive reality in one square inch of the beach at Scarborough than in the whole extent of Hollywood') as his labours were switched from *Kim* to *Oliver Twist* to *The Prince and the Pauper*, then back to *Kim* and something called *Burn, Witch, Burn* (which he flatly refused) before finally, after seven or eight weeks of indecision and inactivity, he was asked by Selznick, now with another studio, to do a script of *Little Lord Fauntleroy*. However, all this time he was being paid nearly $1,000 a week, seeing the sights, shopping and writing nothing for the studio—which if anything increased his sense of unreality.

He took refuge again in home life with the faithful Harold, concerts, boxing and sometimes wrestling matches, and his own work, writing short stories and forging ahead with his current novel. Around Christmas his social life perked up with a brief visit by H. G. Wells, with whom Walpole went to visit Hearst's extraordinary estate at San Simeon, the very bizarreness of which, made up as it was of bits and pieces ransacked from all over Europe, appealed to him. Christmas was spent with old Hollywood friends—Jean Hersholt, Richard Boleslawski, George Cukor—and a lot of time in January with more visitors from England—John Masefield and his wife. And though he admitted to enjoying Hollywood enormously, he seems never to have been in any danger of settling down there in gilded exile as a professional Englishman. He soon became intensely homesick for traditional English food: 'an English breakfast—kippers, fat sausages bursting their skins, fishcakes, kedgeree. For lunch, trout and marmalade pudding. For dinner, roast chicken and Stilton. The only possible American foods are steaks and some soups—everything tasteless, oversauced, greasy.' But also, more important, he resented, like Clive Brook, the waste of time, being overpaid and underworked, and realized, away from it, how intensely he loved England.

The tally of works of art he acquired in Hollywood makes it clear that he did not find Southern California in that respect a cultural desert—on his 1935–6 visit he bought three Cézannes, three Renoirs, two Picassos, a Gauguin, a Braque and a Derain, as well as lots of drawings and lithographs and thousands of dollars' worth of antiquarian books. But with rare exceptions he does not seem to have found the company congenial for very long, and to have missed, for all his early relief at being away from its backbiting, the English literary society he was used to. Also, however well paid the work might be, he chafed at its inefficiency, and the necessity of working over and over even such relatively easy subjects as *Kim*, on which his last few months were spent (with true Hollywood type-casting he was assigned only classy, literary works for adaptation). The one script he was happy with, *Little Lord Fauntleroy*, was the only one he was trusted (by Selznick) to write all by himself, and polished it off in a month. When he left Hollywood for the last time on 5 June 1936, it was with a profound feeling of relief, and even though he continued to cherish some of his Hollywood friendships—it is recorded that among the few essential possessions he took with him to the air-raid shelters during the blitz was a photograph of Boleslawski, who had died young in 1937—he never seems to have been seriously tempted to return.

Just as one would expect, it is tempting to say. But the English in Los Angeles, colony or not, often seem to have reacted in quite unpredictable ways. It was likely to be the most unlikely ones who settled down best and clung least to British exclusiveness. Throughout the 1930s many of them gathered at the famous Garden of Allah hotel, not so much because it was a British preserve (which it certainly was not), as because it was a colourful, convenient and reasonably inexpensive place to live, either in the long-term or for the time being, while getting one's bearings in a strange town. Most of the characters in Sheilah Graham's diverting, slapdash history of the institution are either British visitors or disaffected New Yorkers who reserved the right to complain about Hollywood and deny that they were a part of it, even if in practice they never returned home. 'The Algonquin Round Table gone west and gone soft' was one description—on which might be superimposed an alternative image of the British, like Noël Coward's Uncle Harry, 'giving way at practically every pore'. In other words, it was somewhat self-consciously bohemian, a haven for people who wanted somehow to keep up their connections with the outside world.

The Garden of Allah was at 8150 Sunset Boulevard, right on the border of Hollywood and Beverly Hills, though later redesignated West Hollywood, and was bought by Alla Nazimova as her home when she first arrived in Hollywood in 1918. In 1927 it was turned into an hotel by the addition of twenty-five separate villas in the grounds, round the pool, and began a chequered commercial career that lasted until it was demolished in 1959. It had the advantage of being central to the film-making community, not too expensive, and very free-and-easy in its toleration of eccentric life styles. It recommended itself, therefore, to those who could not yet afford to live elsewhere, or were not sure that they were ready to take the plunge into something more permanent, as well as being a social centre for their friends and like-minded people.

It was obviously a curious mixture. Most of the Garden of Allah stories seem to concern drunkenness and debauchery of various kinds, but at the same time if one wanted to keep oneself to oneself that was also easily possible—it just did not make for such lively copy. Many of the most solid citizens, like Clive Brook and C. Aubrey Smith, came frequently to visit friends at the Garden of Allah, which was also an occasional refuge for Leslie Howard and Ronald Colman. When Laurence Olivier was in Hollywood for the first time, in 1931–2, making not much impression in a number of not very notable films, he was there with his first wife, actress Jill Esmond, and they rented a house. The second time, in 1933, it was strictly to make one film, *Queen Christina*, which he felt he could not turn down, offering as it did a chance to star opposite Garbo. And so, for the six months in question he decided to stay at the Garden of Allah, to emphasize the temporary nature of his return. Unfortunately, in the event he did not stay even that long, since Garbo did not approve of him as her leading man and insisted instead on her old co-star from silent movies, John Gilbert. It is recorded that virtually the only thing Garbo said to Olivier during their brief collaboration was, apropos of nothing in particular, 'Life's a pain anyway.'

Others had happier experiences, at least on the personal level. Frank Lawton, star of *David Copperfield*, was living at the Garden when he persuaded another émigré, Evelyn Laye, to elope with him to Yuma after renewing acquaintance with her in the bungalow of another Garden resident, Ramon Novarro, with whom she was then starring in *One Heavenly Night*. Another from the cast of *David Copperfield*, Elizabeth Allan, also lived at the Garden for some years. There were many occasional visitors from Britain, like the actress Heather Thatcher, famed for her monocle, who always stayed there, and it was much favoured by English ingénues like Virginia Cherrill, briefly Cary Grant's wife, and not-so-ingénues like the impressionist Florence Desmond, who came out to make one movie in 1933.

However, it was not only the theatricals of the English contingent who favoured it. Somerset Maugham, for example, lived there while working at Paramount in the mid-thirties. But this was not a happy time for him as far as work went; he told Adela Rogers St John: 'It's all very well. They send for me in order to get something new into films, to get them out of a rut. But every time I get my foot out of the rut, they shoot it off.' Maugham at this time could count as an émigré even less than his archenemy Hugh Walpole: he spent a shorter period in Hollywood, liked it less, and left with less to show for it, not even a screenplay actually produced. When he returned in the 1940s to write a script for the film of his novel *The Razor's Edge* (a script that, again, was not used) he made even less effort to become a long-term part of Hollywood life. He stayed throughout the writing period with the projected director of the film, George Cukor, and worked in relative isolation from other Hollywood visitors.

Another Englishman who stayed at the Garden of Allah in the 1930s and might (loosely at least) be regarded as an intellectual did, in the event, become much more of a fixture of Hollywood life. This was Charles Laughton, who, with his wife Elsa Lanchester, came and went frequently during the 1930s before settling full-time in Los Angeles in the 1940s. In 1932 the Laughtons made their first trip to Los Angeles for Charles to star in *The Devil and the Deep* with Tallulah Bankhead and Gary Cooper, a script specially written for Laughton by another English émigré of the time, the playwright Benn Levy. When this was delayed he made instead a film of another script by Benn Levy, *The Old Dark House*, based on a novel by J. B. Priestley, which also featured such other British émigrés or visitors as Boris Karloff and Ernest Thesiger, and was directed by the most important British director in Hollywood at this time, James Whale.

For this visit the Laughtons lived in a house in the Hollywood Hills that was rented for them by the studio. And in their experiences one can see some of the social problems that were likely to beset the so-called English colony. To begin with, Laughton, even before his big success as Henry VIII, was that oddity, a character actor who had become a star. One might say that so was George Arliss, but at least Arliss was an old-style English theatrical gentleman, while Laughton's unconventional style and appearance marked him out at once as definitely not the correct cricket-playing type. Consequently, the cricketing set did not feel at home with him, and tended to look down on him as some sort of barbarian, while he had little time for them, regarding them as philistine bores. This may have been part of the reason why he did not get on with Boris Karloff (though there seem to have been remarkably few of his co-stars at this period with whom he did get on). At the same time, Karloff did not approve of James Whale because Whale was, it seems, a terrible snob who, with no particular justification, looked down on Karloff and was very rude about him and his supposed commonness—though in fact Karloff's family background was decidedly grander than Whale's own.

No doubt it seems ludicrous that this sort of social infighting should still have existed on the other side of the world, but it did lend colour to the widespread belief that all the English were obsessed with class and intensely snobbish. Be that as it may, the Laughtons did not make many new friends in Hollywood, though they retained a few, like Benn Levy, from back in England. When they left after five films for him (none for her) it was with no particular sense of regret or desire to return. Indeed, Elsa Lanchester preceded her husband in returning to England, and at once acquired the London flat that was to be their permanent base throughout the 1930s. So, on their return to Hollywood in 1934, for Charles to make *The Barretts of Wimpole Street*, they moved into the obviously more temporary quarters of a bungalow at the Garden of Allah. They continued to stay there whenever they were in Hollywood (which, given his busy career, was quite frequently) until early 1940, when they moved into another rented house and then, after a year and the bombing of their London flat, to a permanent base in Los Angeles, a house in Pacific Palisades.

But then Laughton was obviously a loner in many respects, picking and choosing his friends with no fixed principle. Obsessed with work, he was seldom easy to approach socially, unless his quasi-paternal teacher instincts were aroused, as often occurred with those much younger and simpler than himself, such as the succession of bisexual young men who attracted and sometimes satisfied his sexual interest. He became friendly with some of the Hollywood establishment, among them the Thalbergs, since he respected Irving Thalberg's natural taste and culture, but moved little in smart society. He got on well with a few of the old-guard Britishers, but otherwise seems to have been more at home with fellow Europeans, who were more likely to share his cultural tastes than the Americans and less likely to have snobbish reservations about him than the English.

Some of his associations were rather surprising; he got on well with Erich Pommer, for instance, whom hardly anyone else seems to have been able to manage. They were associated in the production of three films in Britain in the late 1930s, and Laughton starred in 1940 in Pommer's Hollywood production of *They Knew What They Wanted*. And, exceptionally for an English actor, he was able to relate on equal terms with the likes of Jean Renoir and Bertolt Brecht, with both of whom he worked closely in the 1940s, when he himself had become truly an émigré rather than merely a regular commuter.

It is not to denigrate the power and value of most of the English contingent as stars or reliable character actors to say that, beyond their mere presence and maybe a kind of speech-model they provided, they had little creative contribution to make to Hollywood or the American cinema. Though they often, naturally, appeared in films with British settings or subjects, there was no perceptible difference in authenticity or even literacy in most of these films—if the British actors had any ideas of their own or criticisms to offer, these would seem to have been remarkably ineffectual. The conventional image (conventional for Americans, be it said, even more than for Europeans) of European culture face-to-face with transatlantic crassness does not bear examination: films of the 1930s do not seem to be in any way more intelligent or culturally valuable in proportion to the degree of European influence they show—and certainly not to the degree of any specifically British influence. Nor did the writers make a much better showing. True, Hugh Walpole managed to fashion an excellent script for Selznick's production of *David Copperfield*, but many Hollywood script-writers could and did do as well. Otherwise, for the most part, the British émigrés fitted in perfectly with Hollywood and Hollywood accepted them totally: all that might be left to distinguish them was a British accent—part of the stock in trade, like a moustache or a duelling scar—and often not even that. Who remembered, after a while, that Bob Hope had once been English?

Laughton could have made a difference, but, in the 1930s at least, he did not. He was his own man, and contributed his unique character to his roles and his films, but he was too peculiar and unclassifiable to fit into any accepted pattern, or to have any wider impact on Los Angeles life; it was only in the 1940s, with the major influx of European intellectuals, that he came to play a prominent part. Indeed, there is only one Englishman in Hollywood in the

1930s who made a really distinctive contribution, bringing something unmistakably foreign to American sound cinema and making it seem perfectly at home there. This was James Whale, director of *Frankenstein*, *The Old Dark House* (during which he and Laughton did not get on) and several other classics of Gothic cinema. He was, in his own way, as eccentric and unclassifiable a figure as Laughton, which may have been why they failed to establish any fellow feeling, though both were North Countrymen and both homosexuals.

Whale had been, obscurely, an actor in England for eight or nine years before he had his big unexpected success as a stage director with R. C. Sherriff's First World War drama *Journey's End* in 1928. This brought him to New York to direct the American stage production, and then to Hollywood to direct the film version as a 'British talkie' in America, before Britain was properly equipped to make all-talking pictures. Before this happened, he worked with Howard Hughes directing the dialogue sequences in *Hell's Angels* (1930), in which Jean Harlow made an unforgettable impression by suggesting that she 'slip into something more comfortable'. *Journey's End* (1930) was made with an all-British (or, considering the single German character, all-European) cast, recruited entirely on the spot except for the leading player, Colin Clive, who was brought over especially from the London stage cast.

Journey's End was explicitly a British film made, by accident as it were, in a Hollywood studio. When, as a result of its success, Whale was put under contract by Universal, it was obviously taking his Britishness into account, as his first assignment was filming Robert Sherwood's play, *Waterloo Bridge* (1930), the story of an unhappy love affair between an American soldier and a London prostitute during the First World War. He really hit his stride, though, with his second film for Universal, *Frankenstein* (1931). This was, of course, not set in Britain, though based on an English novel and given a couple of English leading actors, Boris Karloff and Colin Clive. But what Whale brought to it was unique in Hollywood and very particularly European: the English tradition of Gothic horror fantasy, the English black sense of humour, and a visual style full of expressionistic lighting effects, bold use of shadows, reflections and wilful distortion. Visually, as a critic remarked of one of his later films, the film 'might have come from UFA a dozen years earlier'—but it certainly would not have been so ruthlessly funny if it had.

The phenomenal success of *Frankenstein* made Whale Universal's top director, and the particular favourite of studio head Carl Laemmle Jr. Though he did not choose to work exclusively in the Gothic horror genre (one of his biggest successes, for instance, was something as thoroughly American as the first sound version of *Showboat* in 1936), his finest and most personal films were in this area or closely related: *The Old Dark House* (1932), *The Invisible Man* (1933), *Bride of Frankenstein* (1935). These starred, as far as possible, the British actors he loved to work with, and are completely unlike anything else made in Hollywood at the time or since. Of course, this was in the first instance because Whale himself had a highly individual talent and a personal style that nobody else could successfully duplicate or emulate—even supposing anyone else had wanted to. But so many elements in the formation of his creative personality go back to his English origins—his theatrical training, his awareness of European art (he had some early training in art, and always exerted a strong influence on the design of his stage and film work, even when he did not carry it out completely himself), his wide reading in English literature, particularly of the humorous and sensational varieties. Indeed, the film-maker he is most readily comparable to is that most English of Englishmen, Alfred Hitchcock, with whom he had many of these traits in common.

In private life Whale would seem—accounts tend to be somewhat hostile and malicious—to have been rather self-consciously grand and snobbish; very much the art collector and cultivated international sophisticate. This pose—insofar as it was a pose—excited the unkinder members of the English colony to reflect unflatteringly on Whale's humble social origins, making discriminations that would mean little to Americans. He certainly lived in showy style, enjoying to the full the high salary he was then getting in Hollywood. In an interview in the *New York Post* in 1936 he said: 'That they should pay such high salaries is beyond ordinary reasoning! Who's worth it? But why not take it? And the architecture! And the furnishings! I can have modernistic designs one day and an antiquated home over night! All the world's made of plaster of Paris!'

His attitude did not endear him to the Laughtons, who had known Whale when he had played Laughton's son in *The Man with Red Hair* on the London stage back in 1928, just before he directed *Journey's End*. They considered him talented but vulgar. Others considered him talented but dangerously indiscreet about his sexual proclivities—and indeed there are vague but persistent rumours that some kind of homosexual scandal was involved in his precipitate retirement from film-making (though not from Hollywood) in 1941, in the midst of filming, ironically perhaps, *They Dare Not Love*. Be that as it may, James Whale's was the most distinctive British presence in the Hollywood film world throughout the 1930s but because he was *sui generis*, he remained isolated, his work coming from nothing and leading to nothing. Clearly he had no difficulty acclimatizing himself to Hollywood, and for a decade Hollywood had no difficulty in using him: he was an English survivor, just more spectacularly, personally talented than most.

At the very end of the 1930s, in 1939, there was a sudden influx of the English. But even if they came over a few months before the beginning of the war in Europe and their migration had nothing directly to do with it, we still tend to think of them as belonging primarily to the wartime generation of émigrés, faced with the same problems, the same kind of divided and contradictory loyalties. They belong, therefore, essentially to the next section of this book. But somewhat before their arrival there were other newcomers to Los Angeles who introduced something noticeably new. The key figure here was Aldous Huxley, the first Englishman of note to settle in Southern California who could credibly be called an intellectual. He was probably the first to approach it in the slightly sceptical, slightly amused, slightly amazed spirit that was to become familiar to foreign residents in the 1950s and 1960s—those who could cope with Hollywood on their own terms and adored it for its exotic, science fiction quality (an attitude neatly adumbrated in Reyner Banham's enthusiastic study *Los Angeles: The Architecture of Four Ecologies*).

Huxley came to Los Angeles largely by chance. When he left Europe in April 1937 it was, by his own cautious account, just to tour America, with no fixed plans, and certainly no definite ideas of settling there. Huxley, his wife Maria, their teenage son Matthew and their philosopher/mystic friend Gerald Heard spent some time first in New York, then motored across the country to pass the summer in Frieda Lawrence's ranch in New Mexico. There Huxley wrote most of *Ends and Means*, found the country fascinating but obscurely hostile, and by September was happy to move on to the more relaxing (?) environment of Los Angeles. Even then they had no particular plans. Hopes of interesting film companies in adapting

Huxley's books were held out by the Los Angeles bookseller Jake Zeitlin, but not surprisingly nothing came of them. He did receive some kind of offer to adapt *The Forsyte Saga* to the screen, but refused.

They rented a small flat in Hollywood, and did the usual round of activities for visiting celebrities: dinner with Charlie Chaplin and Paulette Goddard, trips to the Disney Studios and Mount Wilson Observatory, meetings with Anita Loos and other famous writers now temporarily or permanently settled in Hollywood. The Huxleys had little to do with the English old-guard *per se*, or indeed with the Hollywood side of Hollywood; more in common with non-movie people like the astronomer Edwin Hubble and his wife. After a month or so as tourists they were off again, Huxley and Heard lecturing across America.

At the end of the lecture tour. Huxley still had no definite idea of settling in America, though it was recognized as a possibility. He was swung in the direction of California by the remote chance that a studio might be interested in a film scenario he had written while in Hollywood, and so by February 1938 he and his wife were back— Gerald Heard having already returned. They moved into a small furnished house in Laurel Canyon, saw a few of the friends they had made on the earlier trip, and still talked of leaving in a couple of months, once they had got their son settled in college. But through Anita Loos, Huxley received an offer to write a script based on the life of Madame Curie to be filmed at MGM with Garbo, directed by George Cukor. Contracts were finally signed in July, calling for eight weeks' work for a fee of $15,000. They moved from house to house—Beverly Hills, West Hollywood—and settled down to a quiet social life with a small group of intimate friends, including Gerald Heard, the Hubbles, Anita Loos, Krishnamurti and Christopher Isherwood, who arrived in May 1939. Huxley duly wrote his script for Metro: it was paid for in full, shelved and completely rewritten before a film on the subject finally emerged five years later.

The Huxleys talked of using the film money to return to Europe, but the advantages of the Californian climate for Aldous's health— like Sanary in the summer—had become obvious; they had many friends there and were becoming increasingly cut off from Europe the longer they stayed. And they were independent enough in their ideas to benefit from Los Angeles's unique ability to be all things to all men. If it was still primarily a brash, philistine community, or at least those parts of it connected with the movie business, it also had two major universities, libraries like the Huntington Library in Pasadena, and many inhabitants who had nothing whatever to do with movies and lived their own versions of the cultivated, intellectual life. They could find the stimulation they needed and, when necessary, the privacy for him to write—his first Californian work, *After Many a Summer*, was an early outcome. Heard felt they were if anything too social, too accepting of the unworthier aspects of Los Angeles life, but contact with the outside world, with many different outside worlds, was vital for the ever-curious Huxley.

In April 1939 they moved away from the centre of Los Angeles, westward to Pacific Palisades, an area soon to be much patronized by European intellectual newcomers. They lived with a comfort and enjoyment surprising to many of their friends in a rented house furnished in the most extravagant kitsch taste, which they did little or nothing to moderate in the three years they were there. Little by little, Huxley was insensibly settling in and becoming part of the Los Angeles scene—however improbable a part it did not matter in a city that thrived on improbabilities. He wrote, he read, he improved his failing eyesight by application of the Bates method of muscular re-education, an American speciality. And towards the end of 1939, having just turned forty-five, he accepted another scripting assignment at MGM, an adaptation of *Pride and Prejudice*. Just as he began work on it, war broke out in Europe, thus putting paid—for ever, as it turned out—to any vague ideas the Huxleys might have had of returning. Since the beginning of the year the stream of those who felt that Europe was doomed had been increasing; now, and for the next five or six years, it flowed in only one direction—westward.

7. Hollywood Left and Right

Late in 1934 there was a meeting at the Hollywood Women's Club. The excuse was a reading of a new play by a new writer, Irwin Shaw's *Bury the Dead*, given by no lesser citizens of Hollywood than Fredric March and his wife Florence Eldridge. The real reason was to bring together a lot of people in Hollywood who for one reason or another were interested in the anti-Nazi cause: liberals, communists, intellectuals, Jews.... The play was a strong if naive diatribe against war and in support of democracy, dramatizing the sense of betrayal felt by the dead of the First World War when resurrected to see what the next generation had done with the world. The audience was duly impressed and moved. Then a young Hollywood screenwriter, Donald Ogden Stewart, made a speech urging Hollywood to pull its head out of the sand and take a positive part in the struggle to preserve democracy. 'Let us have no more million-dollar revolving staircases, no more star-filled symposiums of billion-dollar entertainment—but let us have some simple truths, as we have had tonight, some simple truths on a bare stage, against nothing but a plain background.'

At the time such principles were unexceptional, even if people were a little surprised to hear them from Stewart, a former self-confessed playboy and bright young thing who had suddenly undergone a conversion to romantic socialism, if not out-and-out communism. Of course, Hollywood did not take any notice of his exhortations: he himself was then working at MGM on the script of a glossy Joan Crawford vehicle, *No More Ladies* (1935), and went on to his next assignment, *Conquest* (1937), the story of Marie Walewska and Napoleon reworked for Garbo. But it did seem that at least some of Hollywood might be dragged an inch or two into the modern world of grim political reality. A little later Stewart was involved in another, apparently even more successful, rally of the same sort. Two eminent anti-Nazis arrived in Hollywood, Prince

Hubertus von und zu Loewenstein, one of Hitler's most vocal Catholic opponents, and 'Breda', author of *The Brown Book of the Hitler Terror*, and were introduced by Stewart to Hollywood notables, including the Thalbergs, the Selznicks and the Goldwyns, at a reassuringly elegant private dinner party. The result of this was a large white-tie-and-tails dinner at $100 a plate attended by virtually everybody who was anybody in Hollywood, led by the Archbishop of Los Angeles (though he, circumspectly, left early when he was told that Breda was a communist). But then, as Stewart glumly observes in his autobiography, the success of these meetings probably had more to do with the excellence of the champagne and the social impressiveness of an old European title than with any very deeply felt political responses.

In any case, what more could be expected of a movement largely sponsored by writers, in a world where Louis B. Mayer had observed after the political defeat of Upton Sinclair in the 1934 election for Governor of California, 'What does Sinclair know about anything? He's just a writer'? The whole story of Sinclair's bid for office is, in fact, rather interesting as indicative of the real climate of opinion in Hollywood at that time. Sinclair was then a well-known 'left-wing' novelist, sponsor of Eisenstein during his disastrous Mexican venture and biographer of William Fox, the Fox of Twentieth Century-Fox. In fact, he was just an unusually liberal democrat, unusually concerned with labour conditions. His campaign slogan was 'End Poverty in California', and to do this he advocated a degree of federal control of the film industry, increased taxation of the rich, and the recognition of organized labour in its various shapes and forms by the unwilling movie studios. Of course, to virtually all the Hollywood tycoons this was out-and-out Bolshevik revolutionary talk, liable to have blood running in the streets, and they showed a more united front than ever before to stop Sinclair and elect the Republican candidate, one Frank E. Merriam, instead.

Even life-long Democrats like Joseph Schenck rallied in panic to Merriam's cause. The amount of vituperation and outright misrepresentation heaped on Sinclair's head was extraordinary—and so blatant that it seems unthinkable today, when smear tactics have at least to be subtler. The major companies even conspired to make fake newsreels, using material from feature films of delinquents crowding into California to exploit Sinclair's proposed new society, and staged phony interviews with actors straight from Central

Casting pretending to be Bolshevik agitators backing Sinclair or apple-pie American grannies voting for Merriam. This was also the first major instance of professional public relations intervention in American politics—the campaign was placed in the hands of Campaigns Inc., a firm of San Francisco origin that was subsequently to become one of the most powerful and successful PR firms in America. And when you consider that one of the anti-Sinclair campaign's most active instigators in Hollywood was Irving Thalberg, it is evident that such 'left-wing' initiatives as Donald Ogden Stewart's introduction of the distinguished anti-Nazis to Thalberg and his fellow tycoons later the same year were hardly likely to have any positive results.

And Thalberg was always considered, at least within the narrow Hollywood context, as an intellectual. When Sinclair was roundly defeated, it was as much a defeat for intellectual intervention in Hollywood affairs as for proto- or crypto-communism. The fact that a man—or woman—gave any evidence of thinking was an immediate cause for mistrust, and none was mistrusted more than the writers. Especially if they had some sort of foreign or, perhaps even worse, New York background. The first attempts of the writers in Hollywood to get themselves organized, as the Screen Writers' Guild in 1931, had not got very far because the studios stood solid in refusing to recognize it or bargain with it, and it had not succeeded in recruiting enough members to enforce its requirements in any effective way. It had originally been the brainchild of unashamed, self-confessed leftists like John Howard Lawson, liberals like Dudley Nichols, and middle-of-the-roaders like Oliver Garrett, who rendered himself suspect by hanging around with cosmopolitan intellectuals, such as the Viertels. When the Guild was revived and revitalized in 1934, it was largely owing to the influence of a new influx of New York writers with reputations outside Hollywood: Dorothy Parker, Dashiell Hammett, Lillian Hellman, Charles Brackett, Samson Raphaelson.

This, naturally, made it seem more of a menace than ever before to the studio heads, and they promptly retaliated by setting up their own cat's-paw organization, Screen Playwrights, and proposing to blacklist anyone connected with the dreaded Guild. However, even in this they were not really political, or at least, politics always gave way to enlightened self-interest. The attitude could be summed up in the famous Goldwyn story of his violent quarrel with an actor, which climaxed in Goldwyn shouting: 'And furthermore, you dirty double-crossing hypocritical sonofabitch, I don't ever want to see you on this lot again,' and then adding as the actor rushed out, '... unless I need you.' The studios' hostility to the Guild was mainly their idea of self-protection, but if they felt they needed one of the Guild's members they were certainly not going to stand on principle. So, largely because it managed to enlist a lot of really important writers of proven commercial capabilities, the Guild managed to survive, flourish and become eminently respectable and 'establishment' in its turn.

But in general the major figures in Hollywood were not very politically aware. Mayer, Thalberg and De Mille were known to be staunch Republicans; the rest presumably had enough interest to vote in elections, like anyone else, but politics was never allowed to get in the way of business. It was obviously necessary for the movies, as a major American industry, to keep in with both major political parties so that they would never be left totally out in the cold no matter who happened to be governing. But this merely encouraged the tendency, already present in most of the heads of the industry, to consider politics very little except in terms of what would or would not be good for the box-office. Some of them, like dictators in their own domains, admired the style of the European dictators, so that Harry Cohn, head of Columbia, for instance, had his offices decorated along the lines of Mussolini's, but it is doubtful if Cohn could have told anyone even the basic outlines of the Duce's social, economic and political policies—it was all a matter of image, as was perhaps to be expected of the image industry *par excellence*.

This political indeterminacy was, partly at least, a natural result of the way the tycoons had cut themselves off from their own ethnic origins. Most of them, for example, were Jewish; most of them had been born in Eastern or Central Europe, or born of parents from those parts very shortly after their arrival in America. But none of them remained strict orthodox Jews, religiously or socially; most of them took gentile wives and in their determination to become 100 per cent Amerian patriots, all surviving affiliations with the old countries were forgotten. Specifically Jewish causes never did all that well in Hollywood because they did not accord with the tycoon's primary self-image. Ben Hecht in his autobiography recalls an occasion when he tried to persuade David O. Selznick to contribute to an appeal designed to finance a Jewish army in Palestine. Selznick declined on the grounds that he was an American, socially and psychologically, not a Jew. Hecht got

Selznick to nominate three people he could phone and ask whether they considered Selznick an American or a Jew; if one of them said 'American' then Selznick would not have to contribute. Hecht won his gamble, but the fact remained that however others might categorize him, Selznick still considered himself American, not Jewish (and certainly not Russian, though his father was a jeweller from Kiev), and reacted accordingly.

This meant that appeals in Hollywood on behalf of anti-Nazi causes, which one might suppose would have had an excellent chance in a community where so many of the leading figures were, after all, Jewish, in fact fell on deaf ears, at least in the 1930s. Of course, as soon as America entered the war against Germany the situation was very different: then it was American patriotism in play, and no one was slow in rallying behind the Stars and Stripes. But up to that point, there was little automatic sympathy in Hollywood for victims of or refugees from Nazi or any other kind of political oppression in Europe, and all attempts to play on presumed fellow feelings on their behalf were doomed to disappointment.

Consequently, what appear at first glance to be political issues, political decisions, generally turn out to have been considered almost entirely in non-political terms. The Prince von Loewenstein would be fêted, and to a certain extent listened to, not because he was an anti-Nazi, but because he was a prince. Others might be shunned, not so much because they were communists—that was perfectly acceptable provided they were commercially viable—as because they might be trouble-makers in industrial relations, or because as 'intellectuals' they provoked discomfort in their less educated potential employers. Certainly there was no automatic reverence for the intellectual such as would be encountered in many parts of Europe. At best the movies might appreciate the snob value of employing a world-famous writer or artist: the name alone was impressive, indicating that Hollywood could buy anything it wanted—a sort of human equivalent of the Spanish cloisters and French baronial halls from which Hearst pieced together his fantasy castle at San Simeon. But of course, once the name had been bought, it was quite a different matter to allow, say, Maurice Maeterlinck or Salvador Dali to do anything that would validate the name and reputation. It often seemed as though intellectuals in Hollywood were not so much bought as bought off.

Superficially, it might seem that such encounters were between the sophisticated and the naive: all the intellectuals had to do really was take the money and run. But curiously enough, on closer inspection it is more difficult to determine who were actually naive. Certainly, many of the intellectuals in Hollywood, or those who passed as such, seem to have been astonishingly unschooled in the ways of the world, while the supposedly numbskull tycoons they encountered at least had the kind of street wisdom that made them more than a match. One would, for example, back the ignoramus Louis B. Mayer, sobbing over his own Andy Hardy movies, any day over Aldous Huxley, who was surely one of the most intelligent men ever to live in Los Angeles, but a child when it came to money matters or the practical everyday organization of his life. Few indeed were the visitors or settlers who, like Hugh Walpole, could cope with the conditions of life in Hollywood and get exactly what they wanted out of it.

Much the same seems to have been true in the sphere of politics. There was undoubtedly something very simple-minded about the tycoons' attitudes to politics, but such as they were, they were effective: when Hollywood set about seriously blocking Upton Sinclair's election, it succeeded completely. Not that anyone knew or cared anything much about the theoretical basis of Sinclair's policies (simplistic as that itself was): they simply saw him as a threat, and acted accordingly. In comparison, the politics of the 'intelligent' writers seems to be equally naive, but far less effective. It is easy—perhaps too easy—to make fun of the parlour communists, such as Donald Ogden Stewart and Dorothy Parker, who underwent some kind of instant, emotional conversion to the cause of the workers, represented generally if not always specifically by the Soviet Union, and who went on writing nonsense movies and eating and drinking in all the grandest rendezvous of the privileged, even as they agonized over the plight of the have-nots. But at least their feelings, however muddled and at odds with their actions, were basically sincere; as Stewart puts it, quite simply: 'I think we all felt a bit guilty about making all that money and not doing anything about it.'

In theory, this group of left-wing New Yorkers in Hollywood should have provided in every way a bridge between culturally and politically isolationist Hollywood and the influx of European intellectuals and literates during the 1930s. In practice they do not seem to have had much contact, though at least they made it their business to be aware of what was going on in Germany and, later, Spain and to keep others informed through the Anti-Nazi League and other kindred organizations. They also felt themselves to be Hollywood's watchdogs against crypto-fascist groups like Victor McLaglen's Light Horse Cavalry and Guy Empey's Hollywood Hussars, assumed by most people (including, to be fair, the majority of their members) to be no more harmful than the Boy Scouts, allowing a lot of grown men who might have known better to dress up and play soldiers at weekends.

The main point of connection between the New Yorkers and the Europeans was, as might have been expected, Salka Viertel's 'salon' in Santa Monica. Donald Ogden Stewart met her professionally at the most acute period of his political conversion, when, as it happened, he was working at MGM on the *Marie Walewska* script, and found that she was an inescapable part of the deal as Garbo's 'favourite script-writer'. He became for a while a regular visitor to 165 Mabery Road.

Reading of this period in Salka Viertel's memoirs *The Kindness of Strangers*, one receives, by inference at least, a very curious picture of the political atmosphere in Hollywood at the time. The book abounds in sentences like 'Sam [Behrman] arrived, as dear and whimsical as ever, and in spite of the Spanish Civil War, which broke out in July, Hitler's threats, and the appeasement policy of England and France, we finished in a reasonably short time a very good screenplay.' Considering that this is the same *Marie Walewska* screenplay, one in a succession of period pieces that Salka Viertel was working on for Garbo in the Culver City dream factory of MGM, the impression is unavoidable that even for people with as many European connections as the Viertels, what was happening in Europe was little more than a picturesque but distant backdrop to work and romance in Hollywood. (Berthold Viertel was in fact in Europe at this time trying to make films there while Salka slipped insensibly from an affair with Oliver Garrett to an affair with Gottfried Reinhardt.) A little earlier, commenting on her Sunday afternoons, which then regularly included such émigrés or visitors as the French playwright Marcel Achard (working on scripts for Maurice Chevalier), the Schoenbergs, the Russian composer Dimitri Tiomkin and the Polish composer Bronislaw Kaper (then both working at MGM), the English writer Clemence Dane, and Otto Klemperer, the German conductor of the Los Angeles Philharmonic, along with Americans like Johnny Weissmuller, the screen Tarzan, Oscar Levant and Miriam Hopkins, she remarks that, 'Political discussions, verging on personal bitterness, were unavoidable among the Europeans and amazed the Americans. Gottfried participated in them as passionately and prominently as in Ping-Pong.'

So much for that. And yet Salka Viertel was not a silly woman, and as Hollywood writers went she was politically quite active. She was busy in the Screen Writers' Guild in the days when it was considered (by her employer, Thalberg, for instance) as a subversive organization, and was a founder-member of the Anti-Nazi League. And she stuck by her convictions when friends started to be more careful. Lubitsch warned her in 1936 that the Anti-Nazi League was in the control of the communists and therefore he was leaving it. Though she pooh-poohed the idea ('Ernst, what all these people do is sit around their swimming pools, drinking highballs and talking about movies, while the wives complain about their Philipino butlers'), she did believe that the Popular Front was the only way to fight fascism, and she stayed in the League. The Popular Front indeed had permeated her own family. Berthold was an eccentric kind of socialist, she was a 'premature anti-fascist', and their sons Peter, Thomas and Hans were respectively a New Dealer, a Democrat and a Trotskyite.

Even so, she seems to have retained throughout the Thirties her own capacity for surprise at the way politics worked, or did not work, in Los Angeles. The secret seems to have been that life was only some larger, more diffused, and probably less spectacular movie. Understand that, and everything else falls into place. In the 1960s people were to start complaining that elections, especially presidential elections, were fought more on the kind of figure the candidates cut as television personalities than on any even faintly reasoned assessments of the political programmes they stood for (Kennedy is more attractive than Nixon, so Kennedy gets elected). But Hollywood already judged along these lines in the 1930s— everything depended on star quality.

When in 1937 André Malraux visited Hollywood (along with Hemingway and others) to speak on behalf of the Republicans in the Spanish Civil War, his presence in town was carefully advertised by a few select gatherings, such as that at Salka Viertel's which brought a hundred distinguished citizens to hear him and contribute right away some $5,000 to the Republican cause. Once Hollywood had been apprised that it had in its midst a star attraction, a world-famous writer and intellectual, a mass meeting was held at the Shrine Auditorium, packed to the doors with 'stars, producers, writers, doctors, lawyers, teachers, shop clerks, workers from the studios, the Douglas and Lockheed factories, and practically every German refugee in Los Angeles.'

The evening was a triumph—of rhetoric and PR—and brought in a lot more money. But, much more bizarre, at the end of his thank-you speech, when Malraux raised his hand in the clenched-fist communist salute, thousands of ladies in mink, actuated by a keen showbiz sense of occasion, rose in reply clenching their bejewelled hands. And what did it mean to them? No more, probably, than another experience equivalent to weeping over the fates of Luise Rainer and Paul Muni as *echt* Hollywood Chinese peasants in *The Good Earth*.

And yet, in certain respects the why does not matter that much; much more important were the consequences of such ventures. As a direct result of Malraux's visit and that, shortly after, of Hemingway and the left-wing Dutch film-maker Joris Ivens with their film *The Spanish Earth*, fifteen stars (among them Fredric March) gave a thousand dollars each to provide an ambulance and medical supplies for the Republicans. Though the anti-fascist activities of highly-paid New York writers like Donald Ogden Stewart, Dorothy Parker, Sam Behrman, Anita Loos and others may seem rather ridiculous and dilettante, at the same time they did, for whatever reasons, do a lot of good on a personal level, using their best efforts to get distinguished émigrés work in the studios, signing affidavits to assist their immigration, and so on.

While these efforts were not exactly negligible, they amounted to surprisingly little. What strikes one is how marginal the political activities of even the most committed were in Hollywood. Obviously within their own little circles events like the German–Soviet pact of 1939 could cause a major crisis: where did dedicated members of the Anti-Nazi League, who also regarded themselves as communists or fervent Russian sympathizers, stand? Among them, for a while, there were bitter dissensions. But for the rest of Hollywood, insofar as it was aware that anything odd was happening in Europe, the dilemma created by the pact was just one more occasion for making rather cruel fun of the naive fellow travellers.

The House of Representatives Committee on Un-American Activities (HUAC), set up in 1938 to investigate evidence of political infiltration (mostly left-wing) in American life, moved into Hollywood in 1940 to study signs of 'premature anti-fascism' in the movies, and found precious little to excite them. And even in HUAC's witch-hunting heyday, it is interesting to note that throughout all the thousands of pages devoted to the hearings of the Committee after the war on 'Communist Infiltration of the Hollywood Motion-Picture Industry' there is not one clear example of any of these left-wing writers, actors and directors having any influence at all on the content or attitudes of the films being made in Hollywood in the late 1930s and early 1940s. However important the fight against fascism might be in Europe, Hollywood remained secure in its dreams of glamour, romance, escape, and 'Boffo in Cinci'.

It was indeed in every way a foreign country that the émigrés found awaiting them in a frenzy of apathy as the Second World War began in Europe and the trickle westwards became a torrent. Paradise or purgatory? That all depended....

THE FORTIES

8. Gone with the Wind Up?

Surprising that the English should have been first. Even more surprising, perhaps, that they should have been forgiven last. As late as 1979 Naomi Mitchison observed, speaking of her friendship with W. H. Auden: 'It never was the same after he went to America. Somehow it wasn't, you know, with those who weren't in Britain during the war. You couldn't feel the same way towards them: something died.' For a certain generation, evidently, the feeling of betrayal ran deep. And yet the war itself had little to do with the major English migration. Premonitions of it, maybe, and a general disenchantment with the state of Europe. But the only émigré (never a full-time resident of Hollywood, though he worked there intermittently) who frankly admitted to staying in America because he was terrified of the war was the playwright Frederick Lonsdale; he even announced once that he was going on to Japan because everyone there was so yellow they would not notice him.

For the rest, it was a complex of reasons, among which fear of the war—however understandable—played only a small part. Many of them, indeed, spent some time struggling in vain just to get back to England once war broke out. And those who stayed often seem to have arrived with no fixed plans to do so, or to do anything in particular, by a kind of continental drift. Aldous Huxley, as we have seen, arrived by chance, wandered off, came back just for a while because of the climate and the proximity of friends, and stayed on without any real moment of conscious decision. In August 1938 his wife wrote:

> In Sanary Aldous can live only part of the year, the working part; even so, books are lacking. In London he can only live part of the year because of the climate.... California—with its many disadvantages—combines some of the advantages of London and Sanary. Anyway, we can't go on like Lawrence, keep running off in search for the perfect place; it doesn't exist and it seems to me

that at our age we ought at last to have found the tranquillity to stay where we are.

And still they hesitated and planned and changed plans, until the war in Europe virtually made up their minds for them.

There were, of course, good reasons to be depressed by the situation in Europe and wish to get away, other than an immediate 'cowardice' faced with the horrors of war (the 'gone-with-the-wind-up' syndrome). In many ways the Munich crisis of September 1938, with its craven capitulation to Hitler and his territorial expansion at Czechoslovakia's expense, the 'little piece of paper' that was supposed to guarantee 'peace in our time', was much more difficult for committed liberals, or even conventionally patriotic Britons, to swallow than the possible physical dangers of war, if it came. The end of the Spanish Civil War in March 1939, with complete victory for the Falange and everything left-wing intellectuals had been fighting against, was a further reason for feeling that Europe was finished, and nothing good was to be expected or hoped for on that side of the Atlantic.

Moreover, for those who were involved with film-making in Britain, there were some purely local hazards to contend with. The British film industry had been in a precarious state of equilibrium throughout most of the 1930s. The much reviled Quota Act of 1927 had done its job in that it guaranteed a showing for a high proportion of British films in British cinemas—even though in practice this included a lot of quota quickies, which just barely fulfilled the minimum requirements of length and Britishness and let all consideration of quality go by the board. At the other end of the scale, Alexander Korda had hit the jackpot, in 1933, with *The Private Life of Henry VIII*, and had subsequently been pursuing the chimera of a large, profitable, wide-open American market, such as the success of *Henry VIII* seemed to promise. This meant that a number of, by British standards, very expensive films had been made, using a lot of international talent (for Britain too had its émigrés, most of whom found haven for a while in the productions of the émigré Korda), with very variable commercial and artistic success. Oddly, while all this was going on, the British films that were most successful in America tended to be those that were not particularly directed towards America at all, such as the succession of classic thrillers Alfred Hitchcock was making for the modest, middle-of-the-road company Gaumont-British.

For most of its existence, in fact, the British film industry had been all too closely involved with America—fighting off American competition, courting American audiences, hiring American stars (usually falling stars), and trying to attract American money. In 1937, Gaumont-British was being summarily closed down by its new owners, Korda was bringing out some of his most expensive flops (such as *Knight Without Armour*, starring Marlene Dietrich and directed by Jacques Feyder) and things were yet again in a state of ferment and threatened crisis. But it suddenly began to look as though the long-hoped-for arrangement of co-production with America and worthwhile American financial participation in British film production was actually going to come about. Michael Balcon, newly fired from Gaumont-British, was promptly appointed head of a new MGM-British operation, and taken out to Hollywood for indoctrination by Louis B. Mayer. His roots and interests were, however, almost defiantly British, and it is not really surprising that after one production, *A Yank at Oxford* (American director, American star), Balcon was replaced by his second-in-command, Victor Saville, who had always been more amenable to America and American methods. But, in any case, only two more productions were to appear under this banner before, in 1939, the worrying state of affairs in Europe persuaded MGM to close the enterprise down, successful as it had proved (primarily as a way of making what were in effect American films cheaply on location), and take Victor Saville back to Hollywood as a staff producer in Culver City.

Other film-makers, disquieted by the unstable situation of the British film industry, were beginning to look with interest towards Hollywood. They would have done so anyway, war or no war. And if Hollywood offered a receptive market for their talents, why not? Balcon recalls in his autobiography that on a visit to Hollywood earlier in the 1930s he showed Louis B. Mayer his latest production, *Tudor Rose* (1936), a modest historical piece about Lady Jane Grey with no big stars and a young director, Robert Stevenson. Mayer asked him how much it cost, discovered that it was between £30,000 and £40,000, and at once ordered one of his subordinates to 'sign up everyone concerned with this picture'. Nothing came of this, though Robert Stevenson went on later to a long and successful career in Hollywood. But the attractive idea of Hollywood largesse persisted. And though horror stories trickled back, all the same there seemed to be no harm in at least trying one's luck, especially if offered the possibility to make far richer, stranger things than would ever come one's way in England.

Actors, naturally, were in the habit of frequent commuting. Figures such as Charles Laughton, Leslie Howard and Laurence Olivier were as familiar and sought-after in America as in England. Directors, for some reason, seemed to be less flexible. They seldom, in those days at least, travelled for one film; if they travelled at all, it was likely to be for a long period or for keeps. So a trip to Hollywood was considered a serious thing, and liable to be regarded, even before the war, as defection. All the same, as another economic crisis befell the British film industry at the end of 1937, many of the small mushrooming companies went into liquidation, and opportunities for producing anything exceptional became ever fewer and further between. Inevitably, more and more British film-makers began seriously to wonder about their chances in Hollywood. Hitchcock made his first visit to America in 1937, just to New York, and in the wake of critical enthusiasm and gratifying box-office returns for his films, such as *The Thirty-Nine Steps* (1935), offers of work started pouring in. He was, anyway, beginning to feel that, even as the big fish in the small pond of British cinema, he was getting into too much of a routine, rigidly type-cast as a maker of thrillers and effectively prevented from trying anything different.

On his second visit to America, in July 1938, he went to Hollywood for the first time, was fêted as a celebrity visitor and met, among others who had been courting him across the Atlantic, David O. Selznick. Selznick this time made Hitchcock a concrete offer that he could hardly refuse: a four-picture contract at about $40,000 a picture, to start the following month with a film based on the sinking of the *Titanic* and then, as the second project, a version of a book that Hitchcock had already tried himself to buy for filming in England, Daphne du Maurier's new bestseller *Rebecca*. He agreed in principle, but in practice his debut in America was put off for a few months by organizational problems, which first shelved then cancelled the *Titanic* project. Obviously, had he started filming in August 1938 and stayed on in Hollywood he might still have come in for some criticism for not being in England at the beginning of the war, but no doubt far less than actually descended on his head because he did not leave England until well into 1939 and did not start shooting on his first American film, *Rebecca*, until the outbreak of war in Europe.

He was by no means the only British film-worker to go west at this time. Herbert Wilcox had had a distribution arrangement in

America with RKO for his British films, mostly starring his wife-to-be Anna Neagle. They had just made two of their biggest successes together, *Victoria the Great* (1937) and *Sixty Glorious Years* (1938) (both based on episodes in the life of Queen Victoria) and they and RKO felt it was time for them to attack the American market more directly by actually making films in America. At the end of 1938 Wilcox went to Hollywood to make detailed plans for this. A co-production company was set up, and a project for a filmed life of Marie Lloyd was considered, with Cary Grant as co-star. Eventually Grant turned down the idea, and thus enforced a change of plan. What Wilcox came up with was a new version of the Edith Cavell story, about an heroic British nurse in the First World War, which he had already made as a silent with Sybil Thorndike. This being acceptable to all, Anna Neagle was summoned to Hollywood in March 1939 and work began on what was, in effect, a British film made completely in America, *Nurse Edith Cavell* (1939).

When it was initiated it seemed to be a relatively uncontroversial piece. But by the time it was ready for release the Germans had marched into Poland and the Second World War had begun. The isolationist American press—notably the violently anti-British *Chicago Tribune*—denounced it as a cunning piece of pro-British propaganda, shrewdly anticipating the outbreak of war and violating the Neutrality Act. For a while it seemed possible there might be an official directive that it be withdrawn from American distribution, but finally the film's status as propaganda was largely a matter of interpretation—Lord Lothian, the British ambassador, opined diplomatically that while the film did work very effectively to build up sympathy for the British, it could not be quite pinned down as propaganda within the meaning of the Act. The film received some excellent press, as well as hostile, and Anna Neagle was eventually nominated for an Academy Award for her performance. However, Lord Lothian also advised Wilcox to be careful in future productions not to violate the Neutrality Act, and so the next three Wilcox/Neagle films were wholly non-political musical romances—*Irene* (1940), *No No Nanette* (1940) and *Sunny* (1941).

Other British film-makers were also coming, late in 1938 or early in 1939, to feel that in purely professional terms Hollywood was a better bet than England. When, in the middle of 1939, MGM decided to close down their British operation, Victor Saville was in Hollywood conferring on details of release and plans for further production, if any. Since he had the same status in the company as a

127

staff producer in the main studios, and had obviously proved his efficiency in the British operation, he was asked to stay on there and, seeing little prospect for further rewarding work in Britain, agreed to do so. In any case, he had always insisted that though he was a very capable director, his real love and talent was for producing, and at that time a major Hollywood studio was the best place in the world for a producer to produce.

Though Saville, like just about every other Britisher in Hollywood during the early days of the war, did come in for some criticism in Britain on the grounds of 'desertion', his departure, safely before the outbreak of war, was not as controversial as that of some others. Robert Stevenson, for instance, director of *Tudor Rose*, the object of Louis B. Mayer's abortive enthusiasm a few years earlier, was a convinced pacifist engaged, when war broke out, in making small-scale films for Michael Balcon at Ealing, where Balcon had set up operations after leaving MGM. But David O. Selznick, having recently imported Hitchcock from England, was still on the lookout for European talent and offered Stevenson a contract. He decided to take the opportunity, and left for Hollywood with his actress-wife Anna Lee soon after war had been declared. Typically, Selznick never actually employed Stevenson himself, but hired him out to other studios, sometimes as part of a package (like *Jane Eyre*) that he had put together himself. Also, oddly enough, Stevenson the conscientious objector did anyway do his part in the war, in the US Army from 1943 to 1946.

Much more fuss accompanied the 'defection' of Alexander Korda to Hollywood in 1940. Korda, of course, was only a naturalized British subject, and in the somewhat hysterical atmosphere of the 'phoney war' he was therefore all the more suspect. He had all sorts of purely business reasons to be looking outside Britain as the war began. For one thing, since the mini-crisis of 1937 he had been in financial difficulties (more or less the usual ones in his extravagant, hit-or-miss operation). He had one very expensive production, *The Thief of Bagdad*, shooting for several months and still uncompleted when for the moment all film production was stopped in September 1939; even if it was possible to start up again soon, the necessary Middle Eastern locations for the sequences still to be shot would obviously not be available. He also needed finance for new productions, on a scale that was unlikely to be available in Britain, even if the necessary facilities were.

In December 1939 he went to Canada and the United States,

primarily to promote his new, quickly made propaganda piece *The Lion Has Wings*, but also to see his new wife Merle Oberon, who was filming in Hollywood, and discreetly check out the financial possibilities of America. He already had to defend himself against charges in the British press that he was planning to desert, and to explain that his director brother Zoltan, a consumptive, was going to America for his health. In February 1940 he was back in America, however, seeking American financial backing. He received it, to the tune of $3,600,000, but with the proviso that only $400,000 of that could be used to make two relatively small-scale films in Britain; the rest had to be used in America. So the die was cast. In June 1940 he transferred production of *The Thief of Bagdad* to America (the location scenes were shot in the Grand Canyon), and himself stayed there until January 1942.

What, precisely, was he doing there? To begin with, he was making three films, *That Hamilton Woman* (*Lady Hamilton*), *Lydia* and *Jungle Book* (as well as participating in various undefined ways in the production of Lubitsch's *To Be or Not To Be*). The first of these, the only one he directed himself, was obviously (rather too obviously, as it turned out) a piece of pro-British propaganda, wrapped up in historical romance. The other two were straight Hollywood films, the first a remake by Julien Duvivier of his own French classic *Un Carnet de Bal*, retailored to the requirements of a vehicle for Merle Oberon; the second a spectacular based on Kipling that was ready-made as a vehicle for Korda's contract star Sabu. *That Hamilton Woman* was Korda's main overt contribution to the British war effort, telling the story of the love affair between Lord Nelson and Lady Hamilton in a way cunningly designed to attract sympathy for Britain's stand against Nazi Germany (the contemporary relevance of Nelson's long speech to the Admiralty about the impossibility of making peace by appeasing Napoleon was quite evident) while wrapping up the propaganda in a sugar coating.

All the same, the film got into trouble with a Senate committee investigating the neutrality of Hollywood film-makers, and specifically whether any of them could be accused of 'inciting to war' (September 1941). Evidence was given to the committee by representatives of the isolationist, anti-British and pro-German factions in Hollywood, who found indications of what would later be called 'premature anti-fascism' in films by other British émigrés, including Chaplin's *The Great Dictator* and Hitchcock's *Foreign Correspondent*. The hearings did not come to anything, being suspended indefinitely in October 1941, but Korda remained under suspicion, along with Victor Saville, of being a British agent, and Korda was summoned to appear before another committee, the Senate Foreign Relations Committee, on 12 December 1941. This could have been very serious for him, but in the event Japan chose 7 December to attack Pearl Harbor, and so the basis of the suspicions against Korda was rendered irrelevant.

But was Korda in fact a British agent in America? Though the story is not even now totally clear, all the evidence seems to point to his being so. Certainly Korda was a close personal friend of Winston Churchill, and rumours were rife, then and since, that he went to America to continue making 'British' films at the direct request of Churchill. He was also closely associated with William Stephenson, head of the British Security Co-ordination group of British Intelligence, who worked secretly for British interests in America up to America's entry into the war. He seems to have worked for Stephenson, and directly for Churchill, as a secret courier, frequently crossing the Atlantic in conditions of some difficulty and danger. And it would surely be very strange, if the British Government considered him a deserter or in any way traitor to the British cause, that he should have been knighted, for unspecified reasons, in the Birthday Honours list of 1942.

Korda was not the only British émigré to be caught in a crossfire between September 1939 and December 1941. On the one side they were reviled by extremists in Britain for having deserted their country in her hour of need. On the other, they were objects of suspicion in America as likely foreign agents threatening American neutrality. In Hollywood there was a lot of sympathy for the British cause, but none of the major film companies could afford to admit it openly, even if they wished to do so (and anyway most of them agreed on purely practical grounds with Sam Goldwyn's assertion that messages are for Western Union). There was the Neutrality Act still to be considered and, if possible, circumvented with extreme discretion. Hitchcock, in the early days of the war, was particularly upset by his inclusion in a violent attack launched by his old friend and colleague Michael Balcon on the deserters to Hollywood safety. Balcon was subsequently informed, unofficially, that Hitchcock, like Korda, was staying put in Hollywood at the express request of the British Government, since he could do far more for Britain there than he could back home. But the damage had already been done and wounds inflicted that would take a lifetime to heal.

The rest of the British colony got their orders, to much the same effect, in a more roundabout way. The first thing to do when war broke out, obviously, was to contact the British consul in Los Angeles. He said his directives were that British actors and others should stay put and 'not panic'. Shortly afterwards, Herbert Wilcox and Anna Neagle were in Washington for the opening of *Nurse Edith Cavell*; Wilcox saw the ambassador, Lord Lothian, who, when he heard that they intended to return to Britain as soon as they could, told them to stay in America, where they could be more use than they would be in Britain as 'untrained labour'. With younger Britishers (Wilcox was then 48) the question of call-up was also germane. Selznick was worried as early as 23 August 1939 about what would happen in the event of war to the British nationals in the film he was just about to start—*Rebecca*. If Laurence Olivier and George Sanders were ordered back immediately, 'we would be in a fine pickle if they walked out in the middle—not so much of a pickle as Poland, I grant you, but still a pickle.'

But even if deferred, call-up was always a possibility. Laurence Olivier was, in fact, eligible, and like most of his compatriots restive in America. At the outbreak of war he was just beginning shooting on *Rebecca*, and Vivien Leigh, soon to be his wife (though the romance between them was still being kept as secret as possible) was just finishing on another Selznick project, *Gone With the Wind*. 'Staying put', they both went on to other films at MGM, both with a comfortingly British ring to them: he in *Pride and Prejudice* (1940) with a new British import, Greer Garson, and she in a remake of *Waterloo Bridge* (1940). These films completed, they put on an ambitious New York stage production of *Romeo and Juliet*, a singular disaster that closed rapidly, leaving them bereft of the savings they had put into it. A series of further inquiries about the possibility of returning to England received rather negative responses. Duff Cooper, then Minister of Information, continued the line of 'you may be more use where you are'. Ralph Richardson, who was already in the Fleet Air Arm, was consulted about Olivier's chances of getting into it and thought they were slim.

At this point Korda called them in New York and offered them *That Hamilton Woman*, which seemed to be the answer to all their problems, financial and professional. It was to be made quickly and relatively cheaply; it also gave them at last the feeling of doing something for Britain, as well as enabling them to bring over their children by earlier marriages to safety in America. At the end of

August 1940 they also received confirmation of their respective divorces, and so were able at last to marry, with the help of Ronald Colman and his wife Benita Hume in ensuring secrecy.

By this time things had gone from bad to worse in Europe, and as there was now a new British ambassador in Washington, Lord Halifax, the British film colony got together to discuss the situation and deputed Laurence Olivier, Herbert Wilcox, Cary Grant and Cedric Hardwicke to fly to Washington to consult with him. Lord Halifax took the same view as Lord Lothian: unless there were specialized qualifications for aiding the war effort, Britishers should stay where they were, as England, with its food shortages and other trials, could not accommodate 'unnecessary' people. All the same, some were determined. Olivier had managed to obtain a pilot's licence while preparing for and shooting *That Hamilton Woman*, which made his chances for the Fleet Air Arm considerably better, and did at least constitute 'specialized qualifications'. At the end of December 1940 the Oliviers sailed for Europe. Herbert Wilcox and Anna Neagle were not able to follow until August 1941.

Clearly the war had created—for the first time outside press agents' fantasies, it seems—a real sense of community among the British in Hollywood. What had been more or less socially agreeable, according to taste and interests, in seeing other British residents in Los Angeles became suddenly almost a patriotic duty. Unfortunately, the only quasi-official result of this new British sense of togetherness was not too wonderful and was in any case so long held up that it lost any impact it might have had. This was the collaborative film effort *Forever and a Day*, an episodic story of life in Britain through several generations of the same family in the same house, which was produced as a charitable, non-profitmaking venture by RKO in 1941 and used virtually all the British talent then available in Hollywood, as well as many Americans sympathetic to Britain. Episodes were directed by Herbert Wilcox (starring, inevitably Anna Neagle), Victor Saville (starring his old British collaborator Jessie Matthews, borrowed from a disastrous Broadway-bound show for what proved to be her only Hollywood experience), Robert Stevenson and Cedric Hardwicke. Hitchcock prepared an episode with Ida Lupino (another Britisher, though so long in Hollywood one tends to forget it), but at the last moment was unable to direct it, so it was directed by René Clair instead. Other actors involved included Charles Laughton, Ian Hunter, Ray Milland, C. Aubrey Smith, Merle Oberon, Gladys Cooper, Victor

McLaglen, June Duprez, Anna Lee, Roland Young and Dame May Whitty, while among the writers was the improbable combination of Christopher Isherwood, Frederick Lonsdale, Charles Bennett, John Van Druten and C. S. Forester.

Of course, there was always the danger that the film, however innocent of direct propaganda it might be, could be accused of violating the Neutrality Act. However, Herbert Wilcox, who had dreamed up the project, was advised that criticism of this kind might be avoided if the American profits were donated to an American charity, and so it was arranged, the charity chosen being President Roosevelt's personal favourite, the March of Dimes. But one way and another completion of the film was delayed, and then it was virtually shelved. It surfaced finally only in March 1943, by which time its topicality and usefulness to the British war effort were diminished almost to zero.

Other attempts at pro-British propaganda were more successfully managed. Leslie Howard, an on-off member of the British colony in Hollywood, had never really settled in America, even though he regarded America as his second home. When he finished work on what was to prove his last Hollywood film, *Gone With the Wind*, in August 1939, he returned home to England, his departure marked by a rather absurd piece of flag-waving from his agent, who announced that this showed him to be 'typically English; blind, unswerving duty to King and Country, unquestioning response, that's the attitude of every true Britisher.' Be that as it may, in the early days of the war Howard remained very concerned with Anglo-American relations, and from the British side did what he could. For Duff Cooper at the Ministry of Information he prepared a paper based on his knowledge of America and Americans, *Notes on American Propaganda,* in which he outlined his ideas about the usefulness of film:

> I am quite certain that, properly camouflaged, the message we want to deliver can be carried direct to the American people. I regret already the word 'camouflage'. We want to give them facts, supply them with information. After all, most of them are intensely sympathetic to our cause, they are 'rooting' for us, they want us to win. They are vitally interested, morally and humanly, in the drama in which we are taking part. It does not take much more to persuade them that we are the heroes of this drama.

Receiving little or no direct response from the government, who were inclined at this time to put films, propaganda or otherwise, very low on their list of priorities (thinking, for instance, that film studios would be better used if requisitioned for other purposes), in 1940 Howard began work himself on a 'camouflaged' propaganda project, *Pimpernel Smith*, which would help to carry his message, on the strength of his personal popularity, to the great American public.

No doubt a message is likely to be more palatable if embodied in a narrative film without any designs on its spectators. At any rate, that seems to be the principle on which Alfred Hitchcock, that great disapprover of messages, set to work on his 'message' film, *Foreign Correspondent*. When the film opened in August 1940 the New York *Herald Tribune* observed approvingly that it 'blends escapist entertainment with challenging propaganda in film terms'. The 'challenging propaganda' was sufficiently evident for the film to be picked out for suspicious scrutiny by the Senate committee on Hollywood neutrality.

The film, which was quite an expensive one for its time ($1,500,000), came about mainly through a happy meeting between Hitchcock and Walter Wanger, a leading independent producer at that time who had something of a reputation for making serious anti-fascist films—mainly on the strength of the relatively anodyne and non-committal *Blockade* (1938), a romantic melodrama with a Spanish Civil War background. All the same, as an independent he was less worried by the possibility of official disapproval than the major studios, and appreciated the publicity value of stories currently in the news. With this in mind he had bought the screen rights to Vincent Sheean's autobiography *Personal History*, which chronicled Sheean's experiences as a politically concerned correspondent in a Europe under the imminent threat of war. The book, embodying no more than the vaguest idea of a film subject, was handed over to Hitchcock and he set about inventing a film story around it with the aid of two familiar English collaborators, Charles Bennett, who had come over under contract to Universal in 1937, and Joan Harrison, who had come over with Hitchcock in 1939.

The story they came up with could hardly have been more cunningly designed to foster sympathy for Britain under the guise of a typical Hitchcock thriller. The central character is an American journalist who arrives in Europe without any kind of political commitment and gradually, through personal loyalties and the inevitable love interest, becomes involved against his will in the anti-Nazi cause. The conclusion is quite explicit. The hero is broadcasting to America:

JONES: Hello, America. I've been watching a part of the world being blown to pieces. A part of the world as nice as Vermont, Ohio, Virginia, California and Illinois lies ripped up bleeding like a steer in a slaughterhouse. And I've seen things that make the history of the savages read like Pollyanna legend.

ANNOUNCER: We're going to have to postpone the broadcast. *(At this point sirens begin to wail and lights flash as bombs begin to burst outside the studio.)*

JONES: Don't postpone nothing, let's go on as long as we can.

ANNOUNCER: *(To Carol)*: Ma'am, we've got a shelter downstairs.

JONES: How about it, Carol?

CAROL: They're listening in America, Johnny.

JONES: OK. We'll tell them. I can't read the rest of this speech I have because the lights have gone out. So I'll just have to talk off the cuff. All that noise you hear isn't static, it's death coming to London. Yes, they're coming here now. You can hear the bombs falling on the streets and homes. Don't tune me out—hang on—this is a big story—and you're part of it. It's too late now to do anything except stand in the dark and let them come, as if the lights are all out everywhere except in America.
(Music—'America'—begins to play softly in background of speech and continues through end credits.)

JONES: Keep those lights burning, cover them with steel, build them in with guns, build a canopy of battle-ships and bombing planes around them and, hello, America, hang on to your lights, they're the only lights in the world.

Foreign Correspondent was, in fact, the most direct, frankly partisan film about the war to come out of Hollywood before America's own entry into the war, and its very existence gives colour to the story that Hitchcock stayed on in America at the direct instigation of someone high up in the British government. Especially since Hitchcock was already contemplating a companion piece,

Saboteur (1942) which he made after two safely non-political films but before America was committed to the fight against fascism. Indeed one of the intervening films, *Suspicion* (1941) was originally planned to end incongruously with the unscrupulous hero going off to redeem himself, accompanied by some resoundingly anti-Nazi sentiments, as a pilot in the Battle of Britain. (The reasons for the suppression of this particular oddity clearly had more to do with artistic discretion than political pressure.) Even if Hitchcock had not later in the war taken a year off from his highly profitable and successful Hollywood career to make, in doodlebug-plagued London, a couple of propaganda shorts for the Ministry of Information, it would be difficult to suppose that he was happily ensconced in Hollywood as a cowardly deserter from his native land.

Of course, Hitchcock could hardly be considered, any more than any of the other Britishers primarily involved in films, as a politically motivated émigré: of them all, probably only Robert Stevenson had gone to Hollywood, or more precisely had left Britain, on some kind of principle. There were certain practical difficulties in their return to Britain at the beginning of the war (not to mention official advice to stay put), but it was assumed that they all would be likely to return home and do their bit for the war effort as soon as they reasonably could. Most of them did even if, like Hitchcock, they did not choose to stay there permanently. This in itself was enough to separate them decisively from the other, smaller group of Britishers in Los Angeles, who had left Europe in pursuit of some ideal—pacifism usually being an important motive force.

The most important members of this smaller group were Huxley and Heard, soon to be joined by a third, Christopher Isherwood. While Huxley and Heard had somehow drifted into permanent exile, and had settled in Los Angeles more or less by chance, Isherwood was more purposeful. He left Britain in the company of W. H. Auden on 18 January 1939—'the most important literary event since the outbreak of the Spanish Civil War', Cyril Connolly called it, rather bizarrely suggesting that he regarded the Spanish Civil War primarily as a literary event also. If so, from the perspective of 1940 when he made the observation, he was probably not far wrong; at least he seemed to voice the real views of many contemporary intellectuals. Certainly, on the boat to America, Auden and Isherwood finally got round to admitting, to each other and to themselves, that they were bored and disillusioned with left-wing politics and the fight against fascism. Spain was a psychodrama that had somehow gone wrong and now, with a shameful peace precariously established in Central Europe by the Munich agreement and the Spanish Civil War nearing a foregone conclusion, they turned towards the New World for something new to worry about or, preferably, find peace in.

Gerald Heard had found the answers to his psychological and historical questionings in the teachings of Vedanta philosophy as expressed in the life and work of the Swami Prabhavananda, who had been living and teaching quietly in Hollywood (literally in the geographical centre of Hollywood) since 1929. With characteristic reservations, Huxley had followed Heard, at least so far as to take up meditation. Isherwood arrived in America with a numbing sense of his own lack of direction. He had abandoned one faith, his faith in militant socialism, and realized that now—no doubt partly as a result of a former boyfriend's being drafted into the German Army—he had a total emotional revulsion from the whole idea of war, and desperately needed something to hold on to. He and Auden were to an extent lionized in left-wing circles in New York, mainly on account of beliefs they no longer held. Auden seemed well able to cope; he met his lifetime lover Chester Kallman at the beginning of April, and was obviously destined for success in America, of whatever kind. Isherwood, on the other hand, felt 'pure despair'.

At this point he thought of Heard, whom he had met some years before in London, and of Christopher Wood, a friend of his and of Heard's who was then also in Los Angeles. In addition, there was Huxley, whom Isherwood admired but had never met. He wrote to Heard, and was inspired by Heard's reply to set out for California at the beginning of May 1939, in a roundabout fashion by Greyhound bus. Part of the plan—the most practical part—was to find work as a writer somewhere in the movies; he had already written film scripts in England, and another acquaintance out in California, though not for the moment around, was Berthold Viertel, director of one of them, *Little Friend*. (The making of this film was later fictionalized in Isherwood's first American novel *Prater Violet*.)

To begin with, Isherwood settled in the Hollywood Hills, began seeing a lot of Heard, and by July had met both the Swami and the Huxleys. Little by little he, the confirmed atheist, came under the spell of the Swami's teachings and, no doubt more importantly, the Swami himself (nearly all of Isherwood's major decisions in life have been, on his own admission, emotional and very much bound up with personality). For a while he became so engrossed in the Vedanta that E. M. Forster observed wryly to another friend in 1944, apropos of Isherwood's letters, 'How he does go on about God!' though by the next year Isherwood was refusing to join one of Heard's groups because he was 'sick and tired of hearing them yacking about God'.

All the same, throughout the war years he was primarily occupied with coming to terms with his newly acquired religious convictions and deciding how to live with them, in the world or out of it. Not all of the influences on him were so unworldly as Heard and the Swami. At this time he also got to know another unlikely British addition to Los Angeles society, the rich bisexual art patron and would-be poet Edward James, who had arrived in California at about the same time as Isherwood. James expressed a desire to become a disciple of Heard and the Swami, though he was somewhat mistrusted by Heard and Maria Huxley, who could not conceive that someone as rich as he could be spiritually serious, but he also moved with ease among Hollywood high society and the contingent homosexual circles, which also intrigued Isherwood and had little to do with self-denying spirituality.

Huxley, with whom Isherwood rapidly became friendly, especially once he penetrated Huxley's pontifical facade and discovered the good humour and gentleness underneath, was certainly unworldly enough in his way. Anita Loos recalls, for instance, that he was convinced when war broke out that he would have to give up work on the *Pride and Prejudice* script because 'I simply cannot accept all that money [$1,500 a week] to work in a pleasant studio while my family and friends are starving and being bombed in England.' The possibility that he could send most of that money back to England had simply not occurred to him until his wife suggested it. But in other matters he did manage to fit in rather practically with Hollywood: his adaptation of *Pride and Prejudice* was successfully concluded to the satisfaction of MGM, and other scripting work was offered whenever he wanted it. And for all his personal devotion to Heard he remained critical of his intellectual rigidity and stylistic fuzziness. Huxley himself always offered an encouraging example of how to live sensibly both in the special world of Southern California and aside from it.

Huxley stayed put in California throughout the war years, and indeed for the rest of his life. He lived first in Pacific Palisades, then from 1943 to 1947 primarily in the Mojave Desert, at Llano del Rio, with interludes in Beverly Hills when film work offered (on a curious selection of 'suitable' classic adaptations, including *Jane Eyre* for Twentieth Century-Fox and *Alice in Wonderland* for Walt Disney).

But Isherwood grew restless. He moved in various circles besides the Huxley–Heard group—through the Viertels he met many of the German émigrés, and soon took over a house in Amalfi Drive, near where the Huxleys were living at the time and just a short walk from the Viertels, in the centre of what was rapidly to establish itself as the main emigré area in and around Santa Monica. In 1940 he worked on various film scripts, usually just contributing odd scenes and pieces of dialogue to the script-factory, without screen credit. For most of the time he was under contract to MGM, where he had a hand in, among others, *A Woman's Face* (1941), directed by George Cukor and produced by another British émigré, Victor Saville (who at least came in useful by providing a few hints for the character of Chatsworth in *Prater Violet*), and *Free and Easy* (1941), based on Ivor Novello's play *The Truth Game*, the first adaptation of which had been Novello's own principal task when he was in Hollywood ten years earlier.

The agreeable routine—Tuesday lunch with the Huxleys and assorted oriental or pseudo-oriental mystics at Farmer's Market, where all kinds of dietary kinks could be accommodated; Sunday lunch at Anita Loos's in Santa Monica—was interrupted by a series of attacks on runaway intellectuals, in particular Auden and Isherwood, by Cyril Connolly in *Horizon* (though he denied it was meant as an attack), Harold Nicolson in *The Spectator* and Sir Jocelyn Lucas in the House of Commons. If anything Isherwood seems to have been reassured by most of the attacks, though he resented Connolly's. He was, however, feeling that it was time he got his house in order by carrying his by now dedicatedly pacifist reactions to the war a stage further. This he did by first going on a retreat organized by Heard and a group of Quakers at La Verne College, a little way inland from Los Angeles proper, then in October 1941 going to work at the Quaker-run Cooperative College Workshop in Haverford, Pennsylvania, at this time a school for European (chiefly German) refugees to help acclimatize them to the English language and American culture. Here he stayed for nine months, calming the 'terrible psychic restlessness which a war-situation generates', and starting after a long dry period to write again for his own satisfaction.

In July 1942 Isherwood had completed his stint at Haverford and returned to California, with the strong probability that he would be called up for service in a non-combatants' labour camp of some kind. It did not happen before the maximum call-up age was lowered at the end of the year, and meanwhile he began work on a new book, *Prater Violet,* completed a couple of film scripts and continued his Vendantic studies. Despite occasional practical contacts with the film world, he seems at this time to have seen relatively little of the Viertels' circle, and concentrated mainly on working through (if not totally out of) his system the teachings of the Swami Prabhavananda. In 1945, *Prater Violet* completed, he decided definitely that his true vocation was in the world as a writer, rather than in the meditative life as a swami.

In practice, therefore, Isherwood and Huxley were no more specifically a part of émigré society, let alone the alleged British colony, than the more workaday British newcomers to the film world in Hollywood, who, whatever quaint survivals of Britishness they cultivated, very rapidly either faded completely into the landscape, like Hitchcock, or returned to England, like the Oliviers and the Wilcoxes. If there was an exception that proved the rule, it would no doubt be the unpredictable Charles Laughton, who never fitted neatly into any pattern. Though in certain respects he tended to be regarded (and certainly cast) as every American's parody idea of an Englishman, Ruggles of Red Gap for ever, he was in fact far more cosmopolitan in his interests and acquaintances than most of his compatriots, and a sight more intellectual than any of the other British actors around Los Angeles. He had settled happily with his wife Elsa Lanchester in Pacific Palisades, the centre of émigré-land, in 1941, having been unable to return immediately to England at the outbreak of war because of his contract with RKO. But he had been doing everything possible at the American end to help the British war effort. Like just about every other Britisher in Hollywood he was involved in *Forever and a Day*, playing a discreetly drunken English butler, but more to the point, he drove himself unmercifully, once America had entered the war, in aid of the Allied cause, going on long and wearisome tours to sell war bonds, reading in veterans' hospitals and making endless propaganda broadcasts.

In Hollywood, too, his cosmopolitan attitudes were clearly perceptible. He did occasionally appear at the Viertel soirées, and became friendly with a number of distinguished émigrés, several of whom he worked profitably with: Julien Duvivier in *Tales of*

Manhattan (1942), Jean Renoir in *This Land Is Mine* (1943) and Robert Siodmak in *The Suspect* (1945) are the most notable. But the most important relationship, professional and personal, that he had with an émigré was outside the cinema altogether—the three years he spent with Bertolt Brecht assisting the slow gestation and definitive revision of Brecht's play *Galileo*, first performed in Los Angeles in 1947. Before we come to that, however, or Laughton's work with the French film-makers, we must get back to the German exiles we left in Sanary-sur-Mer and see what happened to them with the outbreak of war and how they and other anti-Nazi Europeans finally made their way to Southern California.

9. The New Weimar

For the little knot of distinguished German exiles in Sanary-sur-Mer
things had been reasonably comfortable. As the 1930s progressed,
the colony was gradually augmented by more and more long-term
residents—particularly after the Anschluss made Austria impossible
for liberals and Jews, and then the invasion of Czechoslovakia in
1938 put another, part-German-speaking country out of bounds.
The last major arrival at Sanary was Franz Werfel, who had already
been an occasional visitor but continued to live in Austria until the
Anschluss in March 1938. He was very definitely *persona non grata*
with the Nazis, more because he was Jewish than because of any very
pronounced political bias in his writings. He had, anyway, been
thrown out of the Berlin Akademie der Künste in 1933, along with
Alfred Doeblin, Georg Kaiser and, eventually, Thomas Mann. At
the time of the Anschluss he was abroad, and simply did not go back;
in fact he was ill with a high fever when Austria was overrun, and
later thanked heaven that this cushioned the blow for him. Friends in
France at once found an old mill at Sanary for him and his wife to live
in, and he joined the German community there, at any rate for the
time being.

'For the time being' was rapidly becoming the watchword of the
exiles. Though few dared actually put the worst into words, the
possibility of its happening became ever stronger and closer. In
France, as in Britain, it was still possible, after the Munich
agreement, for natives to put their heads in the sand and pretend to
themselves that it meant 'peace in our time'. For Germans it was not
so easy: most of them had a much clearer idea of Hitler's ambitions
and his capabilities. What they had to rely on was the cowardice or
complacency of the British and French governments—if they
continued the policy of appeasement these two countries might still
provide a safe refuge. But even so, probably not for ever: the more
they gave in to Hitler, the closer came the day when they would have

to face up to him on their own doorstep. So the émigrés did not rely too much on anything. But, for the time being, they stayed.

When the worst began to happen, on 3 September 1939, most of the Sanary crowd were still there, enjoying the late summer. The principal exception was Thomas Mann, who travelled frequently the more he, in his sixties, began to assume the mantle of a grand old man of letters. Earlier in 1939 he had been in America, teaching at Princeton and lecturing all over the States on 'The Problem of Freedom', then in Holland working on *Lotte in Weimar*, then in Zurich, London and finally Stockholm, where he was to be the German representative at a meeting of the International Pen Club. As soon as Britain and France declared war on Germany he left London for America again on board the *Washington*, which had been converted into a sort of refugee ship for hundreds of extra passengers eager to leave Europe while they still had time. At least Mann was going with the certain prospect of a new guest professorship at Princeton during the winter of 1939–40, and was not psychologically unprepared. Early in 1938 he had already been saying to Americans in a speech on 'The Coming Victory of Democracy':

> I believe that for the duration of the present European dark age the centre of Western culture will shift to America. It is my own intention to make my home in your country, and I am convinced that if Europe continues for a while to pursue the same course as in the last two decades, many good Europeans will meet again on American soil.

In this prediction he was right, and, as so often, prescient. At least it enabled him to make the transition to America more gracefully and comfortably than many of his friends and contemporaries, including his brother Heinrich, whom he had last seen in Paris in June 1939. Heinrich Mann was still living in Nice, with his German mistress Nelly Kroeger, and his first act after the outbreak of war was to marry her, so that for better or for worse their lives were definitely linked. As a well-known anti-Nazi and political exile—president, indeed, of the German Popular Front abroad—Heinrich Mann did not run into trouble with the French authorities for having suddenly become an enemy alien, though nominally a Czech citizen: many people in his position, as their equivalents in England, were interned in the slightly hysterical atmosphere that marked the beginning of hostilities. He was also now nearly seventy, and unwilling to leave

France and abandon his daughter Goschi to her fate in Czechoslovakia (not that there was anything he could do about it).

Soon, however, he was persuaded to cable Thomas at Princeton and ask him to use his influence to get him an entry visa for the United States. By this time events were moving fast while the wheels of bureaucracy ground slow, and the German invasion of France took place in May 1940 before anything could be done for him. Though he was already living in that part of France which became for a while the 'neutral' state of the Vichy government, it was laid down in the settlement that anyone the Germans wanted would be extradited. Though extradition proceedings had not yet begun against him Heinrich, as an obvious leader of the anti-Nazi Germans in France, suffered a Vichy campaign of vilification, and had to go into hiding in Marseilles ready to make his escape as soon as the papers came. They finally arrived at the American consulate there in August, but it was already too late for him to leave openly, without the exit visa he had been firmly refused.

There were others in the same predicament. Lion Feuchtwanger's history since the outbreak of war had indeed been decidedly worse. For all his anti-Nazi record, he was promptly interned, released through influence brought to bear by friends in the British government, and then interned again in May 1940, when all German citizens in France were interned, regardless of their political record. In his camp (separated from his wife) he fell seriously ill; a news photograph of him standing behind a barbed wire fence came to the attention of his New York publisher, Benjamin Huebsch, who happily was in a position to go straight to President Roosevelt with it. As a result, a presidential directive went out to all US foreign missions to assist Feuchtwanger in any way they could. Assisting above and beyond the call of duty, the US consul in Marseilles, Hiram Bingham, Jr, actually arranged to have Feuchtwanger kidnapped and reunited with his wife Marta, who had already contrived to escape from her camp.

Getting them out of France was another matter. In Marseilles the Feuchtwangers joined forces with the Werfels, Heinrich Mann and his new wife, and Golo Mann, Thomas's son. Feuchtwanger set about plotting various possibilities of escape, such as a boat to Tunisia. But in the end, with the help of an American Unitarian minister, Hastings Waitstill Sharp, they got on a train heading for the Spanish border, and then made their way across the Pyrenees on foot, passing by Lourdes, where Franz Werfel made a vow that if they got out of it alive he would write about St Bernadette of Lourdes (a vow he later kept in his bestseller *The Song of Bernadette*). From the Pyrenees they went to Barcelona, from Barcelona by train to Madrid, and from Madrid by air (Lufthansa, oddly enough) to Lisbon. There they had to wait for weeks to get on a boat to New York, but finally found room. Feuchtwanger went first, on an American ship, leaving his wife to follow two weeks later, along with the Werfels and assorted Manns, on a Greek steamer, the *Nea Hellas*.

Feuchtwanger arrived in New York on 5 October 1940; the rest of the party on 13 October. Thomas Mann was at this time living, though not teaching, at Princeton again, and came to New York to meet his brother. The arrival was attended with some confusion owing mainly to the conflicting demands of two organizations interested in the exiles: the Emergency Rescue Committee, a generally liberal organization set up by Frank Kingdon with Thomas Mann's help and co-operation, and the Exiled Writers Committee, an offshoot of the extreme left-wing League of American Writers. Both arranged dinners for the new arrivals: Feuchtwanger attended the Exiled Writers Committee's dinner, the rest making their excuses; Thomas Mann spoke at the Emergency Rescue Committee's dinner, and Heinrich Mann and Franz Werfel were present. Already the exiles were learning that to stay clear of trouble in America you had to know who and what your hosts were.

By the time Heinrich arrived, Thomas had spent some time in Southern California, living in a rented cottage on North Rockingham, Brentwood, from the end of June to the beginning of October while he completed his fantastic Indian tale *The Transposed Heads* and began work on the fourth and last volume of the sequence of novels on the life of Joseph. He had already decided that the climate of the West Coast suited him better than the rigours of the east, and had bought a plot of land in Pacific Palisades with a view to building a permanent home there: 'I have what I wanted—the light; the dry, always refreshing warmth; the spaciousness compared to Princeton; the holm oak, eucalyptus, cedar, and palm vegetation; the walks by the ocean which we can reach by car in a few minutes.' Also, there were already friends there—the Walters, the Franks and two of Mann's children, Klaus and Erika Mann.

The house progressed slowly, and Thomas Mann did not finally move from Princeton until 8 April 1941, when the family moved into 1550 San Remo Drive, Pacific Palisades. Heinrich therefore preceded his brother as a long-term Los Angeles resident: almost immediately he was given a contract with Warner Brothers (through the good offices of the Emergency Rescue Committee) and by the middle of November was installed in Hollywood along with several others, including Alfred Doeblin and Leonhard Frank. Their actual duties at their respective studios remained nebulous, though they were required to turn up at their offices by 9 a.m. at Warners, 10 a.m. at Metro and stay until 5 p.m. (or, in practice, 4 p.m.). Doeblin, who had arrived on the same boat as Heinrich Mann, was improbably assigned work on the scripts of *Mrs Miniver* and *Random Harvest,* though it is very doubtful if any of his contributions actually reached the screen. Heinrich Mann was really doing nothing—for $125 a week—and the jobs thought up for the exiled writers, with their mostly minimal English, seem to have been regarded as largely charitable enterprises, brought about by the European Film Fund through the good offices of Thomas Mann and some established German residents of the film colony. These included William Dieterle and his wife Charlotte, and Bruno Frank, a relatively old hand who had been in Hollywood since 1938 and had already successfully adapted *The Hunchback of Notre Dame* for Dieterle; he had even been one of the many to work on *Madame Curie* as a possible vehicle for Garbo.

The European Film Fund was the brain-child of Ernst Lubitsch, Salka Viertel and the agent Paul Kohner, who realized early in October 1939 that many of their old friends and associates, not to mention other, far more distinguished German writers, were likely to become refugees again and need help. Kohner had the reputation of being the most dynamic agent in Hollywood (he had been in America since 1921, when he had come to work for Carl Laemmle at Universal), and once he set his mind to organizing something it was likely to happen fast. On 24 October 1939 a meeting took place at the house of Fritzi Massari, the famous star of operetta and mother of Bruno Frank's wife Elizabeth. The fund was officially set up with a committee consisting of the directors Curtis Bernhardt, William Dieterle and Lothar Mendes, the producer Gottfried Reinhardt, the writers Bruno Frank, Erika Mann, Walter Reisch and Salka Viertel, and the actor Conrad Veidt.

Though, of course, in Hollywood there were always wheels within wheels, subterranean grievances and rivalries (Salka Viertel, for instance, was instantly dismissed from MGM in 1940 merely for bringing in Paul Kohner as her agent to renegotiate her contract), most of the committee members were important people, able to exercise influence in the only way the big companies understood—through the power of their own success. Also, very much to be taken into account, Dieterle's wife Charlotte and Frank's wife Elizabeth were determined and social ladies, prominent in the organization of Hollywood charities, so that they were able to enlist the help of many executive wives and raise funds in the grand traditional style. The immediate result was that, some months before the first important refugees arrived from defeated France, Harry Warner, always the most liberal in his sympathies of all the Hollywood tycoons, had agreed to hire émigré writers at a standard $100 a week to work at Warner Brothers, and Louis B. Mayer, worked on by Kohner and Gottfried Reinhardt, then a contract producer at Metro, had made the same agreement for MGM.

In those days, $100 a week was a living wage and a godsend to strangers in the country with no other visible means of support, but it was nothing compared with what most of the contract writers were getting. Leonhard Frank, in his lightly fictionalized autobiography, *Heart on the Left,* recalls being met on the landing-stage in New York by a man from Warners who gave him an advance of $200 and told him to report to the studio in Hollywood in a week's time. There he found that the writer in the next office to his was earning $3,500 a week and also informed Frank that obviously their bosses judged the value of everything by what they paid for it. So it stood to reason that the studios would not suppose someone they paid a mere $100 a week to be of any use at all. In fact Frank was given nothing at all to do, even for appearances' sake, for the first three months. Then he was assigned the adaptation of a novel called *Danger Signal,* but since all the highest-paid writers in the studio had already laboured on it in vain, it was clear the assignment was not to be taken very seriously.

The pattern of Heinrich Mann's life at the studio, in the office opposite, was much the same. He was, after all, now approaching seventy, and though he had managed to acquire a surprising mastery of written English he could rarely be persuaded actually to speak anything but German, so no doubt his presence at Warners was regarded as even more completely a charitable sinecure.

None of the one-year contracts was renewed. In October 1941 Leonhard Frank and Heinrich Mann were both out of a job, and virtually destitute, along with Alfred Doeblin, who was employed by MGM from 8 October 1940 to 7 October 1941. A couple of later arrivals, Wilhelm Speyer and Walter Mehring, were taken on by MGM in March and April 1941 respectively, but when Mehring's contract expired on 4 April 1942 the scheme for employing refugee writers, even at a minimal wage, came to an end. Other exiles never even held a token job at the film studios, though several of them, like Ludwig Marcuse, were given small grants from the European Film Fund (in Marcuse's case $40 a month). And then there were those, like Feuchtwanger and Werfel, who received sufficient income from their American royalties not to need the work or the grants. Leonhard Frank paints a rather gloomy picture of life in Los Angeles at this time for those surviving on the bare minimum:

> Many Germans had achieved success in Hollywood and had for years been earning enormous salaries, leading the life of dollar millionaires in their luxurious villas. At first they called on Michael [the name Frank gives himself in the book] and drove him out in Cadillacs of the latest model to their magnificent mansions. When they scented that Michael would never become a star in the Hollywood firmament, they cut him dead. A man who earns two hundred thousand dollars in Hollywood does not associate with the man who earns only a hundred thousand. When the year ended and Michael's salary stopped, he was in a good position to discover that in Hollywood money counts and nothing but money. In the eyes of his successful compatriots who met him in the street he was now an incorporeal, invisible ghost...

Frank does not name names, but presumably he is talking mainly about the people who had become completely involved in the film business. Certainly the rest of the German émigrés seem to have stuck very closely together, often meeting socially and self-consciously upholding the idea of Los Angeles as the 'New Weimar'. Nor were all of them at all accommodating to their new environment. During the 1930s Thomas Mann had become very well known in America: he had lectured extensively, toured and (though in a dignified sort of way) done a lot of promotion work on the American publication of his books. Heinrich, on the other hand, refused to go to America to lecture in 1933, or even when his *Henry IV* novels were being published there (and becoming bestsellers) from 1937 on. Now, in the summer of 1941, Heinrich refused to let an English-language version of his war diary be published because he rejected out-of-hand the idea of any editorial changes, even by a publisher as serious and respected as Knopf: he considered himself too distinguished a writer to accept interference of any kind, even in a strange land. In consequence, the formal undertaking Thomas Mann had to sign, to support his brother should he be unable to support himself, when Heinrich and his wife had to go to Mexico in March 1941 in order to return with permanent residents' visas, soon became practically applicable.

For Heinrich Mann, like Leonhard Frank, was one of those who found it difficult if not impossible to work in the Californian wonderland. Frank describes the alarming passage of time in Los Angeles, which 'flew like the passing flash of a colourless bird. A month went by more rapidly than a day of real life elsewhere. After years in Hollywood Michael still felt that he had been there only a few weeks.' He had brought with him a half-finished novel (*Mathilde*), which he continued to work on, slowly and frustratingly:

> Michael found that he needed an enormous amount of energy to go on writing in Hollywood. After the strong, bracing climate of Berlin, which had suited him so well, he found his powers of concentration reduced to a minimum by the tropical enervating heat. It seemed to thin his blood. He told himself there was 'no air in the atmosphere'. Sometimes as he wrote, he panted for that air, driving himself with ruthless energy to chisel from morning to night at a single sentence, only to cross it out again next morning. In Hollywood he lost time, precious time, unrecoverable years.

Mathilde was finally published in 1943, privately by the Pazifischen Press in Los Angeles (one of the very few German texts by exiled writers actually to be published on the spot). Then, after a dry period, he found that the sight of a hideous hand-painted tie in a shop window brought back a whole flood of memories of early days, and he began work on a new novel, *Deutsche Novelle,* first published in English as *The Baroness* in 1950. He was writing it in Los Angeles at the same time that Thomas Mann was working on his *Doctor Faustus*, and he was often a guest in Mann's home when they would each read portions of their respective works in manuscript. Years later Frank was offended when he read in Mann's book *The Genesis of a Novel*, along with praise of his *The Baroness*, some hints that he had been influenced in it by *Doctor Faustus.* But then they tended, no doubt partly because of their precarious situation, to be a touchy lot.

Heinrich Mann had even more to be touchy about. He was now, after October 1941, completely without resources apart from what his brother allowed him and a single payment of $750 from the

Soviet Union on account of the hundreds of thousands of copies of his works sold there. His wife, Nelly, had become a secret drinker and suffered from spells of totally insane behaviour, thereby making herself obnoxious to the rather staid household of Thomas Mann. She also quarrelled with many of Heinrich's other friends, or their wives, notably the insufferable Alma Mahler-Werfel (as she now liked to be known, deliberately slighting her present husband in favour of the previous one).

Heinrich had been making notes since 1940 for a grotesquely comic novel on the subject of the martyred Czech town Lidice; in 1942 he sat down and wrote it, very quickly (he who always needed to work slowly), and it was published in Mexico in 1943. Not only did it have no success and bring in no money, but it was actively disliked by most of the few people who read it, on the grounds that its basic material was too emotionally charged to be treated in such a seemingly perverse and even frivolous way.

Things had indeed been getting worse ever since his seventieth birthday party, celebrated late, on 2 May 1941, after Heinrich and Nelly had returned from Mexico and Thomas from Berkeley where, on the very day of Heinrich's birthday (27 March), he was receiving yet another honorary doctorate. This assembly, which took place in Salka Viertel's house, was perhaps the greatest social gathering in the whole history of the 'New Weimar'. As well as, naturally, Heinrich and Thomas Mann, there were present Feuchtwanger, Werfel (with great difficulty, since Nelly Mann was having one of her worst feuds with Alma Werfel, and it took all of the Feuchtwanger diplomacy to patch things up in time), Doeblin, Marcuse, Bruno Frank, Alfred Neumann, Alfred Polgar and Walter Mehring—all the major literary figures, in fact, except Leonhard Frank (for reasons unknown) and Bertolt Brecht, who was not to arrive in Los Angeles until July 1941. The evening climaxed in an exchange of commendatory speeches between Thomas and Heinrich—apparently a ritual performed every ten years—and a happy anticipation of future splendours for both them and the German community at large.

But, in fact, Heinrich was more or less written out before he arrived in America—as might anyway have been the case with a man of seventy—and the next few years held little for him but poverty, embarrassment and sorrow, especially when Nelly, who had attempted suicide before, actually succeeded on 16 December 1944. Even so it is possible—certainly it was Thomas's opinion—that some of his best writing came in his clipped and elliptical memoirs

Ein Zeitaltar Wird Besichtigt, which he wrote in 1943 and 1944. These were finally published, in the absence of any interest whatever from American publishers, in Stockholm in 1945. His next novel, the satirical *Empfang bei der Welt,* written in 1944 and 1945, did not even attain the dignity of print till six years after his death. His final work, *Der Atem,* an autobiographical work in which he and Thomas appear as the sisters Lydia and Marie-Louise, took him two full years to write, 1945–7, and another two of correction before it was finally published, an obscure and puzzling testament. In these later years, after the death of his wife, his health failed until he became a virtual invalid, and a planned trip back to Europe in April 1950 was frustrated by his death from a stroke in March, a few days before his seventy-ninth birthday.

Though there seems to have been remarkably little jealousy between the two brothers at this point in their lives, it must have been particularly galling for Heinrich to sink into obscurity while his younger brother forged ahead and became indisputably the more famous, important and (it was generally accepted) talented after years in which their relative merits remained an endless subject of debate for German literati. Thomas, in fact, was clearly the more practical of the two, the more politic (as opposed to political) and the better able to adapt himself to his new environment, sell himself and his work. Already in 1939 he had made such a place for himself in America that *Life* magazine had done a major story on him. His books came out in a practically uninterrupted stream: having completed his novella about Goethe, *Lotte in Weimar,* during his first few weeks as a visiting professor at Princeton, he began almost at once on *The Transposed Heads,* written at top speed between January and August 1940. Immediately after that he went on with *Joseph the Provider,* the last of his Joseph tetralogy, and completed it by 4 January 1943, despite all that was happening in the world around him and the necessity to write many political essays and anti-fascist broadcasts, as well as continue to give his lectures as a leading representative of the liberal cause in the West. He then set about considering a contribution to a book offering new fictional interpretations of the Ten Commandments, for which he was to be paid $1,000 (Werfel and Bruno Frank also contributed stories). Thinking about the Old Testament from a slightly different angle, he was inspired to write another novella, *The Tables of the Law,* about Moses, between mid-January and mid-March 1943, before starting at once to plan his next major work, *Doctor Faustus,* on 15 March.

In the extent of the output as well as in its amazing variety, it would be an extraordinary record for anyone, but especially for a man who had turned sixty-five at the beginning of the decade. But Thomas Mann was still, what he had always been, a survivor. He survived this time by accepting, but not too much. Once he had decided to come off the fence about Nazism he became one of its most vocal enemies, and achieved a lot of publicity in America as such. He had the advantage of jobs like the guest professorship at Princeton or the consultancy in Germanic literature to the Library of Congress (at nearly $5,000 a year), posts that were secured for him by friends and admirers, amounting to little more than well-paid sinecures.

And Mann's books sold. Translated immediately on their appearance by his 'official' translator of the time, Helen Lowe-Porter, their publication in English was rarely more than a year behind their publication in German. In particular *Joseph the Provider,* when it appeared in America in 1944, was regarded as his climactic masterpiece by the American public and sold nearly a quarter of a million copies in the first six months; in 1948 the four *Joseph* novels came out in one volume and again the sales were phenomenal. Maybe, as cynics would aver, they came into that category always much favoured by American middlebrows: the famous bore that everyone has to read, or at least buy and have lying around, as a mark of cultural respectability. But also the last *Joseph* volume was particularly likely to appeal to Americans, since a lot of Mann's admiration for Roosevelt, who had entertained him on various occasions at the White House, was apparent in the depiction of Joseph—a Joseph wearing, Mann remarked in his foreword, 'a mask of an American Hermes, a brilliant messenger of shrewdness, whose New Deal is unmistakably reflected in Joseph's magic administration of national economy'.

All the same, whatever subtle influence America might have had on his writing, it was noticeable he did not let it go too far. He did not, for instance, undertake to write any work set in America, and until he embarked on *Doctor Faustus* his fictional writings in America, indeed all his fictions written in exile, were set in the past, remote in time and (except for *Lotte in Weimar*) in space as well. In *Doctor Faustus* he took up the subject he knew he needed to expose, the story of twentieth-century Germany, refracted through the experience of one fictional character, Adrian Leverkühn, a Nietzschean composer who belongs within the Viennese school of ultrachromaticism finally ordered by Schoenberg into the twelve-tone system, and in effect sells his soul to the devil of modern life. The novel, planned from the start as one of considerable size and scope, was actually started on 23 May 1943, and progressed variably: eight chapters in three months, followed by only four in the next six months, and then a gradual process of accumulation through 1944, '45 and '46, interrupted by political disputes and illness (including a successful operation for lung cancer early in 1946). By May 1946 he felt he was nearing its end; he wrote the last words on 29 January 1947.

It was a curious and perhaps not an entirely successful work that had occupied nearly four years of his life—though one that increasingly demands study and respectful attention. Always a meticulous researcher of his works, Mann had needed, writing the story of a composer, to get all the musical details right (even though he had written in his diary: 'Technical musical studies frighten and bore me'), and had therefore cultivated those members of the musical intelligentsia present in Southern California who could help with them. Bruno Walter, the conductor, was an old friend. But he did not know Schoenberg at all well until he began writing *Doctor Faustus*. It was also during this period that he became close with Theodor Adorno, a musical theorist and a leading member of the Institute of Social Research, who had settled in Los Angeles in 1941, and met Stravinsky, who had arrived in 1940 and become, like Schoenberg, a close friend of the Werfels.

It should be emphasized that just because someone was friendly with the Werfels, for instance, it did not necessarily mean that he would be friendly with the Manns. Though the principal members of the German literary world on the Los Angeles scene kept in constant touch with one another and sometimes, on state occasions like Heinrich Mann's seventieth birthday, might all be gathered together in one room, in the practical matters of day-to-day life they tended to fall into several different groups. After the first bout of topical enthusiasm, the German film colony had little to do with them, or they with it, and anyone, like Brecht, who had some kind of deep involvement with one aspect or another of show business was likely to have to make some clear social choices.

Within the literary circles there were three main centres—the homes, naturally, of the three most successful writers, Feuchtwanger, Werfel and Thomas Mann. Mann, a major writer of the twentieth century, as the others were not, was the least social of the three. His life was dedicated to his writing and, to a lesser extent, to his wartime propaganda activities. Feuchtwanger, who, it may be recalled, had even back in Sanary days been the centre of a group rather different from and not altogether compatible with Mann's, arrived in Los Angeles on 28 January 1941. After some slight trouble getting his funds in America released (they were blocked, curiously, because he had been interned in France) and the required trip to Mexico in February to re-enter with a long-term resident's visa, he settled down to a prosperous life as a writer and public figure. First he lived in a rented house in Santa Monica, then in 1943 he moved to a palatial villa at 520 Paseo Miramar in Pacific Palisades, now owned by the University of Southern California and kept up as a sort of Feuchtwanger study centre. The Werfels arrived in Los Angeles a little earlier, at the end of December 1940. At first they lived in the Hollywood Hills, near the Hollywood Bowl, but in 1942 moved to their own house in North Bedford Drive, Beverly Hills, where they lived until Werfel's death in 1945, aged only 55.

Though naturally there was much overlapping of acquaintance, Feuchtwanger's group was conditioned by his well-known left-wing sympathies as well as by his financial standing. His closest friend among his peers in Los Angeles, not altogether surprisingly, was Bertolt Brecht. The Werfels had different interests, in the theatre and in music—Alma Werfel had previously been married to Mahler, a fact that no one was allowed to forget; Franz Werfel was an expert on Verdi—so that in their house one was more likely to encounter Schoenberg, Stravinsky, Bruno Walter, Otto Klemperer and Lotte Lehmann, or Max Reinhardt, S. N. Behrman and other refugees from the theatres of New York and Europe. Because of the whole *Doctor Faust* affair and the importance music and musical studies assumed for many members of the German cultural community at this time, it will be most convenient if we pause at this point to take a look at the musical world in Los Angeles during the 1940s and the importance of the émigrés in it.

Though Los Angeles had its orchestra and its concerts in the Hollywood Bowl, it was not the most obvious place for a musician to migrate to, if migrate he must. A performer might always hope to find work in one of the studio orchestras, and a popular composer might be able to profit somehow from the large amount of music required by the films. But, as we have seen, only the most conservative symphonic composers had much chance in Hollywood—provided always that their music, as well as being melodic and easy on the ear, could be composed to order, with a fluency and speed seldom if ever required elsewhere. The music of Erich Korngold represented about the highest to which film scores could aspire—or at any rate did aspire. The stories of other European composers' attempts to come to terms with Hollywood mostly seem rather comical now, though at the time they were decidedly less humorous to those involved. All the same, Los Angeles did attract distinguished musical émigrés, though more as an agreeable place to live than as an obvious source of income.

It was ironic that of them all it was Schoenberg, in most respects the least approachable musically of any composer in the 1930s, who should have lived there longest and settled in best. His health required the climate of Southern California, but he also had the advantage of being a first-rate teacher, even to those who could not begin to understand his music, and he accepted his lot philosophically. It was a curious stroke of fate that brought to Los Angeles another important émigré, indeed the other most distinguished composer of Schoenberg's generation, when Stravinsky determined to settle in May 1940. Though a French citizen since 1934 and basically domiciled in Paris, he had been very much an international figure for years, visiting the US frequently in the thirties to perform his own music. He had little any more to do with Russia under Stalin's rule, his music was roundly condemned by the Nazis, and a group of deaths in his immediate family circle in 1938 and 1939 (his mother, his wife, his eldest daughter and his sister-in-law) seemed to be reducing drastically the personal hold Europe had on him. In September 1939, shortly after the beginning of the war in Europe, he sailed for America, primarily to give a series of lectures in French at Harvard under the title *The Poetics of Music*. In December he conducted a concert of his music in Los Angeles and had the dubious pleasure of seeing what Walt Disney had made of *The Rite of Spring* in *Fantasia*, then returned east to complete his lectures. He married again in March, and as soon as the lectures were over left for Los Angeles with his new bride. He was to remain there, with occasional interruptions, for the rest of his life.

Again the main reason for the choice was health. Stravinsky had suffered a tubercular infection such as had killed his first wife and daughter, and needed the warmth and dryness. He made up his mind with characteristic speed and finality to embrace America and the American way of life, and in August went into Mexico to re-enter on a residence visa as part of the Russian quota; at once he applied for naturalization. Though he was financially quite successful as a composer and performer of his own works, this was largely on the strength of his earlier music; the music of his neo-classical phase was at the time found by many to be arid and puzzling, and his reputation was at a comparatively low ebb in musical circles. But he found that in America he could live in an orderly fashion, undistracted by the conflicts that were disrupting Europe, and earn a decent living. And he made friends in Los Angeles, mostly among the small group of other émigrés of strong artistic leanings, such as Aldous Huxley, Franz Werfel, the Polish–French composer Alexander Tansman, the French composer/teacher Nadia Boulanger (only briefly present), the Russian actor Vladimir Sokoloff, and the Russian–French painter Eugene Berman. Outside this small circle he did not go about very much, and might just as well have been living anywhere.

Stravinsky, too, had his slightly comical encounters with Hollywood. In 1942 he was approached by Columbia to write the music for a drama of the Norwegian Resistance, *The Commandos Strike at Dawn*. He went off and came back a couple of weeks later with a complete score based on Norwegian folk-tunes. Columbia said that was very nice, but they had not yet begun the film. 'Oh!' said Stravinsky, surprised at this unaccustomed slowness. He collected his cheque and went away. His music was never used for the film, but almost immediately turned up again transformed into a concert piece, *Four Norwegian Moods*. Other works of his during the 1940s that had their origin in abortive film-music commissions were the middle movement of *Ode* (1943), meant as music for a hunting scene in Robert Stevenson's *Jane Eyre*, through an initiative of Orson Welles, who starred in it; the *Scherzo à la Russe* (1944), originally composed for a war film set on the Russian front; and the middle movement of the *Symphony in Three Movements* (1945), composed to accompany Bernadette's vision of the Virgin in *The Song of Bernadette* at the request of Franz Werfel.

Otherwise he had little to do with music in Los Angeles: he turned his hand to light music with a *Tango* (1940) meant for dance band and even as a popular song, without noticeable success, and in 1941 was commissioned by the Werner Janssen Orchestra, a local organization, to write his *Danses Concertantes,* of which he conducted the first performance in Los Angeles on 4 February 1942. In 1944 he received another, more curious commission—to join nine other émigré composers in composing a cycle of brief works on themes from the Book of Genesis. This was the idea of the music publisher and composer Nathaniel Shilkret, who himself wrote the section based on the Creation. Each contributor was to be paid $300 for his piece. Bartok, Hindemith and Prokofiev never completed their sections, but Shilkret was obviously better able to keep after composers based on the West Coast. The work as finally conducted by Werner Janssen in Los Angeles in 1945 consisted of seven choral sections—a *Prelude* by Schoenberg, *Creation* by Shilkret, *Fall of Man* by Tansman, *Cain and Abel* by Milhaud (who was teaching at Mills College), *The Flood* by Castelnuovo-Tadesco, *The Covenant* by Ernst Toch, and *Babel* by Stravinsky—in other words, all the musical émigrés of any distinction California had to offer, except the communist (and therefore presumably atheistic) Hanns Eisler.

Though it seems almost inevitable that Schoenberg and Stravinsky must have met at some time during the 1940s in Los Angeles, curiously enough there appears to be no record of a meeting. Schoenberg had reason to resent Stravinsky, not so much for anything Stravinsky himself had done, but because he had often been used by proponents of traditional tonality as a stick with which to beat Schoenberg and dodecaphony. They had been in contact in the early 1920s, and apparently admired each other, but since then they had grown far apart musically (though Stravinsky was finally, some five years after Schoenberg's death, to come round to the twelve-tone system). In any case, neither of them much frequented musical circles—virtually the only musicians Schoenberg saw regularly were his pupils. At the beginning of the war he was well settled in to teaching at UCLA and began the official proceedings to become an American citizen (at this time he held a Czech passport). His music was being performed a little more, even in Los Angeles, particularly in the special context of the 'Evenings on the Roof' chamber concerts organized by Peter Yates and his pianist-wife Frances Muller in a studio built by Schindler on the roof of their Los Angeles home. He was finding little time for composition, what with teaching and writing and becoming yet again a father, not to mention the work he was constantly being asked to do to help refugees and internees. In the university vacation during the summer of 1941, he at last found time to compose a series of *Variations on a Recitative* for organ, commissioned by a New York publisher, and began another work for organ, a sonata, which was left unfinished. Meanwhile, in April 1941 he and his wife had finally become American citizens.

In April 1942 Schoenberg's old pupil Hanns Eisler arrived in Santa

Monica, where he would live for the next five years, writing music for eight feature films and holding for a time a post as professor of music at USC. Eisler was an old friend of Brecht, who had arrived ten months before and also settled in Santa Monica. They met again at the house of Theodor Adorno, where Eisler's chamber work *Fourteen Ways of Describing Rain*, for the same instrumental combination as Schoenberg's *Pierrot Lunaire* (and ultimately dedicated to Schoenberg) was being performed. As it transpired that Brecht did not know Schoenberg, Eisler determined to take him round to meet the composer, with many dire warnings about his behaviour in Schoenberg's presence. Eisler went in great trepidation lest Brecht should upset the touchy composer with some brusque remark about music, or for that matter lest Schoenberg should offend Brecht with some unthinking criticism of socialism, towards which he was far from sympathetic. But in the event it all went smoothly once the two got on to the unlikely common ground of donkeys, which both of them had had experiences with. Schoenberg charmed Brecht by relating how he had learnt to conserve his energy when climbing a hill from watching how a donkey did it, and Brecht later put this observation into a poem for Schoenberg's seventieth birthday in 1944.

At this time Schoenberg had, as usual, financial worries and Eisler offered him a gift of $300, which Schoenberg was reluctant to take. Eisler suggested he might regard it as payment for some more lessons, but Schoenberg observed drily: 'If you haven't learnt it yet, I can't teach you any more.' Eisler remained one of Schoenberg's most frequent visitors, along with Franz and Alma Werfel. Schoenberg saw something of Thomas Mann, too, first at dinner with Artur Rubinstein, and then at the Werfels in May 1943, when Mann, who was already at work on *Doctor Faustus*, noted in his diary that he 'drew him out a great deal about music and a composer's existence.' Schoenberg had by that time got round to composing once again, the immediate results being a setting for speaker and piano quintet of Byron's 'Ode to Napoleon Buonaparte', his first musical work making a clear political commitment, in that the parallel between Byron's hateful image of Napoleon and the character of Hitler was at the forefront of his mind, and a piano concerto. Both were completed in 1942, though neither achieved performance for more than two years.

Thomas Mann was invited to Schoenberg's sixty-ninth birthday party, and this set off a literary exchange, with Mann sending

Schoenberg *The Magic Mountain* and Schoenberg sending Mann the text of his unfinished oratorio *Jacob's Ladder,* which Mann felt was confused and turgid, and his treatise on harmony, which Mann found equally bizarre in its 'extraordinary mixture of pious tradition and revolution', but fascinating. The relationship continued, steadily if not closely, through Schoenberg's composition of the *Theme and Variations for Wind Orchestra* (first performed in 1944 by Koussevitzky, whom Schoenberg detested, arranged by the composer for full orchestra) and the tribulations, tributes and small triumphs that marked his seventieth birthday and enforced retirement from UCLA.

Mann, of course, was meanwhile working on *Doctor Faustus*, a book to which Schoenberg was very relevant, and Schoenberg's name occurs frequently in *The Genesis of a Novel*. There Mann states that Schoenberg and Adorno, his other great source of material, did not meet each other, and suggests that this was because Schoenberg suspected Adorno's admiration of him was not as uncritical as it might be. Other meetings with Schoenberg that Mann records include a discussion of *Parsifal* with Hanns Eisler in Schoenberg's house, which occasioned a letter from Schoenberg, and a dinner at Gottfried Reinhardt's where Schnabel and Klemperer were also present. For Mann's seventieth birthday in 1945 Schoenberg wrote a double canon for string quartet, of a difficulty verging on unplayability, with a presentation inscription saying: 'It is not without "honest" egotism that I wish we may remain good contemporaries of one another for many years.'

Unfortunately that was not to be. The publication of *Doctor Faustus* in 1947 brought about a serious break between them. The basis of the complaints launched by Schoenberg against Mann's novel remains, it must be admitted, obscure except in terms of Schoenberg's tendency to paranoia where his public recognition was concerned. Mann's novel is, after all, very clearly fiction, not a portrait of any real figure; and while Leverkühn, the composer-character at its centre, is credited with inventing a twelve-note system of composition very much like Schoenberg's own, it is hardly likely that otherwise Schoenberg could have wished to be identified with the character—indeed, he would have had more cause for alarm had he supposed any reader did in fact make such an identification. But it seems that Schoenberg never read the book himself, blaming failing eyesight for his not doing so. Instead he relied on his wife and other friends, particularly Alma Werfel, who, never averse to making trouble, urged him to attack Mann and defend his own reputation. This he did in a devious fashion by concocting a satirical entry from an *Encyclopedia Americana* of 1988, which attributes the invention of the twelve-tone system to Mann and dismissing the 'nobody' Schoenberg's claim to it. This was all silly enough to mystify Mann, who replied that everyone who read the novel was likely to know who invented the system, and it was impossible that the novel could detract in any way from Schoenberg's reputation.

The matter might have been left there. But as it had the makings of a cultural cause célèbre, the *Saturday Review of Literature* asked Schoenberg in October 1948 for a statement about *Doctor Faustus*, then asked Mann for a reply, and published both pieces on 1 January 1949. Schoenberg, spurred on no doubt by supporters with more partisanship than sense, savagely attacked Mann on the rather confused grounds that (a) no one would recognize where Mann had stolen his theory from, and so Schoenberg's credibility would be damaged and (b) that everyone would know, and therefore assume Leverkühn was a portrait of Schoenberg, right down to the insanity induced by syphilitic degeneration. He also complained that an explanatory note added to the novel under pressure only confused the issue still further. Mann replied, with as much dignity and tact as he could muster, that no offence was intended against Schoenberg, who was well known as the real-life author of the twelve-tone technique and clearly had little or nothing to do with the character of Leverkühn in the book, who was, in fact, based much more closely on Nietzsche with hints from Mann himself. He concluded:

> It is a painful drama to see how an important man, in an all too understandable over-irritation because of a life which has wavered between adoration and neglect, almost wilfully burrows into ideas of persecution and theft and loses himself in poisonous quarrels. May he rise above bitterness and mistrust and find peace in the secure consciousness of his greatness and fame!

Before the articles had appeared Schoenberg had already made a personal move towards reconciliation in a letter to Mann that acknowledged his authorship of the *Encyclopedia Americana* article and presented it as an attempt to make Mann conscious of the danger to his reputation Schoenberg felt the book represented. But it was clear there was more to the dispute than appeared on the surface: something concerned with the behind-the-scenes participation of

Adorno in the elaboration of the book. Though Mann was wrong in saying that Schoenberg and Adorno never met in Los Angeles, he was correct in his assertion that Schoenberg did not like Adorno, even though some of Adorno's writings on his music were regarded by Schoenberg's supporters as definitive. When they met they usually quarrelled, and Schoenberg disliked Adorno's opaque style almost as much as his chilly and supercilious personality. Adorno, for his part, though as an ex-pupil of Berg's he was thoroughly committed to the twelve-tone cause and the music of Schoenberg, was unable to warm to the composer (who could admittedly be very spiky and difficult)—certainly not in the way he warmed to Mann, who became a close friend in Los Angeles.

Adorno (the name was that of his Corsican mother, retained in preference to that of his German-Jewish father) had come to America in 1937, persuaded by colleagues from the Frankfurt Institute of Social Research, among them Max Horkheimer, Erich Fromm and Herbert Marcuse, who were themselves to be resettled in New York. In February 1938 he accepted a job as head of the music study section of the office of Radio Research, run by Paul Lazarfeld at Princeton. In 1941, having made himself unpopular by his unwillingness to compromise in any way with, or see any good in, American culture, he moved to Los Angeles, where he would rapidly have much more to complain of. He and Horkheimer, who came with him, soon became very friendly with Thomas Mann, and Mann was one of those permitted to read Adorno's largely unpublished study of Wagner, which did not finally appear in print until 1952. He was highly impressed by it, and even more impressed by Adorno's long essay on Schoenberg, completed in July 1943 and later to form the first half of his *Philosophy of Modern Music* (1949). In this, Adorno's enthusiasm for Schoenberg's music is tempered by his doubts about the dogmatic application of the twelve-tone system by his followers; Schoenberg, if he ever read the essay (which is doubtful) would have found chapter and verse for his suspicions of Adorno as a dedicated disciple.

When Mann needed documentation and technical detail for his novel about a modern German composer, Adorno was the natural person for him to turn to, and his contribution is credited over and over again in *The Genesis of a Novel*, summed up in Mann's dedicatory inscription in Adorno's copy of the first German edition, to 'my privy councillor'. Mann explicitly acknowledged that the whole discussion of the tone-row system invented by Leverkühn is closely based, along with much else in the musical material of the novel, on Adorno's essay. In December 1946 Mann appealed in an apologetic ten-page letter for more help from Adorno, and the result was six weeks' intensive work, in virtual collaboration, on the chapters concerned with the creation of Leverkühn's oratorio, the masterpiece that results from his pact with the devil. At this point Mann even consulted Schoenberg directly on a detail from the oratorio, where originally he had meant the chorus to sing unaccompanied in a non-tempered scale. Schoenberg replied that *he* would not do it, though it was theoretically possible; even in the light of this 'permission from the highest level' Mann decided to drop this particular detail. And it is no doubt significant of the way he perceived relations between Schoenberg and Adorno that while he certainly had to work with Adorno behind Schoenberg's back he also describes his recourse to Schoenberg's advice as behind Adorno's back.

Anyway, the whole affair was most unfortunate, especially between two septuagenarians of such distinction; it was no doubt something of a relief, to Schoenberg at least, when Adorno returned with Horkheimer to Europe in 1949. But this has taken us a long way from the Werfels and their experiences in Hollywood during the war years, let alone from Feuchtwanger, the German left-wingers, and the whole question of the émigré intellectuals' attitude to Germany and Germany's attitude to them.

The Werfels arrived in Los Angeles in a rather similar situation to that of Feuchtwanger: Franz Werfel was a well-known, much-translated and popular writer—in 1940 the comic novel he had written in Sanary, translated as *Embezzled Heaven*, was a Book-of-the-Month-Club selection and became an American bestseller—and certainly not in need of handouts from the film companies or anyone else. At the same time, life in the new country was not immediately simple, and they had the same problems of settling in, establishing legal residence and so on as anyone else. But Werfel spoke fluent English, or 'ersatz English' as S. N. Behrman called it, and he had many devoted friends in Southern California, notably his faithful editor and translator Dr Gustave O. Arlt, who arranged for his first accommodation in Los Angeles and eased his way into Los Angeles social life.

Werfel also had a plan: as soon as he had settled in California he began to carry out his vow, taken in highly emotional circumstances on their journey across the Pyrenees, to write the story of

Bernadette Soubirous, the saint of Lourdes. The book, a straightforward, very slightly fictionalized account of Bernadette's life and visions, was rapidly written, published in Stockholm before the end of the year, and rapidly translated by Ludwig Lewisohn to appear in America early in 1942. It also was a Book-of-the-Month-Club selection, sold an astonishing 350,000 copies, and was immediately bought by Twentieth Century-Fox for filming at the healthy figure of $100,000. It made Werfel one of the most prosperous of the émigrés, enabling him to buy an elegant house in the most fashionable part of Beverly Hills and lead a very comfortable life for his last three years, entertaining his friends and taking refuge from time to time in his favourite hideaway, the Hotel Mirasol in Santa Barbara, to write without distraction.

The Song of Bernadette was not his only big success in America during the war years: there was also *Jacobowsky and the Colonel.* This play, written in some sort of collaboration (what sort remains the subject of much argument) with the American playwright S. N. Behrman, was produced by Theatre Guild on 4 March 1944, and had an enthusiastic reception, settling in for a whole season at the Martin Beck Theatre, followed by a lengthy tour. The best-known account of the play's inception is that contained in Behrman's lively, if in some respects unreliable memoirs *People in a Diary,* written nearly thirty years after the event. According to him, it all took place during a dinner party at the Werfels, attended by Max Reinhardt and his actress-wife Helene Thimig, Ernst Lubitsch, the scriptwriter Charles Brackett, and of course Behrman himself. Werfel, a great raconteur, embarked on the story of a couple he had met or heard of in France, a little Jewish refugee from Paris and the fleeing Polish colonel he falls in with, who make their way across the country together and evade the advancing Nazis with a lot of mutual incomprehension that finally, improbably, turns into mutual respect. Everyone present thought it would make a wonderful play, but Werfel felt he needed the collaboration of a practical American man of the theatre, and Behrman was the obvious choice.

Other accounts are rather different. Gustave Arlt says the dinner party was at Max Reinhardt's house, and that those present were, in addition to himself and his wife, the host and his wife and the Werfels, Reinhardt's son Gottfried and the von Kahlers. Gottfried Reinhardt agrees that it was at his father's house, but includes in the dinner party Behrman, Salka Viertel, Vladimir Horowitz and his wife and the Stravinskys. Salka Viertel lists herself, Gottfried

Reinhardt, Behrman, Erich Korngold and his wife and, after dinner, the Stravinskys, as guests of Max Reinhardt on that occasion.

Whoever was correct—and the very range of names that occurs in the different accounts suggests something of the richness and variety of Los Angeles society at that time—it seems clear that Werfel and Behrman entered into a loosely defined collaboration on the subject, and worked together in harmony for some time, even though Behrman, like so many, did not really get on well with Werfel's wife Alma. He tells, for instance, a horrific story of a dinner party with the Schoenbergs at which she insisted on describing in detail the unreasoning passion virtually every significant artist of the twentieth century—Kokoschka, Gropius, Berg, among others—had felt for her, and then concluded, in front of Werfel, by observing that all the same, the most interesting personality she had ever known was Mahler. But it became apparent that the play as Werfel conceived it—'the comedy of a tragedy', as he labelled it—was something rather different from the slick Broadway product Behrman was shaping it into. Not necessarily better either—even some enthusiasts for Werfel find the character of Marianne, symbol of France, embarrassing, and have their reservations about his determination to underline the comedy's serious significance. But things reached such a point, particularly while Behrman was in New York keeping an eye on the play's production, that the collaborators were hardly communicating and Lawrence Langner, of the Theatre Guild, was asked to be arbitrator. There were arguments about the credits—at one time Werfel got the impression that he was not to be named at all as an author, and finally the formula used was 'An American play by S. N. Behrman, based on the original play by Franz Werfel'. Werfel ended by accepting Behrman's superior know-how of the practicalities of the American theatre, but reserved the right to publish his own version independently, which he did—in German and in a close English translation by Gustave O. Arlt, in 1944, while Behrman's version was still running in New York.

Since, obviously, at this period the English-speaking market was of prime importance for German émigré writers (it was this as much as anything that marked the decisive difference between Thomas Mann's fortunes and those of his brother Heinrich in the 1940s), Werfel's next, and as it turned out his last, work was written in a situation of virtual collaboration, though this time far happier and more to Werfel's taste. He was already a sick man when he began writing his futuristic novel *Star of the Unborn,* and most of it was written in Santa Barbara, where he was accompanied only by Gustave O. Arlt. They shared a suite at the Hotel Mirasol. Werfel wrote the book at high speed in German, and handed it over chapter by chapter for Arlt to translate, in close consultation, so that the English version would be able to come out simultaneously with, or as it happened slightly in advance of, the German original. He continued to work on the book almost up to his death in August 1945, and in fact the very last chapter was left for Arlt to translate by himself after Werfel was dead. Comfortable though he had been in the land of his adoption, he had still not written a work that was clearly American in inspiration. *Star of the Unborn* seems to show in parts the influence of Werfel's readings in English-language science fiction and the related works of Aldous Huxley, but it owes quite as much to Werfel's memories of his childhood in Prague and the Europe to which he would never return.

Although Werfel, like Thomas Mann, subscribed to vaguely liberal political ideas and was perforce anti-Nazi, he was not a political animal and there is hardly any politics in his writing. In this respect he was very different from the third of the emigré triumvirate, Lion Feuchtwanger. Feuchtwanger, for all his riches, remained a committed left-winger and, therefore, despite a degree of social amiability, rather apart from the other émigrés in Los Angeles unless they happened to share his views. But then money permitted him to lead his own life very much as he wanted, to become part of America, and specifically Los Angeles, or not. In many respects he would seem to have been as prepared for America as any of the émigrés; certainly throughout his career he had been fascinated by America and had frequently reverted to the subject, directly and indirectly, in his work. However, he had spent little time in America before he settled there in 1940, and a theoretical interest in a country is often very different from a capacity to experience its actuality. It is notable that Bertolt Brecht, so many of whose pre-war works take place in fanciful imaginary America, ceased to write about America altogether once he was in fact domiciled there.

When he got to America Feuchtwanger, like Mann, was in the midst of a lengthy work set in the Jewish past, his trilogy on the life of Josephus, the first-century historian of the Jewish nation. It is possible that on his arrival he was reminded of the words he had written a decade earlier, in the first volume of the book, reconstructing Josephus's thoughts when first confronted with Rome:

> What these men of the West could give—technology, logic—such things could be learnt. What could not be learnt was the visionary powers of the East, its holiness. Nation and God, man and God were one there. Except that he was an invisible God, incapable of being seen, of being known. One was either in possession of him, or not in possession of him. He, Joseph, possessed it, possessed the unlearnable. And he never doubted that he would learn the other, the technology of the West.

In all events, Feuchtwanger's attitude to the combination he could represent of the unlearnable culture of Europe and the technical know-how of America seems to have been marked by a similar confidence.

Once Feuchtwanger had completed *Josephus and the Emperor*, the final section of the trilogy, he started to work on a novel, various shorter stories, and *The Devil in France*, his highly topical account of his sufferings as an internee and refugee in France (so topical that he felt unable to publish its fourth part because of the repercussions it could have on the lives of those who had aided his escape). *The Devil in France* was first published, in English, shortly after his arrival; in its brief epilogue Feuchtwanger describes himself thus: 'I stand on the brink of old age. [He was, in fact, 57.] My passions are becoming feebler, feebler my discontents, feebler my enthusiasms. ... I have come to realize that the folly and stupidity of mankind are as wild and unfathomable as the Seven Seas. But it has also been granted to me to know that the dam erected by the minority of good and wise men is growing higher and firmer from day to day.' The tone is somewhat melodramatic, and Feuchtwanger went on to belie it with another seventeen years of hard and continuous work, which produced seven novels, two plays, stories and essays and the larger part of a long-considered book on historical fiction, interrupted by his unexpected death on 21 December 1958. Two further books were left unfinished.

Unlike Brecht, Feuchtwanger did not lose literary interest in America (real or imaginary) once he was living there. Though the subjects of his works range as far afield as a fantastic depiction of Hitler's fortune-teller (*Double, Double, Toil and Trouble*, 1941), the story of Joan of Arc (*Simone*, 1943), the history of Marie Antoinette (*The Widow Capet*, 1947), the life of Goya (*This Is the*

Hour, 1950) and of Jean Jacques Rousseau (*'Tis Folly to Be Wise*, 1952), the period of the Crusades in Spain (*Raquel, the Jewess of Toledo*, 1954) and the Biblical story of Jephta (*Jephta and His Daughter*, 1957), he also continued to relate his work to the American reality around him and its historical background. He usually wrote rapidly after a long period of gestation, and though he had been thinking of a novel about the American Revolution since the early 1930s he did not get round to writing *Proud Destiny* until 1944–6, spurred on, as he tells us in the postscript, by the events of the day:

> For decades I have been concerned with the strange fact that such different people as Beaumarchais, Benjamin Franklin, Lafayette, Voltaire, Louis XVI and Marie Antoinette, each for his or her own reasons, had to collaborate in bringing the American Revolution to a successful conclusion, and through it the French Revolution as well. When Roosevelt's America intervened in the war against the European Fascists and supported the Soviet Union's battle against Hitler, the events in France of the 18th century became transparent to me and made the events of my own time radiantly clear.

As an offshoot of that he wrote in 1946 a play about Cotton Mather and the Boston witch-hunts of 1642, *The Devil in Boston*. The relevance of that to contemporary happenings can hardly be missed when we remember that in 1946, in the newly cool situation between America and Russia (not quite yet the Cold War), the House Committee on Un-American Activities was getting into full swing again, investigating the possibilities of communist infiltration in American life. And the following year, Brecht and Eisler, among other friends of Feuchtwanger, were to be called upon to give evidence before it and have to leave the country as a result of its 'witch-hunting'. Though he did not live to write another novel on an American theme, a number of his shorter stories such as *Venice (Texas)*, a fantasia suggested by the history of Venice, California, a model seaside suburb built in 1905, not far from Feuchtwanger's home in Pacific Palisades, had American backgrounds. A large part of *The House of Desdemona, or The Laurels and Limitations of Historical Fiction* (1958) is concerned with the role of the historical novel in America, and at the time of his death he was planning for the first time to put his own experience of contemporary American history into a novel, *Die Sieben Weisen*, which would tell of the experience of German refugees and their American friends in California during the McCarthy era.

While Feuchtwanger was in America, far and away his most enjoyable and fruitful contact among his fellow émigrés was with the friend who was to suffer most dramatically from McCarthyite witch-hunting, Bertolt Brecht. They had known each other well for years, and though Feuchtwanger's own political stance was not as left-wing as Brecht's he sympathized fully with Brecht's views and got on very well with him on a personal level. They had first met in 1919, had collaborated in 1923 on an adaptation of Marlowe's *Edward II* and kept in touch through the early years of exile: Brecht had stayed with Feuchtwanger in Sanary for a while in 1937. When Brecht arrived at the port of Los Angeles on 21 July 1941 he was met at the docks by Marta Feuchtwanger, and Feuchtwanger himself at once became Brecht's adviser, champion and friend in California.

From this renewed friendship came the idea of a new dramatic collaboration. In frustration at his failure to get anything moving or make any money in the theatre or the cinema, Brecht started writing a play called *Jeanne d'Arc 1940* (17 December 1941), which would relate the story of Joan of Arc to contemporary reality by way of visions seen by a girl in modern France. A few days later he had drafted nine scenes, four of them visions, and retitled the play *The Voices*. As a result of reading Feuchtwanger's as yet unpublished *The Devil in France*, which he greatly admired, he thought of Feuchtwanger as a useful collaborator on this play with a similar background. Feuchtwanger was delighted with the idea, which did not crystallize until nearly a year later, in October 1942, when they discussed several possibilities for dramatic collaboration, including another adaptation of an English classic, Heywood's *A Woman Killed with Kindness*.

However, they settled on *The Voices*, which was retitled *St Joan of Vitry*, and then again *The Visions of Simone Machard*. Every day in November, December and January Brecht went to Feuchtwanger's house to work on this text, in an atmosphere of extraordinary agreement and harmony, even though they had to break off each evening in time for Brecht to be at home by 8 p.m., since as 'enemy aliens' they were under a curfew. The collaboration suffered from only one stumbling block: the age of the protagonist. Brecht had trouble motivating her unquestioning patriotism unless she was presented as an innocent child; Feuchtwanger conceived her rather as a naive adolescent who was still able to bring a semi-adult understanding to the events around her. When Brecht had to go to New York for three months their work together was interrupted, and on his return to Santa Monica in May Brecht completed the play by himself according to his concept. Feuchtwanger, perfectly agreeable, went on to turn his concept into the novel *Simone*, which first appeared in an English translation in 1944. Brecht's play was not produced until 1957, but in 1944 Feuchtwanger's novel was bought for filming (which never happened) and he insisted that Brecht have a large share of the money. They remained close friends, able to discuss each other's work as equals (Feuchtwanger, for instance, suggested substantial changes to the original characterization of Grusche in *The Caucasian Chalk Circle* and Brecht made them), until Brecht left for Europe after the hearing of the Un-American Activities Committee on 30 October 1947.

Of all his group of émigrés, Feuchtwanger lasted longest in Southern California. Bruno Frank died in June 1945 and Franz Werfel two months later, both barely outliving Hitler's war in Europe. In November the same year Leonhard Frank gratefully pocketed a cheque from MGM for the film rights of *Carl and Anna* and got on the train for New York with never a backward look. Also in 1945, Alfred Doeblin went straight back to Germany as soon as he could, after barely eking out a living in Los Angeles, even while he was writing his great trilogy *November 1918,* not published until 1948–50 (except for an episode published privately by the Pazifischen Presse in 1944—the only writing he managed to get published in any shape or form during his American exile). In 1947 Brecht and Eisler left, in 1950 Heinrich Mann died, and in 1952 Thomas Mann, disturbed by the changing American political climate, moved to Switzerland and spent his last three years near Zurich.

Feuchtwanger was left more or less alone, but he did not seem to mind too much. Back in 1943, at the UCLA Writers Congress, he had spoken expressively on 'The Working Problems of the Writer in Exile', the 'little, silly annoyances' that tore down the exile's nerves, the impossibility of writing with full expressiveness in a foreign language, and the radical changes being in exile made in the writer's 'inner landscape'. Nevertheless he overcame or circumvented them all, and even managed not to be confronted by witch-hunting committees. He remained a German writer to the end, but one whose acceptance of his new life was almost total.

At the same congress Thomas Mann spoke on 'The Exiled Writer's Relation to his Homeland'. This subject too was significant, for the question became the most vital and disturbing in his latter days in America. Largely this was the result of the complexity of Mann's own responses and the honesty with which, once he had decided to get off the fence, he expressed them. He did not, like many others, take the easy way out by postulating some clear division between the Nazis and the rest, the 'good Germans' who could be absolved from all war guilt. On the contrary, as early as December 1943 he had stated in a letter to Brecht on the possibility of setting up a sort of 'Free German' government-in-exile in America:

> Horrors can and probably still will take place, and they will in turn arouse the world's horror of this nation. Where will we be, if we have prematurely vouched for the victory of the better and higher impulses within Germany?

On 29 May 1945, in a speech on 'Germany and the Germans' delivered to the Library of Congress in Washington, Mann made his position even clearer:

> There are not two Germanies, a good one and an evil one, but only a single one, which turned its best by devilry into bad. Evil Germany, that is the good which has festered, the good in misfortune, in guilt and decline. For this reason it is so impossible for a German-born mind to disown the evil, guilt-laden Germany and to declare: 'I am the good, the noble, the righteous Germany in white, the evil I leave to your extermination.' Nothing of that which I have said to you about Germany or tried fleetingly to point out, came from knowledge dissociated, cool or uninvolved: I have it also in me, I have experienced it in my own body.

All this was honest and uncompromising. But tact was never Thomas Mann's strong point, and that was precisely what was called for next. Instead of responding to an appeal from one Walter von Molo, a German writer and supporter of Hitler, that he should return to help in Germany's post-war reconstruction, with a simple reply pointing out the practical problems of such a move—which, admittedly, would have begged the more serious questions—he wrote a lengthy letter rehearsing again the shame of intellectual support (by von Molo among many others) for Hitler and outlining his own sufferings in exile. It was, naturally, misunderstood and laid Mann open to attacks that were not long in coming, mainly from those who sought to salvage the reputation of the writers who had stayed behind in Germany by proposing the concept of 'inner migration' and suggesting that sticking by one's country in her darkest hour was morally preferable to going into comfortable exile for the duration. Mann's principal attacker, someone named Frank Theiss, even went so far as to say that Mann had lost the right to be called a German writer, and was a dishonourable turncoat spewing forth bitterness and hatred for the land of his birth.

Understandably, all of this did not leave Mann very popular in Germany, especially among ex-Nazis, and he refused all invitations to visit Germany again, insisting that he was now an American citizen and Germany was alien to him. In 1947 *Doctor Faustus* was published in Germany in a very limited Swedish edition which could not, for legal reasons, circulate in Germany; early in 1948 it finally came out in German, to widespread hostility. Its reception in America was quite different. It was a Book-of-the-Month Club selection, with a first printing of more than 100,000, a remarkable number for a book that was esoteric in style and themes, and certainly not aimed at a popular audience, in the measure, say, of a Feuchtwanger or a Werfel. Not surprisingly, popular reviewers thought it obscure, over-solemn and confusing.

The anti-Thomas Mann campaign in Germany continued if anything to intensify, especially after Doeblin added his voice to it. But Heinrich Mann, curiously enough, was the subject of renewed attention, especially in East Germany, where he was offered the post of President of the German Academy of Arts in East Berlin in spring 1949, and where his books continued to sell in huge numbers, though not to his profit in America since money could not be taken out of the Eastern bloc.

In July 1949, after sixteen years out of Germany, Thomas Mann finally decided to visit Western Germany to attend the Goethe celebrations in Frankfurt and Munich and then, in a bold and controversial gesture, to visit East Germany as well for the Goethe celebrations in Weimar. As a result of his experience in Weimar, he encouraged Heinrich to accept the East German invitation, but Heinrich died before he could actually go.

The visit to East Germany did little to help Thomas's position, either in West Germany or in an America increasingly at the mercy of Senator McCarthy and his followers. But that is to carry our story too far ahead, way beyond wartime Hollywood and what the émigrés found to do in it—particularly those émigrés who came to Los Angeles very much on purpose, not because of the climate but because it was, after all, the centre of film-making in the free world; they were film professionals and therefore it seemed the only place to be.

171

10. Hollywood at War

Though, as we have seen, the German colony in Hollywood, or some members of it, were conscious very early of the likely consequences of war in Europe and the need to proffer some kind of help to refugee writers, that was, in fact, about as far as it went. The jobs created by the European Film Fund were regarded from the start as sinecures, lightly dismissed charity that demanded little active involvement on the recipients' part in the actual workings of the Hollywood movie industry. They were grateful, but they were bored and they were lonely: no real film people ever spoke to them, and even their outside social contacts with compatriots in the film world were sharply curtailed once it was clear that they were losers in this town that had time only for winners, that they would never succeed by the only standards which meant anything in Hollywood.

To be fair, this was not quite the personal betrayal many émigrés took it to be. Partly it was born out of fear and suspicion, on both sides—few of the film people felt equal to the company of 'intellectuals', which the new arrivals were, to a man, supposed to be, while the newcomers were intimidated by the riches and the no-nonsense American professionalism of their reluctant hosts. Also, there were the practical problems, working the early hours those in the movie-business did, of keeping up any kind of social contacts with people completely outside their own particular world. There was snobbery too, on both sides—money looked down on poverty, European culture looked down on American brashness and vulgarity. And there was a curious and intricate class system operating in Hollywood, based not only on income but also on a whole mass of imponderables, such as which studio one worked for, and what had been the critical reception and box-office grosses of one's last picture, which strangers, let alone foreigners, could not begin to comprehend.

And so, for the most part, the members of the New Weimar, like the few other artists and musicians of distinction who had coincidentally settled in Southern California, held themselves apart from the movie business, waiting perhaps to be wooed, yet waiting in vain, except for occasional encounters with loners like Chaplin and Garbo. There were few, anyway, who could begin to bridge the gap. The most important meeting-ground was the house of Berthold and Salka Viertel (or, as it more and more obviously became, of Salka Viertel alone). Berthold was a moderately successful film-maker who happened also to be a lyric poet of a distinction all the émigrés could respect. Salka was an important script-writer whose importance, based as it was on her supposed understanding of the Garbo enigma, diminished drastically when Garbo retired from the screen in 1941. Though Gottfried Reinhardt, for some years Salka's lover and surrogate host in her house, was a producer at MGM, the groups that gathered there in the 1940s had less and less to do with movies, and when individuals like Isherwood and Huxley did show a surprising ability to function successfully in a movie context, that had very little to do with the reasons anyone in émigré circles would be likely to cultivate them.

But all this, of course, presupposes that the émigrés were from the start of their Los Angeles sojourn very much on the outside looking in. (If, that is, they would deign to look.) Such was the attitude, or at any rate the situation, of those I have been discussing up to now. But there were many others who were in a very different position, and it is now time to take a further look at them. Some, the early arrivals, were already well established and more or less thoroughly Americanized by the outbreak of the Second World War. Others were to arrive in Los Angeles during the 1940s, as one European calamity followed another, but with one clear intention: to work, somehow, in Hollywood; to work, somehow, in films.

It was hard to say whether, for most of them, their refugee status was more of a good or bad thing. Evidently, as Lang had found on his arrival five years earlier, they were not negotiating from a position of strength, such as a successful and *continuing* career elsewhere would give them, and Hollywood, always respectful and desirous of those who spurned, or seemed to spurn it, could be merciless towards those who were evidently in need of it. On the other hand, there was a histrionically sentimental side that could be exploited: Hollywood loved a drama, and the idea of these heroic refugees, snatched from the jaws of death, was appealing to the dramatic instinct. On a wave of emotion many found it easier to get

173

into Hollywood than they otherwise might have. Robert Florey, who, as an old hand at Hollywood and leading Frenchman-on-the-spot, made himself the main liaison for the French when they arrived, said that he never had any trouble introducing such compatriot directors as Jean Renoir, René Clair, Julien Duvivier and Léonide Moguy to the Directors Guild and getting them made members of it. How successful they were afterwards was, of course, up to them, but at least it was a foot in the door.

To reach that point it was necessary first to get to Hollywood, and this could be more of a problem. To the old immigration quotas, with the obstruction to entry they represented, were added the newly relevant measures taken legally to enforce United States neutrality. Together these represented considerable mistrust on the government's part of the growing stream of foreigners who wanted to enter the country for primarily political reasons. Early in 1940 Roosevelt created an Advisory Committee on Political Refugees, to screen the numerous applications for entry and recommend the most deserving cases (on cultural and moral grounds) for visas. During its first few months of existence it recommended 567 writers, artists and assorted intellectuals for visas, but by October 1940 it had to report that only 40 of these had actually been granted by the State Department. Eventually it recommended that some 3,000 people be granted visas, but well under half that number were actually authorized. Most of those who got as far as Los Angeles did so on temporary visas and had to go through the wearisome and humiliating process of going over into Mexico and waiting there until they could re-enter under some longer-term arrangement.

Then, however sympathetic people in Hollywood were in principle to the refugees (and many were not even that), there were other problems: fear that the newcomers might include subversive elements or even German spies; more immediate fears that they might be taking the bread out of Hollywood residents' mouths. The *New York Times* did a carefully noncommittal story about this in March 1941, emphasizing that though what it called 'Hollywood's refugee problem' had not yet reached alarming proportions, people were already worried: 'Forty or fifty well-known film-workers from middle Europe have been more or less recently employed by the studios—at whose expense doesn't seem quite clear just now—and there are twice or three times that number waiting round on the off-chance that a job will be found for them.' No doubt the parenthetical question of whose expense was aimed in its literal sense at the European Film Fund, which had arranged that about eight writers who were far from being 'well-known film workers', or indeed film-workers at all, should be employed at the (minimal) expense of Warner Brothers and MGM. But it was the more metaphorical senses of the question that gave rise to most worry in Hollywood: were the truly famous film-workers going to take jobs which otherwise would have been done by decent hard-working Americans—Americans, at least, of a few years' seniority?

For there was the rub. Hollywood had always shown an extraordinary propensity for absorbing and making its own talent from wherever it might come. Any sort of pseudo-Hitlerian separation of the sheep from the goats, true-born native Americans from first-generation Americans, childhood immigrants from recent immigrants, would be virtually impossible, and in any case unprofitable. But it seems that in Hollywood it was most frequently those who had only just got over the wall who were most eager to kick down the ladder. One often finds what appear to be extraordinary examples of non-communication and refusal of aid. Victor Saville seemingly did his best to secure work in Hollywood for his former leading lady Jessie Matthews, the biggest star, after all, of Thirties cinema in Britain. As between, say, Jean Renoir and the star of his acclaimed French success *La Bête Humaine*, Jean Gabin, it was a moot point who might have been in a position to help whom. But it really is astonishing that Lilian Harvey, the big star of German cinema throughout the Thirties (and, for a while, big in Hollywood too) should have been in Los Angeles all through the war, along with her producer Erich Pommer, her directors Wilhelm Thiele and Erik Charell, her writers Billy Wilder and Walter Reisch, and that none of them apparently lifted a finger to help her, so that she never made even the smallest appearance in a film and had to find work as a nurse instead. Perhaps this had something to do with her return to Germany when Hitler was already in power.

In this kind of case there was, as well as some possible element of personal animosity—the fact of all being émigrés together did not mean that all old feuds were automatically forgotten—a strong element of show-business ruthlessness to be taken into account. In Hollywood nobody loved a has-been—on the contrary, they were feared and avoided, like some kind of *memento mori*. In 1940, at 34, Lilian Harvey was no longer quite the fresh young ingénue she had been a few years before, and that was reason enough in itself not to employ her: who wanted, after all, to jinx his own picture?

In any case, there was hardly anyone in Hollywood, certainly among the directors, writers and such, who was so secure that he or she could afford to risk very much, or so independent that all decisions were entirely up to him. Few of the émigrés had got to be producers, and none, except Lubitsch for a brief period at Paramount in the 1930s, had achieved the standing of a tycoon in charge of a studio. Erich Pommer, whom we last encountered during his none-too-successful stint as a contract producer with Fox in 1934, had spent the intervening years in England producing for Korda and then making three films for Mayflower, an independent production company he had set up with Charles Laughton. After the last of these, *Jamaica Inn* (1939), which happened also to be the last film Hitchcock made in England before leaving for Hollywood, Pommer found the situation for German émigrés in England becoming more difficult by the minute and, of course, once war had broken out, potentially dangerous, so he decided to try his luck in Hollywood again.

Pommer's first production in Hollywood was a curious crypto-lesbian drama called *Dance, Girl, Dance* (1940), a *film noir* about the private lives of chorus-girls with heavy Germanic overtones that ran into many production difficulties and had no noticeable success when released. His second, much more ambitious venture, was a reunion with Charles Laughton in a film version of Sidney Howard's already twice-filmed play *They Knew What They Wanted* (1940), about an Italian vine-grower who takes on a mail-order bride.

Though Pommer had an independent-producer contract with RKO, the amount of independence he could actually exercise was strictly limited, since all the finance for his films would come from the studio, and if they were not financially successful, the studio could very rapidly rethink the situation. *They Knew What They Wanted*, torn as it was by dissensions between Laughton and his co-star Carole Lombard, Laughton and his director Garson Kanin, and further hampered by the discomfort of the whole crew working on location in the Napa Valley (Pommer had picked up back in Europe a passion for location authenticity), did not turn out very well, and was not a success with the public. The failure of two films in a row virtually finished Pommer's career—he was in no position to help anyone else in Hollywood, and there seems to have been no one in the right sort of position who was ready to help him. Especially, no doubt, since when he was czar of the German film industry he had a reputation for being very imperious and difficult to deal with, and made many enemies who would be more than happy to see him fall on hard times.

He hung on in Hollywood, inactive, till the end of the war, then returned to Germany in 1946 as Film Officer under the Occupation to supervise the revival of the German film industry. Like Korda, he was amazingly unstoppable, and by 1950 was in production again as head of the new International GmbH company, making some of the most famous and commercially successful West German films of the early 1950s, such as *Kinder, Mütter und ein General* (1955). And though his experiences in Hollywood had not for the most part been happy, he could not stay away; in 1956 he returned for a third time, and spent the last ten years of his life there.

Undoubtedly the most personally powerful film émigré in Hollywood in 1940 was the longest-standing resident, Ernst Lubitsch. He had not only been making films continuously there since 1923, but he had had fewer box-office disasters than almost anyone else, and had been producer as well as director for most of his films (whether or not he took a producer credit). He had continued to visit Europe quite frequently and had kept up contacts with European friends and collaborators, so it was only to be expected that he would be one of the earliest people in Hollywood to manifest concern for the way things were going in Europe in 1939 and try to do something to help. This took shape in the European Film Fund. He was able to exert some pressure on behalf of this idea at MGM because he had just made there one of his most famous films, *Ninotchka* (1939), in which Garbo famously laughed, and they were eager to keep him around. His next film, also for MGM, was *The Shop Around the Corner* (1940), another very European subject, set in Budapest and based on a Hungarian play by Nikolaus Laszlo, but a romantic comedy of life in a store with no hint of the troubled state of Europe at the time it was actually made, and with a thoroughly American cast and crew.

It must have seemed that Lubitsch was, in fact, whatever his sympathies and concerns as a private man, just about the last person in Hollywood fitted to give artistic expression to the Nazi menace and the horrors of war. After all, he was famed exclusively for his naughty, light-fantastic comedies, taking place in a Ruritanian never-never Europe, which, since it never existed anyway, could hardly be affected by wartime changes. Except, of course, in the willingness of audiences to suspend disbelief. No doubt aware of this problem, Lubitsch very carefully skirted the issue in the film he made after *The Shop Around the Corner*, running for cover in a remake of one of his old standbys, *Kiss Me Again* (1925), a Sardou comedy tactfully translated in this new version (retitled *That Uncertain Feeling*) from Paris to New York. But Lubitsch's real-life sympathies were not to remain totally unexpressed, and late in 1941 he made what seemed at the time one of his few dramatic miscalculations when he began work on a dark comedy, *To Be or Not to Be*, based on an original story by himself and Melchior Lengyel concerning a group of actors during the German invasion of Poland. It began shooting on 6 November 1941, and finished 23 December, i.e., after Pearl Harbor and the entry of the US into the Second World War. This change of situation brought about a radical change of mood in the American public, and so what might have been acceptable before—the belittlement of Hitler and the Nazis by way of a sometimes almost farcical comedy—suddenly became hard to swallow and seemed in more than dubious taste.

Criticism, made generally uncomfortable by the film, centred on one line: that in which Sig Ruman, playing a German general, says of Jack Benny, a ham Shakespearian actor: 'What he did to Shakespeare, we are now doing to Poland.' Walter Reisch, émigré writer who had scripted *That Uncertain Feeling* and a friend of Lubitsch, records that the night of the film's sneak preview the film went very well until that line came up; the audience seemed to be shaken and offended by it, and were from then on thrown out of their good mood. Afterwards, at a party that included Reisch, Wilder, Charles Brackett, Korda, Henry Blanke and S. N. Behrman, Lubitsch's wife finally dared to suggest that the line be cut. She was backed up by everyone else there, and it was evident from the reactions of other people in the nightclub that Lubitsch had, at least in terms of the sensibilities of that moment, made a grave error. However, he refused to change the line in question, and even a couple of years later bothered to answer a criticism of his next (completely non-political) film, *Heaven Can Wait* (1943), which alleged that the 'Berlin-born director' of *To Be or Not to Be* had made a 'callous, tasteless effort to find fun in the bombing of Warsaw' like this:

> When in *To Be or Not to Be* I have referred to the destruction of Warsaw I have shown it in all seriousness; the commentation under the shots of the devastated Warsaw speaks for itself and cannot leave any doubt in the spectator's mind what my point of

view and attitude is towards those acts of horror. What I have satirized in this picture are the Nazis and their ridiculous ideology. I have also satirized the attitude of actors who always remain actors regardless how dangerous the situation might be, which I believe is a true observation.

Never have I said in a picture anything derogative about Poland or the Poles. On the contrary I have portrayed them as a gallant people who do not cry on other people's shoulders in their misery but even in the darkest day never lost courage and ingenuity or their sense of humour.

It can be argued if the tragedy of Poland realistically portrayed as in *To Be or Not to Be* can be merged with satire. I believe it can be and so do the audience which I observed during a screening of *To Be or Not to Be;* but this is a matter of debate and everyone is entitled to his point of view...

Clearly, none of his European friends believed for a moment that he was insensitive to the sufferings of the Poles, let alone in any sense pro-Nazi. And a viewing of *To Be or Not to Be* today vindicates his point of view. But the whole story does provide some evidence of the touchy situation in which émigrés were likely to find themselves. Or rather, the series of touchy situations: first, the problems of having some sort of political commitment in circumstances that were supposed to be neutral, and then, for the Germans at least, the rather different problems of being an 'enemy alien' in a country newly in the grip of war hysteria and chauvinistic patriotism. Lubitsch, of course, had long been a naturalized American, and did not have to bother with curfews for aliens and other such minor irritations; he even became an air-raid warden, and was observed by Laurence Olivier delivering angry instructions to a black-out offender in the heaviest imaginable German accent. But clearly that did not save him from suspicion and hostility on account of his German background, however remote it might be.

Lubitsch had for long been almost completely Americanized, though as we have observed, carefully retaining his 'Europeanness' as a saleable commodity, something which made his films that little bit different and special for American audiences. Even though his source material was usually European—often a half-forgotten Hungarian, French or German play—he liked to have it worked over, under his direction, by a cunning combination of European and American talent: the writing team of Billy Wilder and Charles Brackett, with whom he worked on *Bluebeard's Eighth Wife* and *Ninotchka*, is a good example. Thus, even professionally, he contrived to keep a foot in both camps, making the most of his dual heritage and experience. In this he was very different from Fritz Lang, his nearest competitor among the German émigrés in fame and Hollywood success. Though Lang obviously retained unconsciously a lot of the ideas about film-making he had acquired or developed during his German days, on a conscious level his determination from the outset seems to have been to become an American film-maker with no apparent hint of foreignness in his work.

The foreignness is there all the same, very much so in the two films he made after *Fury*, *You Only Live Once* (1937) and *You and Me* (1938). The first, with its powerful Germanic chiaroscuro and its glum view of the human condition as a trap from which only death can extricate one, fitted into a cycle of dark social dramas of the late 1930s, such as *They Won't Forget*, and was, like *Fury*, a box-office success. *You and Me*, Lang's only attempt at comedy in America, seems to have been intended as an American equivalent of a Brecht *Lehrstück*, explaining light-heartedly the purely economic lesson that crime does not pay; it was even originally intended to have a complete score of songs by Kurt Weill, Brecht's former collaborator on *The Threepenny Opera*, though in the event Weill, a recent arrival from Europe, left Hollywood for New York halfway through the picture, and so contributed only one song. Apart from its sheer oddity, the film is rather a muddle and fails to make any clear effect, so not surprisingly it was a box-office failure, and Lang was out of work for the following two years.

When he returned, it was through a project he had been developing, significantly entitled *Americana*, which was to present a panoramic sweep of American history in terms of the Western, that most American of genres. Nothing came of this idea directly, but because of it Darryl Zanuck offered Lang a Western to direct at Twentieth Century-Fox. It was a sequel to one of the big successes of 1939, Henry King's *Jesse James*, was in colour, and was called *The Return of Frank James* (1940). It was in every way, therefore, as distant as could be from any lingering idea people in Hollywood might have of Lang as a German director: even visually, with the soft, warm tints of Technicolor in the wide open spaces of the West, it is a radical break with his past. (Even so, it is interesting that Lang, discussing the film much later with Peter Bogdanovich, makes the explanatory point about his interest in it that 'the Western is not only the history of this country, it is what the Saga of the Nibelungen is for the European'.) From this film he went directly on to another Western, *Western Union*, early in 1941, and on the strength of these two all-American successes found himself re-established and again in a position to do something he really wanted to reflect the current situation in Europe.

With *Man Hunt* (1941), at least, we have to take it on trust that it was basically something he really wanted to do. Certainly he never subsequently struck any attitudes about it, and did make it clear that this was not a project he himself nurtured, but one which was offered to him in the form of a finished script by the studio. Nor can one suppose that Twentieth Century-Fox, though of a relatively liberal disposition under the rule of Zanuck, had any political ideal in mind when they undertook the production. It was no doubt simply that the book upon which it was based, *Rogue Male* by Geoffrey Household, had been something of a bestseller and seemed to have the makings of an effective film thriller. All the same, it concerned an unsuccessful attempt on the life of a Central European dictator, presumably Hitler, and the problems that subsequently befall the would-be assassin. Even in still-neutral America, such a story had to have some believable location, and the opportunity to make it into an explicitly anti-Nazi film was too good to be missed. This was still more than six months before Pearl Harbor, but Zanuck did not interfere, except to warn Lang not to put in too many swastikas—a warning Lang firmly ignored, on the ground that dramatic effect required that part of the film's significance to be crystal clear.

The result is that *Man Hunt*, though perhaps too slow, moody and atmospheric to be wholly successful as a thriller, remains one of the most explicitly anti-Nazi films to be made in America before her entry into the war: something that later helped to build Lang's dubious reputation of 'premature anti-fascist' as well as consorter with open communists. That he had innocently signed in the Thirties, like many other people in Hollywood, a couple of petitions and appeals, which subsequently proved to emanate from communist-front organizations, was still to come. He had yet to get out of his Twentieth Century-Fox contract, and after illness, real no doubt but convenient, had taken him off two further films he did not want to make, he succeeded in doing so.

By now it was the middle of 1942, and among the various offers Lang had was one, rather persistently reiterated, from an independent producer called Arnold Pressburger, whom Lang had known slightly for some years. Pressburger's activities had been much more international than Lang's: he had begun in Germany in the 1920s, moved his operations to Britain in 1930 and Paris in 1937 and, having fled from France in 1940, had just succeeded in producing in Hollywood a very odd film indeed, Sternberg's reworking of the old whorehouse melodrama *The Shanghai Gesture* (1941). Clearly he was not the man to shy away from bizarre projects, and Lang felt he had found just the right thing when he read the newspaper accounts of the assassination of Heydrich, Nazi 'protector' of Czechoslovakia.

To help him develop the idea, he looked to another recent arrival, a writer totally inexperienced in American film-writing, but one for whom he had a great admiration dating back to his early days in Germany: Bertolt Brecht. It was the genesis of what was eventually to become *Hangmen Also Die* (1943). This, the only major screen-writing job that Brecht did in America, has been the subject of so many conflicting accounts, so much indignation and recrimination, that it is very hard now to disentangle the truth. It all started with Brecht's arrival in America, from Vladivostok on 21 July 1941: some say that Lang, along with Feuchtwanger, sponsored his admission; others say that Brecht and Lang had never met before their first Hollywood contact. However that may be, at least Brecht, unlike most of the grander German literary émigrés, was really interested in the film-making side of Los Angeles. He was a practising dramatic writer in a place which, theoretically at least, was a great market for dramatic writing, and he wanted to continue to exercise his craft as well as to make a living. His English was not bad, though on the whole he refused to use it except when absolutely necessary. He had already sketched out (in German) a variety of possible film-treatments on subjects as unlikely as *Lady Macbeth of the Yards*, *Caesar's Last Day*, and *Fear and Misery of the Third Reich*, as well as apparently being paid in late 1941 to work on something called *Bermuda Troubles* at MGM—a project that seems to have come to nothing.

Thus when Lang suggested early in May 1942 that they collaborate on a dramatic version of the Heydrich story he did not need a lot of persuading. He and Lang worked together every day, Brecht's principles (political and dramaturgic) working with, and sometimes against, Lang's show-business know-how and constant appeals to audience-acceptability. And at least it was money. Lang asked him how much he hoped to be paid for his work on the script, and he wondered tentatively whether $3,000 would be too much to ask. Lang announced he was going to ask for $5,000, but when the time came to negotiate in early July he asked Pressburger for only $3,500, which Pressburger, adept at filming on a shoestring, still tried to cut down, though finally acceding to Lang's urgings that despite the deficiencies of Brecht's English he was the ideal man for the job because of his specialized political knowledge. It was, however, also agreed that an American collaborator on the script should be sought—preferably one who spoke fluent German and was socially and politically amenable. A young socialist playwright called John Wexley was chosen—he had just had a *succès d'estime* with a death-cell drama *The Last Mile*, his German was excellent, and he was a member of the Communist Party, a fact that later got him into more trouble than Brecht, who never was.

Wexley first appears in Brecht's diaries on 5 August; Brecht notes that Wexley was being paid $1,500 a week. There was evidently some mutual mistrust: Brecht and Wexley would discuss a scene, then Wexley would write it, and Brecht got the distinct impression that Wexley did not want him to see what had been written. But things seem to have been patched up, and for a couple of months the collaboration went quite smoothly, with Wexley apparently acting as a moderator between the rather impractical Brecht, interested mainly in his crowd scenes and the epic aspects of the story, and Lang, who was determined that however serious the film's message, it had to work first of all as a thriller if it was going to work at all. Brecht's chief satisfaction was that he and Wexley were writing an 'ideal script', full of epical niceties, as well as the bread-and-butter Hollywood script they were being paid for. But in mid-October Wexley told Brecht that Lang had made a big scene with him about their ignoring the commercial basics, which did not seem to bode too well for the chances of the 'ideal script', when and if they were able to finish it.

At the beginning of November Brecht was informed the film was now shooting, and on a visit to the studio discovered that some things he had thrown out of the script were back in and being shot. Later he blamed Wexley, who had, he alleged, 'sold out for two weekly pay-cheques of $30,000' (which one suspects to have been an infuriated slip of the pen for '$3,000'). Lang's version is rather different. He claims that at the end of October he was still expecting to start shooting in a month's time. They had at that point a script of some 280 typed pages (nearly double the length of an average 100-

minute film) and were just getting down to the necessary job of pruning and revision when Pressburger informed him that owing to unforeseen circumstances they must start shooting in a week. Lang claims that he did the best he could in the circumstances, cutting without upsetting the balance and interest of the original more than could be avoided.

But this was not the last of the disputes. Brecht and Wexley next found themselves at loggerheads over the issue (vital in Hollywood) of screen credits. Wexley suddenly insisted that, since he had written the English script, he should get sole screen credit for it. Whatever Lang's attitude in keeping the balance between his writers and his producer (no doubt from Brecht's point of view he was too conciliatory towards Pressburger, though this tough practicality may also have been to the ultimate good of the film), in this dispute he seems, from his own account at least, to have been very much on Brecht's side. He maintained before the Screen Writers' Guild, and continued to maintain ever afterwards, that Wexley's job was almost entirely translating what Brecht wrote (sometimes, he added, far too literally) and that Brecht should have at least equal credit. The Guild was inclined, as usual, to take the side of an American writer and Guild-member against an outsider, and so Wexley got sole credit for the screenplay with 'adaptation and original story' credited jointly to Brecht and Lang. (Oddly enough, this partisan attitude still persists. Hitchcock himself went before the Guild's arbitrators to secure screen credit on *Torn Curtain* for the British writers he had brought in completely to rewrite the script, but the Guild insisted on attributing sole credit to the original writer involved, Bryan Moore.)

That, anyway, was how Lang told it; Brecht, inevitably, had a conflicting story. According to him, Lang and Pressburger wanted him to have no credit at all on the film (though why is not explained), and Wexley was encouraged by them to maintain that he had hardly even met Brecht. Whatever the truth, Brecht and Hanns Eisler, who had composed the score for the film, strongly protested the Guild's decision, but in vain; apparently Brecht and Lang never had any communication afterwards.

All the same, whatever the screen credits say, Brecht's mark is all over *Hangmen Also Die* (Lang claimed that at least 90 per cent of what was used in the script came directly from Brecht). At the time this would not have been so apparent, in that Brecht was known hardly at all to the English-speaking public—even his biggest commercial success, *The Threepenny Opera*, was known only from a short-lived New York production in 1933 (America did not become really conscious of it until 1954, when Marc Blitzstein's somewhat modified translation of it was done in New York with Lotte Lenya as Jenny). Consequently it is understandable that Brecht's name, anywhere on the credits, would have meant nothing. But today, it is possible at once to see Brecht's savage humour in some of the verbal manipulation that goes on in the scenes involving translation from German to Czech, Brecht's teaching tone in the Professor's meticulous explanation to his daughter of how information spreads as far as the Gestapo through the most innocent of confidences, and Brecht's heritage of Expressionist stage-craft in the scene where the news of Heydrich's death spreads chorically through a darkened cinema. There are hints of the famous alienation-effect in the film's attitude to its characters. As Lang observed later:

> We didn't want analyses of characters, we simply schematized into those who resist and those who organize, those who aspire to freedom but have not yet found or chosen the means of action, and finally the collaborators, the genuine enemy of the people like Czaka... For me, psychology is not in the talking, it is in the action, in the movement, the gestures. In *Hangmen Also Die* there is a great deal of detail that makes the personalities come alive... It is the behaviourisms which create the character.

Naturally, Brecht was not satisfied with any of this. Not even the final song, 'Never Surrender', written on 13 December to music by Eisler (part of a score for which, incidentally, Eisler was nominated for an Oscar), which has seemed to at least one competent judge 'even in English pure Brecht', was done to his liking. He complained that Lang had brought in some Tin Pan Alley hack at great expense ($500) to travesty what he originally wrote, then put together something incoherent himself from the various versions. In the lines

> Brother—the time has come!
> Brother—work to be done!
> Take hold of the invisible torch, and pass it on!

he complained that an invisible torch was unlikely to attract much attention, and preferred his original 'flag'. Now it is not so easy as it might appear to say who is right and wrong in all this—even if we accept the Brecht diary account as gospel. It is obviously a clash between two ways of thinking: the Hollywood way, as represented by Lang, and the way of a European *littérateur*, as represented by

Brecht. Lang was not alone in his standards—indeed, he was probably more open to and understanding of other attitudes than most people of power then in Hollywood. Brecht was absolutely typical of the émigré German literary community in his refusal to take any real notice of Hollywood's practical requirements, to regard them in effect as beneath his notice. But he too was more flexible than most; at least he did make a serious attempt to work in and with Hollywood. And while the European concept of a script as a literary entity that should be finished (in its 'ideal form') as the work of the writer or writers, and only then, maybe, subject to discussion and modification, had a lot to recommend it in an ideal world, it could hardly be expected to work with Hollywood deadlines and Hollywood's financial investment in movies as a strictly commercial proposition. Nor does it have much to do with the idea of the film as essentially a director's medium: we may now consider that *Hangmen Also Die* would have emerged, come what may, as a Lang film rather than a Brecht film, but Brecht would never have accepted that.

So, even with goodwill on both sides, Hollywood and the émigré literary community were probably fated to misunderstand each other. If Brecht, a practised if difficult man of the theatre, could not come to terms with Hollywood and its ways, how was it likely that, say, Thomas Mann or Arnold Schoenberg or Herbert Marcuse were going to? In any case, most of the evidence suggests that they did not really want to. There was certainly an element of cultural elitism, which encouraged many of them to speak English as seldom as possible—even when they could speak it quite passably—and to keep themselves to themselves, preferring the society of Germans, even Germans they did not particularly like, to that of other nationalities.

Brecht, at least, though fairly discouraged by *Hangmen Also Die* from any ideas he might have had of the American cinema as a field of endeavour into which he could enter as a full partner or even a personal creator, did stay on in Los Angeles until it became politic for him to move, and did continue with the struggle to function somehow in American show-business. It seems that the only other occasion he actually had anything to do with films again in America was in 1947 when he was called in to do some uncredited rewrites on Lewis Milestone's film of the Erich Maria Remarque novel *Arch of Triumph* (partly because he was at that time trying to talk Milestone into collaborating on a film of *The Tales of Hoffmann*, but also because Charles Laughton was one of its three émigré stars, along with Charles Boyer and Ingrid Bergman). But his principal 'American' work in these years was *Galileo*, a play he had completed in German in 1939: the version staged in 1943 at the Zurich Schauspielhaus, where most of his works of the American period— *Mother Courage, The Good Woman of Setzuan, Herr Puntila*— were also premiered. In 1945–7, he worked it over and translated it into English, in collaboration with Charles Laughton, for an eventual production by himself and Joseph Losey at the Coronet Theatre, Los Angeles, in August 1947.

However, during his Los Angeles years Brecht was constantly busy—writing, trying to set up productions of his old and new work, trying to sell film stories to producers just in order to make a living, and more actively in touch with others of the émigré group in Los Angeles and New York than almost anyone else. Early in 1943, after completing his part of *Hangmen Also Die*, Brecht spent nearly four months in New York, discussing the possibility of a New York production (in collaboration with Kurt Weill, now permanently settled in New York) of *The Good Woman of Setzuan*, working further on an adaptation of *The Duchess of Malfi* for Elisabeth Bergner (finally staged in 1946), co-operating with Wieland Herzfelde, founder of the Tribune for German Literature and Art in America, on the setting-up of a new publishing house for German literature to be called Aurora, and planning a stage version of Hasek's *Good Soldier Schweik* stories for Peter Lorre. Back in Santa Monica, he continued to see Eisler, Lorre and Berthold Viertel regularly, as well as the actor Fritz Kortner and, on occasion, Feuchtwanger, though Brecht put the finishing touches to *The Visions of Simone Machard* alone.

In August 1943 Brecht was deeply involved in the idea of setting up a National Committee for a Free Germany, a sort of informal approximation to or prototype for a 'Free German' government in the United States already mentioned in connection with Thomas Mann's doubts on the subject. The organization was actually mooted on 1 August, in a meeting at the Viertels attended by Heinrich and Thomas Mann, Feuchtwanger, Marcuse, Bruno Frank and Hans Reichenbach, as well as Brecht and Berthold Viertel. At that point they laid out and signed a declaration insisting on a clear distinction between the Nazi government and the German people and looking forward to a strong democracy in post-war Germany. Thomas Mann was dubious from the start, and almost immediately

187

withdrew his signature, on the grounds that the declaration was liable to misinterpretation by America as 'patriotic' and offering a loophole for Germans to dissociate themselves all too easily from war-guilt. Brecht, who never had much sympathy with Thomas Mann at the best of times, felt that in this he was merely being cowardly and a lackey to American public opinion as represented by the most chauvinistic elements of the Press.

Other splits in the unity of the German émigrés in Los Angeles became evident later in the year. Alfred Doeblin's sixty-fifth birthday was celebrated with a party organized by Helene Wiegel at which Heinrich Mann, Brecht, Kortner, Alexander Granach and Peter Lorre among others paid tribute to the man and his work. It ended with Doeblin replying in a speech that urged the restitution of strong religious standards and by implication insulted most of the atheistic guests. The National Committee for a Free Germany continued to cause argument: later in August a New York group tried to place it on a firmer footing, and offered Thomas Mann the presidency, which he of course refused on the advice of the State Department. Brecht was further incensed when, he notes in his journal, he found that, not content with washing his hands of the whole matter, Mann had been spreading gossip that Brecht and his leftish faction were persisting with this 'subversive' activity, against the interests of the American government, on direct orders from Moscow. Brecht observed bitterly in his journal that apparently Mann found it impossible to imagine doing anything, even against Hitler, without orders, and could only conceive of Germany as a prosperous book-buying public.

Brecht also continued to see quite a bit of Adorno, Marcuse and other members of the former Frankfurt Institute of Social Research, now largely relocated in Los Angeles. Though quite friendly on a personal level, his attitude was somewhat ambiguous, in that at the same time he continued to use them and their activities as raw material for his long-gestating, never finished *Tui-Novel*, a satire on the follies of intellectuals he had been working at, on and off, since 1934. The end of the year saw him in New York once more, planning a Broadway version of *The Caucasian Chalk Circle*, helped by Luise Rainer, working with Eric Bentley on an English version of *Fear and Misery of the Third Reich*, to be called at his suggestion *The Private Life of the Master Race*, and finally, none too willingly, renewing the appeal to Thomas Mann, who 'has the ear of America more fully than anyone else among us', to aid rather than obstruct the unity of the German exiles in the planning of a new democratic Germany. Mann continued to be evasive—the time was not right, they should be as unobtrusive as possible and do nothing that might offend America—and Brecht summed up his feelings in a savage poem: 'When Nobel Prize-Winner Thomas Mann Granted to the Americans and the English the Right to Chastise the German People Ten Years Long for the Crimes of the Hitler Regime'.

Early in 1944 Brecht got to know Charles Laughton well, and had a series of conversations with him about the *Schweik* play, which had by then been completed and gone through two drafts of translation, the first under the sponsorship of Peter Lorre, though all ideas of a stage production starring him had apparently been dropped. During the year, in the intervals between working on *The Caucasian Chalk Circle*, making some translations from the Chinese and discussing with Hanns Eisler and Paul Dessau the possibilities of music and epic theatre in combination, Brecht saw Laughton with increasing frequency and by December they had agreed to work on a new English version of *Galileo* for Laughton. Though he had become a member of the Council for a Democratic Germany when it was eventually set up (including no really famous people except himself and Berthold Viertel), Brecht was increasingly sceptical of its usefulness, and, ironically, tended more and more to the Thomas Mann view of the right attitude to take on German war-guilt and the 'good Germans', though for the opposite reason. He felt that German imperialism went far further than just the Nazis, including the whole German bourgeoisie, and that it would very soon be time for the proletarians to help themselves. At the same time, he worked fitfully on a version of the *Communist Manifesto* in German hexameters, drafted various outline film treatments, for America or for Germany (after the German surrender in May 1945), and urged Laughton on to complete work on the English text of *Galileo*.

Though the end of the war in Europe encouraged new plans for possible work in Germany, Brecht seems to have had no immediate urge himself to return. At last something appeared to be moving for him in America—the *Galileo* project especially, but also the eventual production of *The Private Life of the Master Race* (by Berthold Viertel after Brecht had been unable to agree with his old associate Erwin Piscator on the details of the production) for the labour unions in New York, with the émigré actor Albert Bassermann and his wife Else in leading roles, on 12 June 1945. Also the long-delayed adaptation of *The Duchess of Malfi* was complete and ready to be staged. On 2 December *Galileo* too was finished, and everyone concerned seemed very happy with it, except for the practicalities of actually staging it. Orson Welles was interested, but money was a problem. Paul Czinner, Elisabeth Bergner's husband, was also interested, but there the problem was a personal one between him and Laughton. And Laughton's agent kept interfering to cause further complications. In consequence there was no chance of the play's being performed during 1946, and Brecht was forced to kick his heels and wait.

It was not till the autumn of 1946 that things started to happen again. First, Elisabeth Bergner finally got round to doing Brecht's adaptation of *The Duchess of Malfi* in Boston and New York, under the direction (very conservative and un-Brechtian) of the English scholar George Rylands. Though as far as Brecht's creative work and reputation were concerned this made little difference, it was in a general way encouraging. And back on the coast *Galileo* was slowly moving forward. Laughton had been fully occupied with films, including a moderately interesting one, *The Suspect* (1945), a tale of wife-murder in Edwardian London directed by Robert Siodmak, and negotiations with Welles and his current backer Mike Todd had proceeded, mainly by indirection. It seems that Welles really wanted to do the play, after his fashion, but equally that his fashion was far removed from what Brecht and Laughton had in mind.

By June 1946 things had come to a head when Welles wanted Todd eliminated from the arrangement (contracts notwithstanding) and to be given a completely free hand in the direction of the play, planned for some unspecified time in the future with some unspecified financial backing other than Todd's. Laughton was incensed by this, and told Welles so in no uncertain terms; consequently Welles removed himself from the scene for good. It was not surprising that Brecht began to listen to offers from Berlin and plan a trip to Zurich the following year.

But *Galileo* was still there, and early in 1947 a definitive production arrangement was actually made. A company called Pelican Productions was being set up in Los Angeles by the American actor-manager Norman Lloyd (later producer of Alfred Hitchcock's television series) and the Russian-American producer John Houseman, formerly co-director with Orson Welles of the Mercury Theatre. They had adequate, if not lavish financial backing, the lease of the small, relatively uncommercial Coronet Theatre in Hollywood, and a seriousness of purpose both Brecht and Laughton found congenial. The director chosen to work under Brecht's guidance was Joseph Losey, a young left-winger who had worked on *Living Newspaper* and had made documentary films with Hanns Eisler in New York. The play was to be the company's second production, following Thornton Wilder's *The Skin of Our Teeth*, and the rehearsals proceeded slowly, interrupted from time to time by Brecht's volcanic fits of anger and Laughton's bouts of nervousness and self-doubt. There were moments when Brecht found nothing right, not even the costumes by his wife, Helene Wiegel, and there were various hirings and firings along the way before everyone was satisfied. And Brecht was, all the time, keeping other irons in the fire: the possibility of returning to the Berlin theatre with Piscator; a film project with Peter Lorre in Switzerland; the plan to visit Zurich, for which purposes he and Helene Weigel had got exit and re-entry visas.

On 21 July *Galileo* opened, and was a triumph—at least as far as anything theatrical could be called a triumph in the Los Angeles of those days, considered as it was the back of beyond in terms of 'serious' American theatre, which stood or fell by its showing in New York. It was scheduled to run for a month, then go to New York, but since the national reviews were not as good as the local ones, the backer decided to delay the New York run until the production had been revised to make it more lively and colourful, and Laughton had elected not to eschew all suspicion of flamboyance and hamminess quite so vigorously. Other problems were also looming.

The House Committee on Un-American Activities began its most savage series of hearings yet in May. Brecht's political sympathies were hardly in question; Losey was regarded as a possibly dangerous left-wing sympathizer; and even Laughton, of no noticeable political interests, was advised to be very careful about what he said in public, and even what mail he received, while working on the play. Obviously Brecht's days in America were numbered, and as it turned out, by the time the play opened in New York on 7 December, he had left forever, and the 'Un-American' witch-hunt was getting into full swing.

But that is to anticipate. We must go back first and find out what was happening to other German émigrés in Hollywood. After his break with Brecht over *Hangmen Also Die*, Lang toyed with the idea of returning to his roots in silent German cinema with a new adaptation of the classic monster story *The Golem*, set in the ghetto of Prague. But in the event *Hangmen Also Die*, if no runaway commercial success, was favourably received, and on the strength of it he was offered another anti-Nazi thriller to direct by Paramount. This was *Ministry of Fear* (1944), based on a Graham Greene novel he had wanted to buy himself, so he agreed without looking at the script, which proved to have been concocted by his producer, and so was not subject to modification. In consequence, Lang claimed to have had no interest in the film, and merely did a routine professional job on it, but curiously enough it emerges as a very characteristic work, haunted with the shadows of Mabuse's nightmare world; not perhaps a very serious anti-Nazi film, in that the Nazis are really just 'them', the evil villains who could be anybody. But the fact remains that they are identified as Nazis, this was the time of America at war, and no doubt Lang still wanted to make some kind of statement on the subject, even if by way of a traditional, commercial thriller.

In effect, Lang had gone back into that American cinema of which he had made himself so determinedly a part right from the moment of his arrival. On a conscious level there is nothing to distinguish the rest of his Hollywood work from that of any other American film-maker, of whatever origins. There is no greater interest in German subjects (one more thriller with a background of the fight against Nazism, *Cloak and Dagger*, after the war, proves nothing one way or the other), no greater tendency to work with European émigrés (Lilli Palmer is in *Cloak and Dagger*; apparently she was forced on him and he hated working with her). But on the subconscious level Lang offers a perfect illustration of the influence German cinema had on Americans.

His very next two films after *Ministry of Fear, The Woman in the Window* (1944) and *Scarlet Street* (1945), as remote from the war as could possibly be, are unmistakably in the classic tradition of the Germanic *film noir*, which was one of the dominant genres in Hollywood during the Forties. Both of them are perverse triangle dramas in which an innocent Edward G. Robinson is entrapped by trashy femme fatale Joan Bennett with the complicity of sadistic criminal Dan Duryea. Both of them are studies of sexual obsession and degradation such as might have come straight out of Germany in the 1920s, the world of Wedekind and Heinrich Mann's *Blue Angel* (not to mention Sternberg's). And both of them, for all their nominal American settings (and respective origins in an American novel and a French play), take place in an imaginary night-country of stifling studio sets and rain-washed studio exteriors lit to create to the full that *Stimmung* so beloved of the silent German cinema. Whatever Lang deliberately meant to do (and since he produced *Scarlet Street* as well as directing he must have had pretty much of a free hand) the German in him would out—to the enormous benefit of the American cinema in general as well as just his own personal expression.

I have suggested that the *film noir* was the major contribution of the German cinema to the American during the 1940s. Certainly it is true that the major examples of the genre were nearly all made by German émigrés—though that, as will be seen, is by no means all they did. If one makes the sketchiest possible list it is bound to include at least, as well as the Lang films mentioned, Preminger's *Laura* (1944) and *Fallen Angel* (1945), Wilder's *Double Indemnity* (1944), *The Lost Weekend* (1945) and *Sunset Boulevard* (1950), Siodmak's *Phantom Lady* (1944), *The Suspect* (1945), *The Spiral Staircase* (1945), *The Dark Mirror* (1946) and *Cry of the City* (1948), John Brahm's *The Lodger* (1944), *Hangover Square* (1945) and *The Locket* (1946), Dieterle's *Love Letters* (1945) and *Portrait of Jennie* (1949), Ophuls's *Caught* (1949) and *The Reckless Moment* (1949), Ulmer's *The Strange Woman* (1946) and several more. There are of course other films, often by directors of European origin other than German, that fit into the same category: notably Hitchcock's *Notorious* (1946), Charles Vidor's *Gilda* (1946), Welles's *The Lady from Shanghai* (1948), Litvak's *Sorry, Wrong Number* (1948), Milestone's *The Strange Love of Martha Ivers* (1946) and Tay Garnett's *The Postman Always Rings Twice* (1946). But it was certainly the German contribution that shaped the form and style of the films.

One might wonder why such an apparently gloomy kind of film would exert the appeal it evidently did during the war years, when everything must have seemed so dark in the real world and the cinema was finding unprecedented popularity mainly as a ready form of escape. Such questions seldom if ever lend themselves to simple, unequivocal answers. It is notable, however, that during periods of external political and economic stress, there has usually been a fashion for horror films and sinister psychological dramas. The 1920s in Germany, time of runaway inflation and slow uncomfortable economic recovery, were also the time of *The Cabinet of Doctor Caligari* and its children; the 1930s in America, the era of the Depression, brought forth the original sound

Frankenstein, Dracula and their sequels; the 1940s saw a revival of the classic horror film in the works of Val Lewton as well as the heyday of the *film noir*; the 1950s, with the Cold War and the nuclear threat, produced a new vogue for horror films in Europe, particularly the Hammer horrors in Britain. In each case, the popularity of the kind of film cited decreased as things got better in the world outside. Presumably, the explanation has something to do with the necessity of exorcizing real terrors by a sort of visualized confrontation with them on a fantasy level: if one can purge the fearful emotions vicariously it makes them easier to keep under control in the real world.

Be that as it may, this kind of dark psychological drama had a tremendous vogue in America in the 1940s, and film-makers of German origin were often called upon to supply the demand. Maybe it was assumed that with their German background they should already be expert in this sort of thing. But if so, like many pieces of Hollywood type-casting, this was based on a misapprehension—the same kind of automatic slotting-in that made most of the German actors in Hollywood at this time, however Jewish or generally anti-Nazi, into stereotypical screen Nazis. However, it worked. Several careers that had been lagging suddenly sprang to life. Otto Preminger, who had gone off to New York to lick his wounds after his last innings with Zanuck over the film of *Kidnapped* in 1937, had been directing a variety of plays, comedy and drama, on stage, and when the German star of one of them, *Margin for Error*, decided in October 1939, a few weeks before the play opened in New York, to take off back to Germany Preminger was persuaded himself to take over the role, which he did with great success. Thus it was that when he got another call from Hollywood, it was not as a director, but as an actor, to play (naturally) the role of a Nazi officer in *The Pied Piper* (1942). Fox then wanted him to repeat his stage role in the film of *Margin for Error*, but he refused unless they let him direct the film as well. Finally he talked them into it (his old enemy Zanuck being away at the war) by offering to take only his actor's fee and direct the film for nothing. So it was that he returned to Hollywood as a director by the back door, and after one more mild emotional drama and being relegated by Zanuck on his return to just producing, became involved with *Laura*.

Even that was not straightforward: strangely enough, for one of the most famous and influential films of the decade, its development was fraught with uncertainties, changes of direction and failures of conviction. As a producer, Preminger found and developed the property (from a novel by Vera Caspary), then ran into endless difficulties getting his script approved for production, getting the cast he wanted (particularly casting Clifton Webb, regarded mainly as a light comedian, against type as the insanely jealous murderer), and finding a suitable director. Even when Rouben Mamoulian was chosen as director, things did not go smoothly, and before long Preminger replaced him. The finished film was not liked in the studio, and lots of retakes, changing the whole ending, were ordered and carried out before Zanuck decided that the original ending was best and Preminger's first version was released. Evidently, it struck an immediate chord in the film-going public, and played the most important part in setting off a whole series of films about neurosis, psychoanalysis, obsession and madness.

In this it was not alone. It was almost exactly contemporary with *Double Indemnity, The Woman in the Window* and *Phantom Lady*, all playing on the same sort of theme, set in the same sort of world, and all by film-makers of German origin. We have seen how Lang got to *Woman in the Window*; the routes of Billy Wilder and Robert Siodmak to *Double Indemnity* and *Phantom Lady* respectively were far more devious and unpredictable. Wilder had put in his time starving in Hollywood in the early 1930s, before combining his writing talents happily with those of Charles Brackett, an American refugee from the Broadway stage: like a number of émigrés, he found the best way to success was by minimizing his foreignness and assimilating himself as completely as possible to the American scene. All the same, his first big success as a writer was working for his old German friend Lubitsch on *Bluebeard's Eighth Wife* in 1938, a typical piece of old-Europe-for-American-consumption.

It was also a comedy, as indeed was most of Wilder's previous work: he had no connections whatever with the 'haunted screen' era of German cinema, and was socially and professionally appreciated largely for his famous irreverent Berlin sense of humour. Once the partnership with Brackett was established, he continued to work regularly in this vein, with comic scripts for Mitchell Leisen (*Midnight*), Lubitsch (*Ninotchka*) and Howard Hawks (*Ball of Fire*). But at the same time he struck out in a more serious form with two more screenplays for Mitchell Leisen, *Arise My Love* (1940) and *Hold Back the Dawn* (1941), both based on aspects of the European struggle against fascism and the predicament of the émigré. For their period, they can both be regarded as rather bold, though, as with other films of the same touchy era, it now takes a real effort of historical reconstruction to see exactly how. *Arise My Love* is one of Hollywood's few attempts to treat the Spanish Civil War, but it is used (rather non-committally) as the background to the beginning of a romance between an anti-fascist flyer and a girl reporter, both Americans in Europe. Further events in the world of politics (the German invasion of Poland; the German occupation of Paris) impinge somewhat on their mostly rather light-hearted love story, and they do end by both dedicating themselves wholeheartedly to the fight against fascism from America. No doubt the romantic plot was the only way the rest of the film could be smuggled past the guardians of America's neutrality early in 1940, but it all seems pretty innocuous today.

Hold Back the Dawn is rather a different matter. For one thing it takes place right on the United States' doorstep, in one of those towns on the Mexican border where refugees congregated and waited, often in vain, for the desperately needed American visas. The hero, a handsome Rumanian playboy-dancer down on his luck (Charles Boyer, cast obviously according to the Hollywood theory of total interchangeability among those puzzling Europeans) is advised by his former European dancing partner (Paulette Goddard, cast presumably according to the alternative Hollywood principle of use whoever you happen to have under contract first) to find an American woman who can be duped into marrying him and thereby automatically get a visa. The plot, of course, goes awry, in that he actually falls in love with the dull spinster he traps (Olivia de Havilland), but then has troubles convincing her of this, troubles with the border officials, and even troubles with the film director he is telling the whole story to in order to raise a quick $800. Again, the background remains finally just that: a background to the fairly conventional romantic triangle at the centre of the movie. But all the same it is a piece of good topical journalism, using some of Wilder's own experience in entering America and that of his less fortunate friends to construct a mechanism for the plot and insinuate some ideas into the heads of his audience subliminally while on a conscious level they are being merely entertained.

Though *Hold Back the Dawn* embodied some of Wilder's own ideas and experiences and in a measure did some of the things he wanted to do in the cinema, he felt that the script had been butchered, particularly after the flat refusal of Boyer to play a scene in which the character addressed a despairing monologue to a cockroach. He determined that it was time he and Brackett took the next step towards control of their own writing and how it reached the screen. They had to become a producer-writer-director team. Brackett was not at first eager, and there were obstacles in the way; but bit by bit they got closer to this ideal, finally reaching it with *The Lost Weekend* in 1946.

The first move was to get Wilder back into the director's chair, and this, after writing just one more script, *Ball of Fire*, they achieved with *The Major and the Minor* (1942), a comedy story about a mature woman who disguises herself as a thirteen-year-old in order to ride the railway half fare. Wilder was always convinced that Paramount let him go ahead with the idea largely in the hope that it would be a disaster and he would get all these ideas of producing and directing out of his system. He was secretly terrified it might be, and confided his fears to Lubitsch, who thereupon arranged a surprise party on the set the first day of shooting, which was attended by all the émigré directors he could round up, including Dupont, Dieterle, Michael Curtiz, Henry Koster and William Wyler. Thus sent off in confusing style, Wilder managed to make the film one of the surprise successes of the year, and was now well on his way.

Wilder was a very sociable and ebullient man. His wife, Judith Iribe (step-daughter of the French artist Paul Iribe, who had been a set designer for De Mille at Paramount), was not. Though her circle of friends included Europeans, such as Joe and Mia May, in the main she was much less internationally minded than Wilder, who remained socially at the centre of cosmopolitan Hollywood, where Europeans mixed with transplanted New Yorkers and there was a constant ferment of ideas. The next property that he was given to write and direct belonged very much to this area of Hollywood history: *Five Graves to Cairo*, suitably updated to the German invasion of North Africa. On close inspection this proves to be none other than a new version of our old friend *Hotel Imperial*, based on a Lajos Biro play and already twice filmed in Hollywood, first produced by Pommer, directed by Mauritz Stiller and starring Pola Negri in 1926, then, after an abortive attempt produced by Lubitsch to star Marlene Dietrich and Charles Boyer in 1936, reworked by Robert Florey as a vehicle for yet another émigré would-be Hollywood star, Isa Miranda, in 1939. In Wilder's version an extra topical touch is added by making one of the German characters into Rommel and having him played spectacularly by Erich von Stroheim.

The film was timely, unpretentious and successful within its limits. However, with the next project, which happened to be *Double Indemnity*, Wilder ran into trouble on every side, starting with his partner Brackett, who read the James M. Cain novelette on which it was to be based and flatly refused to have anything to do with such a disgusting story. Again, the studio did not like it (it was sordid and cynical), and just about every possible actor in Hollywood (as well as a number of frankly impossible) turned down the lead role of a nice ordinary insurance salesman who, through his obsession with a calculating, no-good woman, gets involved in fraud and murder. It was a time when people felt that to play that kind of role would ruin a star's image for ever. But probably the most nerve-racking problem of all was the collaborator Wilder chose for this script: Raymond Chandler.

Chandler was another émigré of a sort, but about as far removed from Wilder in background and character as could be imagined. He was half-English in origin, had been educated at an English public school and had come out to the West Coast in his early twenties to work as a bank clerk. Then, after a spell in the Canadian Army in the First World War, he became an auditor for a group of oil companies, which he continued as until the early 1930s. He began writing detective thrillers around 1933, and finally started selling his writings to pulp magazines, such as *Black Mask*, when he was in his mid-forties. As so often in the history of Los Angeles, it was his outsider's eye that had found something distinctive and extraordinary in the area—and in his case something rancid and rotten at the core. The detective hero of his books, hard-drinking, tough, apparently disillusioned Philip Marlowe, actually figures as a sort of crusader on behalf of primitive purity and integrity ('Down these mean streets a man must go who is not himself mean, who is neither tarnished nor afraid....') and the corrupt world in which he operates is captured in the terse, highly evocative descriptive writing of a number of novels that were just beginning to become famous in 1943, when his collaboration with Wilder began. (*The Big Sleep* was published in 1939, *Farewell My Lovely* in 1940, *The High Window* in 1942, *The Lady in the Lake* in 1943; all of them were to be filmed in the wake of *Double Indemnity*, between 1944 and 1947.)

It was this intense, acrid vision of Southern California (as influential in the 1940s as David Hockney's non-committal, strung-out images of Los Angeles streets, houses and pools would be in the

1970s) that fascinated Wilder and which he wanted to get somehow on film. One European outsider could very well understand another's reactions. Personally, however, Chandler and Wilder could not seem to understand each other at all. At any rate, their collaboration was full of difficulties and arguments, apologies and mutual recriminations—more unreasonable it would seem on Chandler's part than on Wilder's, since though Chandler seems to have been (and sometimes admitted that he was) exceptionally well treated, he loved ever afterwards to vent his paranoia in blistering attacks on Hollywood's cavalier treatment of writers in general and himself in particular.

All the same, the film that resulted from this improbable collaboration was a triumph for all concerned. If it began as and remains a fascinated foreigner's view of Los Angeles, the view had such power and conviction that it imposed itself immediately on natives and near-natives, giving them terms of reference. And the view was backed up with a lot of very precise documentation. When the insurance man and his girlfriend have to meet secretly in a grimly impersonal supermarket, that supermarket is exactly observed as never before on screen—possibly because locals, or any Americans, would take such a thing for granted. It takes a foreigner to find the bizarre at the heart of the ordinary—or for that matter to pick out the ordinary in an environment such as Los Angeles, which is by European standards almost wholly bizarre.

And for all its idiomatic local colour, the film remains in many respects very much in the black German tradition: it does not abandon expressionist lighting, the strongly dramatic use of shadows and such, but instead manages to persuade us to accept them as real, normal even, so convincing is the special world the film creates. In Wilder's next film, *The Lost Weekend*, in which he and Brackett finally established themselves as a writer-producer-director team, the world is still a haunted night-world, this time of an alcoholic in New York. Right at the end of our period, in 1950, Wilder made another classic *film noir* in *Sunset Boulevard*, which brings to bear on the Hollywood of the film-makers the same mordant outsider's eye he had previously, in *Double Indemnity*, directed towards a Los Angeles that had nothing whatever to do with the movie industry. Interestingly enough, even at the period of *Sunset Boulevard* Wilder was still having trouble with the conventions of foreignness—and for that matter, the conventions of Americanness. The story concerns a rich and rather mad has-been movie star, who still lives in the past when she was one of the most important people in Hollywood, and the young unemployed movie writer she seduces and to an extent buys into being her lover and supporting her fantasy. Conventional people in Hollywood were outraged, not so much by the story itself (though that too) as by the idea that either, let alone both, the principals should be American. Now if she were some foreign vamp, or he, like Boyer in *Hold Back the Dawn*, a European gigolo of a background as indeterminate as his morals, that would be all right, that would be believable. But Wilder was hitting (in the opinion of Louis B. Mayer, who knew about such things) at the heart of Hollywood, which was to say the heart of America. Give these foreigners an inch, and they take a mile...

Not that Wilder remained exclusively in the special, specially German world of the *film noir*. For there are other things which are just as specially, if a trifle less conventionally, German: notably the sort of comedy of sexual innuendo Lubitsch had been peddling for years and the bitter irony that usually lay behind Lubitsch's comedy of sexual manners. The two films Wilder made between *The Lost Weekend* and *Sunset Boulevard* were both, in their very different ways, manifestations of the German spirit. *The Emperor Waltz* (1948) is a soggy piece of whimsy about a gramophone salesman in Germany who falls in love with a countess while his dog falls for her bitch—a rather Lubitsch-like notion that is handled with anything but Lubitsch-like lightness of touch.

A Foreign Affair (1948) is another matter—equally un-American, but un-American in this case because of its supposed cynicism, the other side of *The Emperor Waltz*'s arch sentimentality. It is a sharp satirical comedy set in Berlin under the Occupation, which points the finger at the muddles and corruptions of American army officialdom as much as at the 'moral malaria' carried over to the American forces by the decadent Europe they are occupying and fraternizing with. The Defense Department did not like the film too much, but its message of a happy medium somewhere between the spinsterish investigating Congresswoman (played by Jean Arthur) and the cool, corrupt nightclub singer, embodiment of war-weary Europe (played, but of course, by Marlene Dietrich) made a lot of sense, at a time when, with investigative committees burgeoning on all sides, at home and abroad, common sense and moderation were not exactly the order of the day.

By this date in his career, and indeed throughout his time as a film director as well as writer, Wilder had represented such a compromise in his own person. He remained foreign enough to be colourful, and maybe also for his mind to work in a way that marked him off as something apart from 'real Americans', but at the same time he had been around long enough, and had observed closely enough, to know just how far he could go without becoming unacceptable to American tastes. He had, in other words, become an American film-maker, though with Continental trimmings. It is hard to tell without hindsight just how we would assess his Americanness if we were to see his films without knowing something of their maker's history. And indeed, since Americanness itself, especially as applied within the American cinema, is such a conglomerate, one can only wonder at the temerity of any committee in assuming that it could readily judge of what did and what did not constitute an un-American activity.

The Americanness of the films of other film-makers of Germanic origin is equally arguable—film-makers who functioned with the greatest success in Hollywood during the 1940s, and showed a similar or even more pronounced penchant for the *film noir*. I am thinking particularly of two whose careers somewhat paralleled Wilder's—Robert Siodmak and John Brahm. Siodmak had followed the same track as Wilder, from Germany after Hitler's takeover to France and then from there (some years later than Wilder, as he was more successful making films in France) to America. Though Siodmak had been quite a well-known director in France, when he arrived in Hollywood just after the fall of Paris, he was among many immigrants, some much more distinguished, none of whom found things easy. He was looking round desperately for a job until finally he went to see Henry Blanke, a producer at Warners, whom he had known some time before. Blanke said he might be able to do something if Siodmak had an original story or something in the way of a property to sell.

Siodmak went home to puzzle over the problem, and the next day woke up with a complete story in his head. He sent this off to Blanke, who put it to Warners. They liked it, but they still did not want him as a director. He tried to hold out and make it a condition he should direct his own story, but finally they made him a take-it-or-leave-it offer he could not afford to refuse, so he sold the story (eventually filmed as *Conflict*, directed by another émigré, Curtis Bernhardt) and went back to looking for a job as a director.

Finally, through his brother Curt, who had come to Hollywood a couple of years previously, he was offered a job at Paramount on a Dorothy Lamour picture, only to discover when he reported for work that the producer who hired him had suddenly left. However, he managed to hang on with a two-year contract, and eventually got to direct five B features, three for Paramount and two on loan-out, none of them any different from the routine Hollywood product of the time. Nor was the film he was offered by Universal when his Paramount contract ended: it was *Son of Dracula* (1943), the latest in a long line of dilutions Universal had been churning out since 1930. His wife encouraged him to take it, he needed the money, and so he did, and made a good enough job of it to be offered a Universal contract and the dubious privilege of directing one of the company's top, if least manoeuvrable, stars, Maria Montez, in *Cobra Woman* (1944), an agreeably idiotic confection in which she played twin sisters, one good, one bad, princesses of a lost island civilization in the South Seas.

It was at this time that Siodmak met by chance another emigré, Joan Harrison, who had come out from England to work as Hitchcock's personal assistant and script-writer on *Rebecca* and then, after a couple more films with Hitchcock, had decided to branch out on her own as a producer. She had a property, in the shape of *Phantom Lady*, a mystery story by William Irish, a favourite writer of Hitchcock's and author of the story he later used for *Rear Window*. She and Siodmak hit it off very well, and she persuaded Universal to let her use him as director on the new film, which was to be made on a low budget but aimed at a better distribution than a B feature. In it, for the first time, Siodmak got a chance to develop a characteristic *film noir* atmosphere. The story concerns a man wrongly accused of murdering his wife, who has to find the strange woman with whom he spent the evening in question in order to establish his alibi, and it takes us through the seamy night-side of New York (all re-created in the classic European style on studio sets) with a story of neurosis, insanity and murder. The film, too, is nearly all atmosphere—almost half is made without dialogue or even incidental music, and imagination and invention constantly stand in for things that could not be literally done because of the limitations of the budget. *Phantom Lady* proved to be successful beyond expectations, and laid the foundations of a profitable Hollywood career for both Siodmak, who stayed on at Universal, and Joan Harrison, who went to Twentieth Century-Fox to produce another *film noir*, *Dark Waters*.

Much was made at the time of *Phantom Lady*'s remarkable 'realism' and precise observation of the American urban scene. Nowadays this seems to be largely beside the point. The film is certainly not realistic in the sense of the shot-on-the-street-where-it-really-happened cycle of the early 1950s. Rather it takes place in a dark fantasy world, which is so powerfully projected that it never occurs to us to question it. In this it places itself very much in a European tradition, and there are a number of specific points where it seems to be making conscious reference to the silent German cinema—particularly in the episode with the mad sculptor who seems to echo *The Hands of Orlac*.

Certainly it placed Siodmak at once as a maker of moody, atmospheric psychological thrillers. Sometimes there are explicitly period-pieces like *The Suspect* (1945, with Charles Laughton playing a London wife-murderer obviously based on Crippen) and *The Spiral Staircase* (1945); or sometimes, like *Christmas Holiday* (a solitary attempt in 1944 to give Deanna Durbin a serious role as the wife of a neurotic killer) or *The Dark Mirror* (1946, Olivia de Havilland as twins, one sane, one mad) taking place in the usual *film noir* never-never land. But even when they are supposed to be realistic depictions of criminal life as it was actually lived in America—*The Killers*, *Cry of the City*, *Criss Cross*—the way the atmosphere is evoked is much more important than the documentary details. The feeling of the sleazy dance hall in *Criss Cross* (1949), summoned up with an absolute minimum of 'fact', and the maximum use of lights piercing the darkness and refracted in the steam of the outside courtyard; the erratic course of the doomed small-time crook in *Cry of the City* (1948), scattered with bizarre encounters, such as that with the giant masseuse; the laconic prologue of *The Killers* (1946), in which the gunmen come to get their victim in a rundown diner—all of these have much more to do with the tone and tempo of European cinema than the action-based narrative drive of classic American film-making.

Though it seemed that Siodmak, once given his chance, acclimatized to working in Hollywood as successfully as any émigré, apparently he did not feel that this was so. He did not have much good to say about any of his American films after *The Dark Mirror* in 1946: even *Cry of the City*, a remarkable film one would think by any standards, he regarded as not bad but not really his sort of film (he said he hated locations), and when he had the chance to head off for Europe in 1951 to make a jolly pirate film for Burt

Lancaster, he took it and never returned. Nor, for that matter, did he ever make anything in France or Germany to match his best American films. Obviously it was the perfect combination of time and place, and talent and fashion that allowed him the opportunity to excel in the émigré genre *par excellence*.

John Brahm's career peaked at much the same time, in much the same way, if also much more briefly. In fact, Brahm managed to make noteworthy films for only about three years, from 1943 to 1946. Unlike Wilder and Siodmak, he came from Germany via London rather than Paris, though apparently he did spend a year of inactivity in Paris on his way to London after the Reichstag fire in 1933. He came from a theatrical family in Germany: his father was an actor and his uncle, Otto Brahm, an important impresario. As Hans Brahm he had already become a leading theatre director in his twenties, and was directing in Berlin at the Lessing Theatre in 1933 (at the age of 40). He began again in Britain as a production supervisor in films, and in 1935 made what seems to have been his first film as a director, a remake of *Broken Blossoms*, supposedly supervised by Griffith, and starring his wife, Dolly Haas, in the Lillian Gish role. In London he attracted the attention of David O. Selznick's agent brother Myron, and went to Hollywood in 1937. There he was regularly in work making a weird variety of crime films, comedies, dramas and even musicals; often B features and with nothing to distinguish them from a host of other routine Hollywood films, except perhaps for *The Undying Monster* (1942), an atmospheric horror B feature about a werewolf on the prowl in a happily synthetic studio Cornwall.

In 1943, fresh from directing Sonja Henie in a skating musical, he got the chance to make a film at Fox with Laird Cregar, a young character actor then having a great success in sinister and neurotic roles. The result was *The Lodger* (1944), a powerfully Germanic re-creation of Jack the Ripper's career in Victorian London (via a novel previously filmed by Hitchcock), which at once made Brahm a name to reckon with. His next four films remained within *film noir* territory. *Guest in the House* (1944), which he co-directed with Lewis Milestone, was about a paranoid young woman upsetting a normal middle-class household; *Hangover Square* (1945) featured a schizophrenic composer (again Laird Cregar in Victorian London) whose alter ego runs around murdering people; *The Locket* (1946) was another study in morbid feminine psychology; and *The Brasher Doubloon* (1947) was perhaps the most authentically Chandlerian of Chandler adaptations, based on his novel *The High Window*. Soon afterwards Brahm went back to Europe, to work on an Italian-made Maria Montez vehicle. From then on he made nothing of any note, either in America or in Europe, until 1955, when he abandoned theatrical features for television, where he became one of the most prolific directors for ten years or so. Again, though Brahm does not seem, any more than Siodmak, to have been regarded, or to have regarded himself, as an exotic on the Hollywood scene, he reached his peak in the heyday of the *film noir*, and faded very rapidly from fame when the vogue passed, lacking perhaps the adaptability of a Preminger to change with the changing times, or perhaps the luck of a Preminger in coming up with a big success in another genre at just the right moment to renew his career.

Otto Preminger's career after *Laura* (1944) provides, in fact, the most complete example of émigré adaptation to Hollywood. The essence of this, of course, is to be adaptable in the first place, and that is arguably achieved (beyond a certain point) only by second-rate creators with no marked creative personality of personal style to cause trouble. Compared with the other German film-makers we have been considering, Preminger has given much less evidence of individuality in his films, of being more than a capable, impersonal craftsman (his much publicized private personality is something else again).

After *Laura* it was no doubt natural that Preminger should revert to the *film noir* from time to time, as long as it remained popular, and so he did in *Fallen Angel* (1945), *Whirlpool* (1949), *Where the Sidewalk Ends* (1950) and—a belated example—*Angel Face* (1952). But they are scattered among a lot of other films that relate to them in no perceptible way (except perhaps for a certain heaviness in all, which we might unkindly label Teutonic). *Royal Scandal* (1945) and *That Lady in Ermine* (1948), both more Lubitsch than Preminger and made respectively under his close supervision and in his shoes; *Centennial Summer* (1946), a piece of musical Americana; *Forever Amber* (1947), an elaborately upholstered piece of costume tushery; *Daisy Kenyon* (1947), a Joan Crawford vehicle; and *The Fan* (1949), an adaptation of Wilde's *Lady Windermere's Fan*. And once Preminger ceased to be a contract director for a major studio and became an independent producer-director in 1953, when theoretically he was free to do much more of what he wanted to do, consistency was even less apparent. He would no doubt have functioned in much the same way in the German or French film industry had he been there instead because, without strong national characteristics, he was able to take on whatever protective covering seemed politic at any given time.

In this he stands primarily as the most famous and successful of a whole group of émigrés, among them Henry Koster, Curtis Bernhardt and Douglas Sirk, who from the start could and did turn their hands to almost anything with equal (albeit artistically modest) success. At first glance it might seem that William Dieterle also belongs to this category—certainly his output was enormous and very varied—but many capable, disinterested observers did not think so. Brecht found his biographical films of the 1930s 'progressive and humanistic and—what in itself is quite revolutionary in the American commercial film—intelligent', and E. A. Dupont wrote that Dieterle was 'the only director in Hollywood who often put his reputation at stake for works of art'.

Nowadays, perhaps we do not think so highly of films like *The Story of Louis Pasteur* (1936) or *The Life of Emile Zola* (1937), with their solidly 'improving' scripts and their fussy, actorly central performances by Paul Muni—they represent a rather old-fashioned and much more naive Hollywood view of 'culture', determinedly literary and responsible. But at least it is clear they were risky propositions and they aimed earnestly at art, even if they did not always quite achieve it (the best is *Juarez* of 1939, a model of cinematic construction and political fair-mindedness). It is, anyway, some testimony to their stature that in 1940 *Juarez*, *Zola* and Dieterle's Spanish Civil War film *Blockade* (another example of bold intentions rather than serious achievement) were singled out as subversive and communistic by Martin A. Dies, congressional witch-hunter of the era.

But Dieterle was, in any case, more of a true artist than these films might seem to indicate. His finest works throughout his career were in fact those which dealt in fantasy, the supernatural or psychological drama of the *film noir* type, and were more distinctively Germanic in treatment. He co-directed with Reinhardt the film version of Reinhardt's stage spectacular *A Midsummer Night's Dream* (1935), and made in 1939 perhaps the most genuinely Reinhardtian film ever, *The Hunchback of Notre Dame* with Charles Laughton in the title role: in it Reinhardt's ideas about the management of crowds, the creation of atmosphere and so on were perfectly realized in cinematic terms. *All That Money Can Buy* (1941), an American Faust story, and *Portrait of Jennie* (1949), a story of time-travelling and love conquering death, are the finest of his supernatural subjects, and *Love Letters* (1945), about an amnesiac murderess and her great love, is a model *film noir*, obsessed and extravagantly romantic in its doom-laden atmosphere.

However, Dieterle's reputation was and has remained curiously indeterminate. He did direct films in Germany before he came to Hollywood in 1930, but he was much better known as a star actor, with Reinhardt in the theatre and as Murnau's Faust on film. He also, incidentally, appeared in early, German-made films by such other eventual émigrés as Kurt (later Curtis) Bernhardt and Michael Kertész (later Curtiz) during the 1920s. He came over to star in and/or direct German versions of early American sound films, and stayed on just to direct, but with no particular reputation to live up to or live down. During the 1930s and 1940s he was seldom regarded as one of the great artists of the American cinema, but more generally he had the reputation as one of the leading ambassadors of European culture in California. As we have seen, he and his wife Charlotte were socially prominent in cultural activities, and more likely to be on friendly terms with the notable literary and musical figures transplanted to Los Angeles than were any of the other specifically film-oriented émigrés. In all of this, though professionally lodged deep in the heart of Hollywood, he really belongs much more happily among the cultured minority who, whatever their links with film-making, made important contributions to, and took full advantage of, the extraordinary intellectual and aesthetic possibilities of life in Los Angeles during the war years.

11. What We Are Fighting For

One of the most extraordinary things about the Second World War was that it actually made culture patriotic. The arts, by some mysterious process, suddenly became a vitally important part of what we were supposed to be fighting for. Of course, a lot of artists were directly enlisted, and the arts took on a different aspect in battledress. Some very improbable film-makers found themselves helping the war effort by making army training films or contributing to Frank Capra's 'Why We Fight' series: George Cukor preceded the neo-Victorian melodrama of *Gaslight* (1944) with a training film on *Resistance and Ohm's Law* (which he alleges he never understood), while Lubitsch was waylaid in 1942 by a short for Capra's unit called *Know Your Enemy: Germany*.

But more to the point than these eccentric excursions was the sudden access of interest in such formerly esoteric pursuits as ballet, opera and 'serious' music. These became suitable things to be done in factories and taken to the battle sector to entertain the troops—or as near to the frontline as could be contrived. Of course, in order to be accepted in this way, they had to be democratized and humanized—a process that usually found its way to the screen in the form of embarrassingly coy disputes on Bach versus Boogie, and generally ended in an uneasy alliance with Leopold Stokowski in twinkling support of Deanna Durbin, Jose Iturbi playing boogie-woogie or, on the other side of the coin, the MGM regulars of *Thousands Cheer* all getting together for a rousing 'Hymn to Peace' by Shostakovich at the fadeout. And then there was Disney's great 1940 extravaganza *Fantasia* (with Stokowski again). Whatever purists might say about it—Stravinsky was none too happy at having *The Rite of Spring* accompanied by a battle of the dinosaurs, but he pocketed the money anyway—it popularized classical music as nothing else had done before, as well as presenting the art of Oskar Fischinger and Kay Nielsen to a mass public.

But the entry of America into the war seemed in some way mysteriously to dramatize this tendency: the message was, you don't have to be stuffy or weird in order to enjoy good art; indeed, you are probably failing in your patriotic duty if you do not make some positive effort. This in its turn changed the atmosphere and attitude in Hollywood. Not radically, for it takes more than a major war to change procedures in the dream factory, but subtly, in little but perceptible ways. As often as not it entailed merely a slight retooling of the standard models. The Good Neighbour policy meant that it was politic as well as popular to give familiar subjects a Pan-American twist in film after film with titles like *That Night in Rio, Weekend in Havana, Carnival in Costa Rica*, and encouraged the importation of talents as improbably various as Carmen Miranda (who was anyway Portuguese, not Brazilian) and Luis Buñuel.

Similarly, routine putting-on-a-show stories could come to involve a symphony orchestra; psychological dramas might be stretched to include dream sequences by Dali or some passable imitation; subjects like *The Picture of Dorian Gray* or *Bel-Ami*, which, in the original novels, featured works of art, could be the occasion for commissioning notable artists to special creation. In the case of *Bel-Ami*, indeed, the director held a limited competition, of which more later, involving a dozen of the world's leading artists of more or less surrealistic inclinations. And producers of routine thrillers and us-and-them melodramas and period swashbucklers suddenly found themselves impelled to employ those cultivated Europeans to give a touch of literary and visual class, or to make key characters 'longhair' artists, writers and musicians. These 'longhairs' were no longer regarded as necessarily crazed merely because of their artistic calling. They certainly might be—like Laird Cregar killing people in the intervals of labouring over his piano concerto in *Hangover Square*—but John Garfield as a tough violinist of working-class origins in *Humoresque* is carefully presented as all-man, and Paul Henreid as the cellist (of all things!) in *Deception* is by far the sanest character around.

In the social life of Hollywood this made little difference. Visiting celebrities were lionized, whatever their sphere of activity, provided the visit was brief. But then it had always been so. During the war years the rank and file of the film community were probably little if at all more aware that there were present in their midst such enormously distinguished people as Schoenberg, Stravinsky and Thomas and Heinrich Mann. Or, if they did encounter them, it was with no awareness of who or what they were. Shelley Winters recalls that her father met Brecht playing open-air chess in downtown Washington Park one day and brought him home for the evening. Afterwards her mother said that he seemed like a nice man, and she wondered what he did: 'I think he is some kind of jeweller: when I asked him he said he made jewels for poor people.' Susan Sontag's parents knew many important musical figures, but she took their presence absolutely for granted and only later realized whom she had vaguely, not very interestedly known. There were many who knew Schoenberg as a ferocious tennis player who had something indeterminate to do with music, and it is recorded that one evening at Ira Gershwin's, a rich society hostess distinguished herself by trying to rope Schoenberg into the after-dinner entertainments with 'Give us a tune, Arnold....'

Professionally, and on the borders of professionalism, things were slightly different. The event that pinpointed this difference was the 1943 Writers' Congress held at UCLA. The cover of the book of its proceedings sports (a trifle improbably) a drawing of a helmeted soldier typing with his rifle by his side lying across the completed pages, and describes the volume as 'An American war book presented by 1500 writers and scholars who participated in the panels and seminars held October 1–3, 1943, under the sponsorship of the Hollywood Writers' Mobilization and the University of California.' The tone is maintained very firmly in the preface:

> By [1943], the writer knew that, in an age of mass aspiration and mass effort, he could not stand remote and alone. The teacher, the student knew this too. The soldier fought in regiments. The worker was part of the team on the assembly line. The scholar and writer also needed that strengthening of the spirit which comes from identity with the labour of others.

It is noted that there was in 1941 a writers' conference sponsored by the Screen Writers' Guild and the Authors' League of America, to discuss purely economic and creative problems. But:

> The intervening years had brought with them new compulsions and obligations. Under stress of wartime demands, the Hollywood Writers' Mobilization had been organized by the guilds of the radio, screen and newspaper, enlisting thousands of writers, readers, publicists, cartoonists, songwriters for duty to our nation and our allies. Inevitably, the new conference could have but one aim—to formulate a program of action for this army!

'To learn to write for the war effort,' stated the Mobilization's first report. (And *writing* meant communication through word, picture or music.)

'To mobilize all writers to dedicate their creative abilities to the winning of the war.' (And *writers* meant craftsmen with instrumental skill to reach vast audiences through air wave, screen, print, forum.)

All of this obviously points to the new attitude that prevailed—or at any rate to the new attitude that was being enthusiastically encouraged. The congress, it was stated, 'belonged to anyone sincerely pledged to prosecuting the war against the AXIS enemy,' and though there is dark talk about 'those forces in this country which fear nothing so much as the free interchange of ideas among people of good will', and their attempts to sabotage the congress, the organizers briskly fought back: 'There would be no room for the defeatist, the cynic, the special pleader for partisan politics, the appeaser, the diversionist.'

Though the jargon is oppressive, it does seem in fact to reflect the way that a lot of artists in the midst of a war (though in Los Angeles far removed from any actual fighting) did feel and react. And the way that a sizeable part of the public began to react to them. A lot of the thinking was naively propagandistic—writers' mobilization was likely to be primarily for composing direct propaganda rather than recognizing the enduring value of great writing, great music, great art as something to be preserved and encouraged irrespective of its immediate value, if any, to the war effort. But some of the battledress glamour and air of responsibility with which the mobilized arts were invested rubbed off elsewhere. And indeed, not all of those involved in the Writers' Congress felt it incumbent on them to assume quite the same Dig-for-Victory tone.

Naturally, as leading writers in exile on the spot Thomas Mann and Lion Feuchtwanger both spoke in the section devoted to 'Writers in Exile'. Mann discussed 'The Exiled Writer's Relation to His Homeland', which he felt was ambiguous, opting himself never to return to Germany even after the forces of democracy had (hopefully) won. Feuchtwanger spoke on 'The Working Problems of the Writer in Exile', which he put, no doubt slightly to the surprise of many of his hearers, in an historical context going right back to Ovid by way of Victor Hugo, Heinrich Heine, Dante and Li Tai Po. It is noticeable, in fact, that the foreigners involved in the Congress tended to take an altogether wider, more philosophical view of the discontents. Mann says to the Americans in his audience

'... when you see the emblem of American sovereignty, the Stars and Stripes, you are perhaps not naively patriotic enough that your heart beats with pride in your throat and that you break into loud hurrahs. You are critical people and you know that these colours must conceal many human weaknesses and inadequacies and perhaps even corruption...' But to hear how the rest of them carried on one would never suppose it.

But at least the Congress signalled a certain awareness on the part of Hollywood that Los Angeles had its quota of people who had suffered more directly than most Americans from the war and the events leading up to it, who had distinguished themselves in many fields beyond Hollywood's usual horizons, and who could in some way, direct or indirect, contribute to and enrich the life and work of the area. Emigrés were not only shunted off into an annex of the proceedings dedicated specifically to émigré problems—in other sections of the Congress, too, they figured prominently. The Dutch film-maker Joris Ivens for instance, talked about the documentary and morale; Hanns Eisler and Darius Milhaud discussed respectively the prejudices that held back Hollywood studios from experimenting in film scores with new musical styles and materials, and the particular fashions in which the French cinema's use of music might point the way to America.

It should be noted here that Ivens and Milhaud were more in the nature of distinguished visitors to Los Angeles—Milhaud from Mills College and Ivens from New York, where he had been working for the previous six years on documentaries, mostly for official agencies like the Department of Agriculture and the War Department. When Ivens tried the next year to make a Hollywood film, a drama of the free Norwegian merchant service to be called *Woman of the Sea* and starring Garbo, the project got nowhere, partly but not entirely because Garbo, despite the writing participation of her favourite script-writer, Salka Viertel, would have nothing to do with it. Instead Ivens went off to Australia to make a film for the dock unions there, then to a succession of communist countries where the political climate was more congenial than it had become in McCarthyite America. Milhaud went back to France as soon as he was able to after the war.

And while visitors, as ever, were likely to be treated with an often slightly mystified respect, those actually on Hollywood's doorstep or in the pay of a Hollywood studio could easily be overlooked. The story of Luis Buñuel is instructive in this respect. Buñuel, after making with Dali the two most famous surrealist films, *Un Chien Andalou* (1928) and *L'Age d'Or* (1930), belonged to that segment of the surrealist movement which, when the uneasy alliance between surrealism and communism broke down in 1933, chose to remain officially a communist rather than a surrealist. He had been in Spain at the beginning of the Spanish Civil War, and had made and/or supervised various films for the Republican cause, which would hardly endear him to the Falangist victors. In 1938 he was sent by the Republican government to Hollywood where he worked at MGM on a film, *Cargo of Innocence*, about Spanish children being taken to safety in Russia—a subject that, on the face of it, seems an unlikely choice for MGM. In the event the film was cancelled when the situation in Spain took a turn for the worse.

This, and the sudden end of the war in Spain, left Buñuel in Los Angeles without work or prospects, and with a wife and young son to support (his second son was born in America in 1940). In this predicament, not surprisingly, no one in Hollywood came to his rescue, apart from Chaplin who bought some gags from him for possible use in *The Great Dictator*. Clearly no one else in Hollywood had heard of him, and one political refugee was much like another, while one from Spain did not even have the possible advantage of Jewish-American connections. Instead, it was the film section of the Museum of Modern Art in New York, and specifically Iris Barry, British-born curator of the Film Library, who offered him a job (and temporarily a home) selecting American and foreign documentaries conceivably suitable for Latin America, and re-editing them with new soundtracks in Spanish or Portuguese (and sometimes in French and English too). Buñuel himself tends to be evasive and dismissive about his work at the Museum between 1939 and 1943, but it seems from the accounts of others that it often involved a radical reshaping of the materials at his disposal into new and personal creations.

However, Buñuel was a member of a team, working in relative obscurity and anonymity. Fortunately so, for though, of course, the film staff of the Museum knew exactly who he was and what he had done, this knowledge had evidently not percolated through to the Board of Trustees, loaded as it was with great establishment names like Rockefeller, Ford, Goodyear, Guggenheim and Luce. But in 1942 Dali made something of a sensation with the publication of his autobiography *The Secret Life of Salvador Dali*, in the course of which he wrote about Buñuel's role in the creation of that famous work of blasphemy *L'Age d'Or* and, incidentally, Buñuel's one-time membership in the French Communist Party. News of this reached Archbishop (later Cardinal) Spellman first, and he came to create a stormy scene in Iris Barry's office demanding Buñuel's instant dismissal. In any case there was around this time a considerable, though gradual, weeding-out of communists and ex-communists from the Museum's staff, and no doubt that also had a lot to do with it. But there does seem to be a certain irony in the idea that his authorship of *L'Age d'Or*, a vital element in his being asked to work at the Museum of Modern Art in the first place, should also be the immediate cause of his dismissal four years later.

Buñuel set out philosophically for Hollywood again, this time under contract to Warners as producer for a series of Spanish-language versions of the films they were then planning. Finally, no specially shot Spanish-language versions materialized, but instead Buñuel supervised the Spanish dubbing on Warner films and worked on his own ideas. Obviously his mind still ran along surrealist lines: in Los Angeles he met again his old friend from Paris, Man Ray, American-French surrealist in the Twenties, who had been drawn to Los Angeles, like so many others on leaving occupied France, because 'It was like some place in the South of France with its palm-bordered streets and low stucco dwellings. Somewhat more prim, less rambling, but the same radiant sunshine.' Together they wrote a scenario, *The Sewer of Los Angeles*, which took place entirely on a gigantic dunghill between a freeway and a desert. Not, perhaps, the most practical subject for Hollywood production, and, of course, it was never made.

Not all Buñuel's projects were so impractical. Another script, *Goya and the Duchess of Alba*, was written (or re-written from a long-standing project) in a form that Buñuel hoped would be suitable for Paramount, though he found no takers. At Warners he expressed a desire to direct a gangster film, and did actually work on a horror film, *The Beast with Five Fingers*, designed for Peter Lorre and eventually directed by Robert Florey, who used some ideas of Buñuel's in the scenes where the severed hand crawls around like some obscene white insect, terrorizing the hero and driving him to insane acts.

Buñuel seems to have done his routine work at the studio efficiently, been paid well for it, and lived a totally anonymous life in Los Angeles, occupying a bungalow like thousands of others, driving his children to the beach (which he loathed) and himself to

Antelope Valley, an inland hunting-ground he enjoyed, and, for all his business associates, remaining completely unknown as a famous surrealist artist or a film-maker who had already made three experimental classics. It does not seem to be recorded whether he saw anything of Dali in the months of 1944–5 when Dali was visiting Hollywood to work on the dream sequence for Hitchcock's *Spellbound* and an abortive animated short called *Destino* for Disney, but on balance it seems unlikely. Occasionally he saw the handful of other people who would have any notion who he was— Man Ray, Aldous Huxley, Alexander Calder—but for the most part he and his family kept themselves to themselves and were happy to do so. His second arrival in Hollywood created no stir; his departure in 1946, lured down to Mexico by the renewed possibility of making films, perhaps even his own personal films, made not the slightest ripple. He simply refused to take a pay cut in the post-war recession and left, and that was that.

Not that Buñuel attempted to make any mark in the cultural life of the community—if he ever had any desire to, he had learnt his lesson. The case of Max Reinhardt was more unfortunate, or seemed so, because it was much more public. Reinhardt, it may be remembered, had arrived in California with a big splash of publicity in 1934 to stage *A Midsummer Night's Dream* for the California Festival Association, and had then, amid even greater publicity, made the film version in collaboration with Dieterle for Warners. This was supposed to lead to great things, including several more films. But when the film failed to recoup its large costs and did not do too well with the critics either, nothing more came of those plans, and Reinhardt went back to Europe to continue his direction of the Salzburg Festival Theatre in a still-democratic Austria. Since he had his hands full there in 1936 he did not himself direct the California Festival production of one of the classics in his repertory, *Everyman*, which was instead directed by a former pupil of his, Johannes Poulsen.

At the end of the year Reinhardt returned to New York to direct a lavish English-language production of Werfel's *The Eternal Road*, with music by Kurt Weill, at Manhattan Opera House, which had some success and ran for 153 performances. There was still talk of other film plans—a *Twelfth Night* to be produced by William Randolph Hearst's company with Marion Davies as Viola, for instance—but Reinhardt was not back in America again until March 1938, when the Austrian Anschluss made him a political refugee, too, and, as it turned out, an American resident until his death in 1943.

For most of this time Reinhardt was in Los Angeles. But in much less grand circumstances than before. He directed an English-language version of *Faust* Part I, which was much like his renowned Salzburg production, for the California Festival at the Pilgrimage Theatre, Los Angeles, and the Civic Auditorium, San Francisco, but for some mysterious reason the public seemed indifferent and this was the last season of the California Festival Association. More immediately and practically, on 26 June 1938 he opened the Max Reinhardt Workshop of Stage, Screen and Radio, a school for young hopefuls in the heart of Hollywood, at 4939 Sunset Boulevard. It was a way of capitalizing on his fame and experience as a director when the opportunities to direct were lacking. The Workshop offered a surprisingly wide variety of courses, and the teachers during the first year included, as well as Reinhardt himself, who directed the main showpiece studio performances, an international constellation of talent including Erich Wolfgang Korngold on stage music and musical scoring, Paul Muni and Basil Rathbone on acting, Rudolph Maté on experimental camera and lighting, Samson Raphaelson on playwriting and John Huston on screen playwriting. 'To Hollywood', said the prospectus, 'a cosmopolis and climate uniquely adapted to a theatrical Workshop, which can unite every dramatic form of expression, both spectacular and intimate, Max Reinhardt brings a rich heritage of traditions gleaned from the cultural centers of the world, sympathetically tempered with true understanding of present day requirements.'

To begin with, the Workshop was quite successful. The first production, Maeterlinck's *Sister Beatrice*, was admired and later taken to Santa Barbara. In December 1938 Reinhardt went off to the East Coast to direct a new play by Thornton Wilder, *The Merchant of Yonkers*, which unfortunately met with little success when it opened in New York and closed after 39 performances. (Later, rewritten as *The Matchmaker* and then transformed into the musical *Hello Dolly!*, it was amply to make up for this first unenthusiastic reception.) He returned to Hollywood and busied himself instead with the Workshop, directing students in *Six Characters in Search of an Author*, *The Servant with Two Masters*, *A Midsummer Night's Dream*, *Everyman* and a semi-professional production of *Too Many Husbands*, a musical version of Somerset Maugham's *Home and Beauty*, with music by Bronislaw Kaper, at the Belasco Theatre, Los

Angeles, in January 1940. But though this amounted to putting a brave face on things (even braver when Reinhardt took over the grandly renamed Max Reinhardt Theatre on Wilshire Boulevard at Fairfax in 1941), it was a sad comedown. Salka Viertel describes the students as 'inexperienced beginners unaware of the artistic importance of their master', and confirms that: 'The Workshop, with its young, raw and inexperienced students, made it impossible to stage unforgettable performances.'

Nor was Reinhardt very practical as a businessman. Though the Workshop was primarily a business enterprise, he could never square his ideals with taking on moneyed impossibles or refusing those he considered really talented even if it meant giving them scholarships the school could ill afford. Nevertheless, few who were subsequently to make a name for themselves seem to have passed through the school (its most notable pupil was probably Nanette Fabray), and surviving production photographs do not leave a happy impression. By the middle of 1940 Reinhardt himself was in serious financial difficulties, and had to dispose of his large house in Maravilla Drive, along with a lot of his furniture and artworks. Though the Workshop hobbled on for a while, he turned his attention more and more to the possibilities of a Broadway comeback.

Salvation, as it proved, was at hand. After the failure of *Too Many Husbands* he had decided that Los Angeles was the worst city in the world for theatre, but he still had hopes for New York, and early in 1942 he started making serious plans for setting up there a repertory theatre company on the European model, in collaboration with Harold Clurman and Stella Adler. They worked out personnel, repertory (plays by Odets, Irwin Shaw, Marc Blitzstein, John Howard Lawson and others, plus revivals of Shaw and O'Neill and selections from lesser-known European theatre) and management: all they needed was the finance. Which, of course, was not forthcoming.

But at this point Reinhardt was offered the job of directing for the New Opera Company in New York a new version of the Strauss operetta *Die Fledermaus* under the title of *Rosalinda*. He was given a free hand and a generous budget, and Korngold, who had worked on his 1927 version back in Europe, to do the new musical arrangements. It opened on 28 October 1942, and was an immediate hit, running in various theatres till some months after Reinhardt's death. It was stylish and easy to take and 'so European'. Audiences loved it, and Reinhardt's name was magic again. Not, unfortunately, magic enough to carry his next production, a sort of pilot for the repertory theatre he was still planning in the shape of an anti-war play by Irwin Shaw called *Sons and Soldiers*, starring two young actors soon to be famous, Gregory Peck and Geraldine Fitzgerald, along with Stella Adler and Karl Malden. It was not, perhaps, the ideal time for an anti-war play, and for that matter the play itself was not very good. Reinhardt himself saw the production's failure as partly an effect of the American passion for type-casting: everyone asked him why didn't he do something else nice and frothy like *Rosalinda*, and he had visions of becoming a 'specialist in musicals' for the American theatre public. But since this type of work was all that was on offer, he took it, and began to work on a second production for the New Opera Company, this time a new version of Offenbach's *La Belle Hélène* called *Helen Goes to Troy*.

On 9 September 1943 Reinhardt had a seventieth birthday celebration attended by a number of old friends in and around New York, among them Carl Zuckmayer, Ferenc Molnar and Kurt Weill. During the night of 30 October he died in his sleep in his suite at the Gladstone Hotel, leaving *Helen Goes to Troy* hardly begun.

It may well be coincidence, but the spectacular decline in Reinhardt's fame and fortune after his definitive arrival in Los Angeles in 1938 does seem to have something to do with his new status as a political exile. Of course the relative failure of his last and, as it turned out, only Hollywood film cannot have helped matters, given that, then as now, in Hollywood you are only as good as your last movie. But had Reinhardt at that stage in his career chosen rather than been forced to settle in America he could probably have weathered that and continued to be sought after as the famed European director. Being in enforced exile was a different matter—it put people one down in a town where that was the last thing you could afford to be.

In this context, the principal French film émigrés seem to have done remarkably well. They were no doubt just as financially dependent on working in Hollywood as anyone else, but somehow they contrived to keep Hollywood unaware of it. No doubt also the decent or more-than-decent successes their films enjoyed helped things along, though it occasionally took some time before they were able properly to establish themselves. But basically it seems to have been more a matter of psychology: it is much easier somehow to be exiled, by your own choice, rather than out of desperate necessity, from a defeated country than to be exiled from a country that is at war with the country in which you have settled and which has deprived you of citizenship and made you in a very real sense a stateless person. In any case, some of the French were in Hollywood on unarguably official business. René Clair and Julien Duvivier, for example, had been dispatched with the producer Jean Lévy-Strauss by the Ministry of Information of the defeated French government with the aim of founding a French centre of production in the United States. With this eventual possibility in mind, Clair had arranged a contract that he rather curiously describes as to make a film for Columbia or RKO—an improbable choice of alternatives at the best of times. After the armistice of 25 June 1940 he was free to set off, and made his way laboriously across Southern France and Spain to meet Duvivier and Lévy-Strauss in Lisbon. There was some six weeks' delay while his visa for America was held up (finally it was issued on the personal intervention of the playwright Robert Sherwood with Sumner Welles and Harry Hopkins), and then they were on a ship bound for New York. Clair, with his wife and son, was welcomed with open arms and warm hospitality by Sherwood on the quay, and sent off to Hollywood in reasonable style as soon as possible.

At this stage, Clair could still have gone back: the United States after all was neutral, and so, nominally, was the unoccupied part of France ruled by the Vichy government. He nearly did return; he was told that he was to be deprived of his French nationality according to a Vichy law affecting all those who had left France after the armistice and all his property forfeited to the State. But fortunately his brother, who was in the French Army in Morocco, was able to go to Vichy, rally some powerful friends, and argue that the law did not apply in that, after all, he had gone only in fulfilment of a contract signed some months before the armistice.

Jean Renoir, who arrived in America later, on 31 December 1940, found himself in rather similar circumstances. He had been called up at the outbreak of war, and drafted to the army film service. At this time Italy was not yet at war with France, and it transpired that Mussolini had seen *La Grande Illusion*, admired it very much, and wanted its director to give a course of lectures at the Centro Sperimentale in Rome. As the French government was willing to do anything to oblige and preserve Italian neutrality, Renoir was at once officially posted to Rome, started to teach at the Centro and at the same time began work on a Franco–Italian film version of *Tosca*.

But then he got into some minor trouble with German interests in Rome and was advised by the French Consul to leave on the next train. Back with Dido, his secretary/companion, in a Paris hourly awaiting German invasion, he decided to keep right on going, hired a car, and set off slowly for the South. Halfway there he received a message from his old friend Robert Flaherty in America telling him that an American visa was waiting for him at the consulate in Nice. There was also the prospect of a contract with Twentieth Century-Fox if he could get an essential exit permit from the French government. Meanwhile the cultural offices of the Vichy government tried to persuade him to stay—rather curiously, considering the strongly leftish attitudes of some of his films of the Thirties, particularly *La Vie est à Nous*, a propaganda film made at the request of the French Communist Party, and *La Marseillaise*, also an enterprise of the Popular Front—promising him complete freedom to make whatever films he wanted.

The route of Renoir and his wife-to-be to America was rather more circuitous than Clair's. They finally took a boat from Marseilles to Algeria, went from there to Morocco, and from Morocco to Lisbon, where they had the regulation wait (even though already equipped with visas) before finally getting on an American boat. Renoir found he was sharing a cabin with Antoine de Saint-Exupéry, famous flier and author of *Wind, Sand and Stars*. Like Clair, Renoir and Dido proceeded almost immediately from New York to Hollywood, taking Saint-Exupéry with them, though Renoir notes that when they settled in Hollywood they hardly saw anything of him, although he was living with them, because he worked all night (on his book *Vol de Nuit*) and slept all day. However, they remained close, and planned together a film version of *Wind, Sand and Stars* which never got anywhere, despite several shared ordeals-by-agent. Renoir had signed his contract with Fox, and settled down to the complicated business of making his first American film. Perversely, in Zanuck's eyes, he wanted it to be in every sense an American film; he emphatically did not want to become an expert in stage Frenchmen with berets and pointed beards, or cardboard mock-ups of a Hollywood-fantasy Paris.

Clair had some of the same problems, but reacted in a very different way. At least in his case it was recognizable that all his films took place in a personal fantasy, René Clair-land, of no specific time, no specific place. It might as well be America as anywhere else, if producers could be persuaded to see that. He tried to interest

Universal in a scenario he had recently written in Paris, *Rue de la Gaieté*, reworked for Deanna Durbin and W. C. Fields. Joe Pasternak, Deanna Durbin's regular producer, had some doubts about it, and proposed instead a subject by Norman Krasna, *Flame of New Orleans*, as a vehicle for Marlene Dietrich.

Clair discovered that he could work very well with Krasna, he liked the idea of a story set in New Orleans, that surviving corner of la Nouvelle France (though the film was made, of course, entirely in Universal Studios), and was able to work again with a couple of his old collaborators from France, the cameraman Rudolph Maté and the costume designer René Hubert. All this side of the film consequently went very well, but according to Marlene Dietrich, Clair had trouble fitting in with American expectations of the warm, human interest a director was virtually required to take in the families of his crew—he struck them as cold and autocratic. Nor, when it came out in 1941, was the film a success; indeed, charming as it is today, it was a box-office disaster. The red carpet that had been rolled out for the famed European director of *The Ghost Goes West* was abruptly rolled back. For months he was religiously shunned by the studios, except for an urgent request to take over Hitchcock's episode in the tribute-to-Britain *Forever and a Day*, and sought refuge, philosophically, in writing a novella called *De fil en aiguille*.

And, naturally, looking for a film subject. One of the books his agents sent him was a novel by Thorne Smith, *The Passionate Witch*. It seemed to have the nugget of an idea for a film, in the notion of an ordinary uncomplicated American unknowingly marrying a witch, and he set to work to construct his own scenario on this basis. At this point he came in contact with Hollywood's number one francophile, Preston Sturges. Sturges, as well as being at that point the new wonder-boy of Paramount, now that he had finally got to direct his own screen plays, was the owner of the Players Club, a bar-restaurant (with eventually a miniature theatre on top) a short distance along Sunset Boulevard from the Garden of Allah. This seems always to have been more of a self-indulgence for Sturges than a serious business venture. This was particularly so during the war, when it became the home-from-home of the emigrant French community, who all too often left their bills unpaid. Renoir speaks rather disdainfully of the 'Hollywood Resistance Movement' centred there: 'The heroic utterances of French émigrés seem to me in bad taste ... Wonderfully victorious attacks on Vichy were launched from that Sunset Strip café. It is not

hard to be a hero when the enemy is 10,000 kilometres away.'
However, Sturges immediately offered to take Clair's script idea
to Paramount. Paramount saw in it possibilities for their new, as yet
somewhat undefined star sensation Veronica Lake, and Clair was off
again, this time heading towards the triumph of *I Married a Witch*.

Meanwhile, the third major figure of the French cinema, Julien
Duvivier, was doing little better at the beginning of his wartime
stopover in America. At the time that Clair had first broached the
idea of the French film centre in America, Giraudoux, then head of
the film office of the French Ministry of Information, had agreed
enthusiastically, but first assigned Duvivier to make an all-out
patriotic celebration of French life and culture at the Victorine
Studios in Nice. Finally entitled *Un tel Père et Fils*, it began
shooting on 10 December 1939, and finished just before the fall of
France. It was shipped instantly to New York, where editing was
completed and it had a successful run more or less throughout the
war, being updated from time to time with insertions of new
newsreel material and added scenes of the sufferings of occupied
France shot by Duvivier with Michèle Morgan, one of the original
stars and at the time also in exile. It was not shown in France until
after the liberation, by which time it seemed merely quaint, not to
say tactless, in that it happened to have cast in heroic roles three
actors who subsequently became notorious collaborators.

Duvivier, like Renoir, was temporarily involved in an Italo–
French co-production project, but negotiations were cut short by
Mussolini's declaration of war on France, and he too set off to meet
Clair in Lisbon and set sail for America. He had the advantage of
having worked in Hollywood before: as a result of the enormous
success of his mid-Thirties films, especially *Pépé le Moko* (instantly
remade in Hollywood with Charles Boyer as *Algiers*) and *Un Carnet
de Bal*, he was invited to come on an MGM contract in 1938. He
directed a few scenes of the MGM spectacular *Marie Antoinette*, just
to feel his way in an American studio, then made *The Great Waltz*
(1938), one of MGM's biggest successes of that era. He had been
impressed with the technical efficiency and resources of Hollywood,
but chafed at working under factory conditions so different from the
power and responsibility a director enjoyed in Europe; pocketing
his large salary he had returned to France.

But at least Duvivier was not an unknown quantity in
Hollywood, and Hollywood was not an unknown quantity to him.
He had even learnt to make himself understood in English, which

was more than Renoir could claim. But for the moment things looked rather bleak: he was in New York with his wife, his son, the reels of *Un tel Père et Fils*, and no money or prospects. As it happened the producer Paul Graetz was also in New York, took charge of the film's completion and exploitation, and put Duvivier under contract. Then he met Alexander Korda, who was looking for a suitable vehicle for his wife Merle Oberon, fresh from her triumph in *Wuthering Heights*, and hit upon the idea of remaking *Un Carnet de Bal*.

This had been, and was in the new version, *Lydia* (1941), an episode film framing various love stories in the reunion of an old woman with all the men she had danced with as noted on a dance card of long ago. *Lydia* was received with critical respect and public apathy, but it did give Duvivier a new foothold in American cinema, and marked him—American 'type-casting' again—as a specialist in episode films, so that two of the three other films he made in America during the war, *Tales of Manhattan* (1942) and *Flesh and Fantasy* (1943), were also films in episodes. Both of them also starred Charles Boyer (get a Frenchman to direct a Frenchman) and Edward G. Robinson, along with assorted émigrés (Charles Laughton in the first, the perennially English C. Aubrey Smith and Dame May Whitty in the second) and Hollywood regulars. *Flesh and Fantasy* also boasted the most notable Hollywood score by the Polish-French émigré composer Alexandre Tansman.

The last and least successful of Duvivier's American films was a French Resistance story, *The Imposter* (1944), starring a visibly uncomfortable Jean Gabin (yet another wartime refugee) in a somewhat lunatic tale about a condemned murderer who escapes the guillotine during the bombardment, joins the Resistance and redeems himself with an heroic death among the Free French in Africa. It was, in fact, an exact demonstration of just the kind of film Renoir was determined not to make in America. Not very surprisingly, after this disaster (which Duvivier brought on his own head, as he worked from his own script, inspired remotely by his big success of 1935, *La Bandéra*), Duvivier found no further work in Hollywood and headed back to France for good, as soon as he could after the war.

Renoir, unlike Clair or Duvivier, firmly resisted all temptations to fall in with Hollywood expectations. When he was offered 'French stories' he refused, and also explained to Zanuck that if films made in the conventional Hollywood fashion were wanted, it was folly to

223

employ him. The only point of employing him was to get something
different, something that any capable Hollywood craftsman could
not give. Eventually he got his way. He was assigned *Swamp Water*,
a purely American subject by the Southern novelist Vereen Bell,
scripted by John Ford's favourite screenwriter Dudley Nichols, and
set in the primitive Okefenokee Swamp between Georgia and
Florida. Renoir's first stipulation was that as much as possible of the
film must be shot on location—a practice virtually unheard-of then,
when the studios prided themselves on being able to reproduce any
place in the world on their own back lots. However, having gone
thus far with this obviously insane Frenchman, Zanuck decided to
go that much further, and Renoir set off with his relatively unknown
cast, his crew and with Dido, his soon-to-be-wife (who happened to
be Brazilian) to act as interpreter.

The filming went quite well, except for a sticky moment when
Renoir was informed from Hollywood that he was to be removed
from direction of the film because he was too slow and was falling
behind schedule. But that order was countermanded the next day
when Zanuck had seen the material shot thus far and decided it was
good enough to give Renoir a little rope to work in his own way.
And Renoir at least had the advantage of being temperamentally quite
unlike the crisp, correct Clair. For all his lack of English, which
was speedily remedied, he was warm and happy and approachable,
and his casts and crews always adored him; when he first arrived
on set after the news had come through of his reinstatement
on *Swamp Water*, he got a spontaneous round of applause.

In Hollywood the Renoirs had settled in as though for a long stay.
He says in his autobiography that in his naivety he just somehow
assumed that his large Fox salary would go on for ever. And he very
soon developed a real love of the place. He arrived with romantic
notions that, despite all his common sense told him to the contrary,
it would still be in some way the Hollywood of Valentino and he
would meet fabled creatures like Mae Murray and Gloria Swanson
on the streets. He did in fact get to know Lillian Gish and for a short
while lived next door to her, but otherwise he soon recognized
where his fantasy and reality parted company. But it did not seem to
bother him as he could obviously cope with the reality, too. He
remained throughout his life, despite periods of great unhappiness
with Hollywood and with America in general, a staunch defender of
Los Angeles, with its beauty and bizarreness, against the rival claims
of other American cities, particularly New York, which he always

regarded as a sort of Hell's kitchen, to be visited briefly and only because of friends strange enough to like living there. In fact, though he spent most of the 1950s working in France, he seems always to have regarded Los Angeles as his home, and retired there to live out his last few years.

For the present, however, he continued to balance fantasy and reality, by buying a rambling house in a once-fashionable area, which had originally been built by Agnes Ayres, Valentino's co-star in *The Sheik*, who was for a time as carried away by him off-screen as on, so that the house, for Renoir at least, gave off all kinds of romantic vibrations. Settled there, he got down to work with Dudley Nichols on his second American film, *This Land Is Mine* (1943), this time for RKO. It was, to be sure, a 'French subject', but one particularly dear to his heart at this time, if only as a reaction to the over-simplifications of the Players Club heroes: what it was really like living in France under the Occupation, what the choices for individual Frenchmen really were, and how no one in real danger would choose to be a hero until he had tried everything else first. The hero of the script, a timid schoolteacher who is gradually forced into an heroic action saving the life of a member of the Resistance, was played by Charles Laughton, who became a close personal friend of Renoir, as of so many other European exiles in Hollywood; indeed, he was one of the witnesses when Renoir and the faithful Dido finally got married.

Renoir was certainly very happy working with Laughton. It no doubt helped that Laughton's most prized possession was 'The Judgement of Paris', a large and important canvas by Renoir's father—one could, after all, communicate with a man like that. Inevitably, like all directors working with Laughton, he had to cope with one of Laughton's famous bouts of uncertainty and creative block. On this occasion Laughton could not *feel* the scene where his character sees from his prison window an old teacher of his and has to establish contact by just calling his name. Laughton complained that he could not see the man: where was he? Renoir, practically, replied: 'Right there, in your mind', and Laughton, relieved, announced he was immediately ready to do the scene. The film was shot at top speed, well within schedule and budget, and had a satisfactory commercial career in America, though Renoir subsequently came to see it as essentially a *pièce d'occasion*, which should never have been shown in France, outside its own immediate context and intended audience.

After completing it Renoir responded to the appeals of the Office of War Information in New York and his friends Burgess Meredith and Philip Dunne, who were then working for it, to come and supervise a short army training film, *Salute to France* (1944), which was intended to familiarize soldiers likely soon to find themselves in France with the local customs. Kurt Weill wrote the music for it, and presumably it would have served its purpose—though there is some doubt whether it was ever actually shown to the troops, like Lubitsch's equivalent picture of Germany and the Germans, which was shelved and reshot and shelved again. In any case, Renoir later declared that there was very little of him in it.

In Hollywood his position was comfortable, if not all that secure—comfortable because he was never starving and seems always to have had films offered to him that he could turn down; insecure because he persisted in doing precisely that, and working only on projects that appealed to him. Some of the projects did not come to anything—the idea of filming Mary Webb's novel *Precious Bane* with Ingrid Bergman in the lead, for instance, which she liked but Selznick, who had her under contract, didn't. (Instead Selznick proposed that Renoir direct her in *Joan of Arc*, an idea which appalled him.) Another which fell by the wayside was a new version of Gorky's *The Lower Depths*, which Renoir had already filmed in France, but this time with the locale moved to the industrial area of East Los Angeles.

In general, despite *This Land Is Mine*, Renoir persisted in wanting to make American-American films, though socially he kept close to French circles in Los Angeles, which clustered round Charles Boyer's home and that of the brothers Hakim—Raymond and Robert—film producers in exile who had already worked with Duvivier (*Pépé le Moko*) and Renoir (*La Bête Humaine*) in France. The Hakims' was the main meeting-place of Renoir, Duvivier and Clair, and ironically it was through them that Renoir got to make his most completely American film, *The Southerner* (1945). They had the rights of a novel called *Hold Autumn in Your Hand*, which concerned the struggles of a young farmer in Texas in setting up on his own with land and weather and circumstance against him. There was already a script in existence, but everyone deferred to Renoir's ideas and wishes, and he wrote his own script (with the unofficial but vital help of William Faulkner). He also assembled his own cast (selecting for the lead, when the star first envisaged, Joel McCrea, dropped out, Zachary Scott, who had played mainly suave villains up to then), worked with Eugene Lourié, who had designed *La Grande Illusion*, *La Bête Humaine* and *La Règle du Jeu* for him in France, and selected his own locations in the San Joaquin Valley not far from Los Angeles, but a million miles from Hollywood.

In fact, Renoir always subsequently maintained, in the face of French critics who wanted him to bewail the need to compromise with the Hollywood system, that he contrived to have almost absolute freedom in and control over his American films. If he made mistakes, they were his own mistakes, and he would have made them just as much in Paris as in Hollywood. *The Southerner* was certainly no mistake: it was his most unequivocally successful film in America.

Many thought that his two subsequent films were mistakes, however. He had wanted since silent days to adapt Mirbeau's once rather daring novel *The Diary of a Chambermaid* to the screen; he came back to the idea when looking for something he could do with Paulette Goddard, someone who as a personality delighted him as much as her then husband Burgess Meredith. Meredith produced the film, wrote it with Renoir, and starred in it with Paulette Goddard. It was played as a deliberately studio-bound artificial comedy, which, with its quirky and unpredictable changes of pace and mood, left American audiences mystified when it came out in 1946. It was 'very European' with a vengeance—if not actually, despite its nominal French setting, very French. It must be said, however, that the film has worn well; its detachment from the expectations of the time now stands it in very good stead.

The detachment was not altogether happy for Renoir. He had visited France in 1945 and been disturbed by a sense of not belonging any more. Not completely American, he was certainly no longer completely French, and found French attitudes at that time—defiant or apologetic about the Occupation, over-wary of the émigrés who were now returning and often downright hostile towards them—rather unnerving. Some of the sense of disorientation creeps into *The Diary of a Chambermaid* (1946), and even more into his last Hollywood film, *The Woman on the Beach*, made in 1946. Mitchell Wilson's novel *None So Blind*, on which it is based, is a fairly conventional psychological thriller, but in his mood of the time Renoir picked out of it the theme of human solitude and the difficulty of communication. He consequently made—in complete freedom—a film that was by his own account strangely lacking in external happening, a rather gloomy and abstract mood piece. Even with Joan Bennett, then at the peak of her career with the two best of her Lang films in the recent past, to recommend it, the film had a disastrous preview in Santa Barbara. Renoir lost his nerve and, entirely of his own volition, reshot most of it, depriving it, in his own later opinion, of most of its quality and coherence in the process.

The film, consequently no doubt, was a total commercial disaster, and though Renoir was under contract to make two further films for RKO, they immediately bought him out. It was to be the last time he made a film in America, though he did not realize it then. He had hopes of setting up production of a novel by Rumer Godden, *The River*, which he had fallen in love with and optioned, with a major Hollywood company, but no one was interested in India without a tiger-hunt or the Taj Mahal. When he went off to India to make the film it was with entirely independent finance (from a Beverly Hills florist with ambitions to be a film producer).

At the time of his departure Renoir made some rather bitter statements. Evidently, though there was not yet, early in 1947, any question of a blacklist, his professional associations ten years earlier with the French Communist Party and the Popular Front were not exactly in his favour any more in the changing climate of the post-war years. When he returned it was as a grand old man, no longer practising as a film-maker, and all was forgiven. He did not bear grudges. In his autobiography he quotes Darryl Zanuck, who said of him after he had left: 'Renoir has a lot of talent, but he's not one of us.' It could be an epitaph on a whole émigré generation.

Certainly the same could be said, or could have been said, of René Clair. Even though, despite lacking Renoir's human touch, he contrived to do more consistently well in Hollywood than ever Renoir did. Partly it was the luck of finding, after the misfortune of *Flame of New Orleans*, the perfect mediator between his own private world and the great American public. *I Married a Witch* was, in a fashion not altogether dissimilar from *The Diary of a Chambermaid*, not specifically an American film nor recognizably a French film. The difference was that it was happy and charming, able to ingratiate itself with an audience of whom Clair had found the measure. In a word, it was a Clair film, equally at home in America as anywhere else: snail-like, he carried his world round on his back. The film was helped by the presence in it of Veronica Lake, and helped her to become a major star. After initial resistance to casting her at all, Clair accepted that she had comic talents he had never suspected and generously apologized to her, though strangely enough, after Sturges's *Sullivan's Travels* and *I Married a Witch*, she never got the chance to play comedy again. Clair was also totally delighted with working for a big studio, and drew every possible benefit from all the technical advantages of the situation.

He now knew where he was in Hollywood. He knew pretty well what would go in America, and it was mainly a question of finding the right subject and persuading the producers that he was right. He worked for a while on a free adaptation of *Le Voyage de M. Périchon*, transposed to America, and on an original subject by himself and Robert Pirosh, who had collaborated with him on the script of *I Married a Witch*. But Paramount, oddly, had their heart set on him directing a lavish Technicolor version of Daphne du Maurier's *Frenchman's Creek* (what's in a name?) with Joan Fontaine, and that somehow he could not see.

While things again hung fire the Allied landings in North Africa took place, and though Clair, like other exiles, such as Renoir and Saint-Exupéry (with whom Clair was also very friendly), had carefully stayed clear of the warring French factions in America, he wanted to be involved in the French war effort at a less political level, and wrote to the French mission in Washington offering his services. The reply was an invitation to go to Algiers to organize the film service of the Free French army. He wanted to know what materials and equipment would be at his disposal, and received the answer that for the moment there were none, but on 10 October 1943 he was given the rank of Lieutenant-Colonel in the French army. He was to be given a credit of $100,000 to equip his unit, and was all set to depart for Algiers in January 1944, to be ready to film the historic events of the Allied reconquest of France, when he discovered that nothing had been done, nothing purchased and he would arrive in North Africa completely unprepared.

That was the effective end of that project, but meanwhile he had found another subject in a short play by Lord Dunsany, plus an original scenario on a kindred topic—the predicament of a man who finds that he knows what is going to happen tomorrow and at first enjoys it, until he finds his own death predicted and has to do all in his power to avoid it. Paramount did not care for the idea, so Clair arranged to take it elsewhere, to an independent producer called Arnold Pressburger. Clair worked on the script with Dudley Nichols, who should by this time have been used to working with the French after his stint with Renoir. Dick Powell starred in *It Happened Tomorrow* (1944) and it remained Clair's own favourite among his American films. While he was shooting it in the early months of 1944 he was expecting any moment to go to Europe to film the Normandy landings, whenever they should occur, but the authorities remained unable or unwilling to organize anything, and meanwhile his wife was taken seriously ill and had to have a serious operation in New York. By the time this was over D-Day had already occurred, unrecorded by the French cinema, and the Clairs returned to Hollywood with no immediate commitments of any kind.

At this point, Lévy-Strauss revived the idea, which had originally been Clair's, of an American-based French production company to involve himself, Clair, Duvivier and, this time, Lewis Milestone, the Russian-born director of *All Quiet on the Western Front*. This seemed to Clair like a good arrangement, so he agreed and began preparing his first independent production. He was interested in the possibility of *Arsenic and Old Lace*—rather surprisingly, since one would have thought it offered little scope for his own personal contribution—but Capra had acquired the rights first, which might be regarded as quid pro quo, since Capra had originally owned the rights to the materials of *It Happened Tomorrow* but had proved unable to get a workable script out of them.

Instead, Clair turned to a subject that was, or could be made into, something in rather the same vein of murderous comedy, Agatha Christie's *Ten Little Niggers*. The nursery rhyme, of course, was changed for American purposes to 'Ten Little Indians' and the film finally titled *And Then There Were None*. Working again with Dudley Nichols, Clair fashioned from this unlikely material a funny thriller with various whimsical setpieces, which remind one that in his methods and attitudes to the film he is not, after all, so far from Hitchcock.

While Clair was preparing the film, Lévy-Strauss died; Duvivier, who was not, as noted, having too prosperous a time in Hollywood, was offered the chance to make a film in Europe and left; and the intended production company subsequently collapsed. Since Clair had the property all ready to go, it was easy enough to make a deal with Fox for this particular film, which Clair produced as well as directed. The agreement was made at the end of 1944, and the film came out in September 1945, to a generally favourable press and considerable success at the box-office. It was generally felt, however, and not least by Clair himself, that the film was a lot less distinctive and personal than his earlier American films.

In any case, he was homesick. He was finally able to return to France, for a brief visit, in July 1945, and found himself overwhelmed with proposals that he should work again in France. The most interesting came from Pathé, who had just set up a co-production deal with RKO. In October Clair returned to his home in Beverly Hills to reflect, and started work on a scenario with a background of French film-making in silent days, eventually to be called *Le Silence est d'Or*. He came to an agreement with Pathé and RKO that the film should be made in French with an English version (scripted with Robert Pirosh), which would avoid dubbing or subtitles by having a commentary on the action delivered by the principal character. Clair had originally thought of the subject as a dramatic comedy for Raimu, but Raimu was in such poor health that he was persuaded to cast Maurice Chevalier instead, with a consequent extensive reworking of the script to accommodate Chevalier's very different personality. On 14 October 1946 Clair started shooting the film in Paris—the first completed film he would have made in France and in French for twelve years. Though he continued to commute for a further year or two between Paris and Beverly Hills, he found none of the American projects offered to him at all interesting, and in 1948 his return to France became permanent: he was back where he belonged.

The French as a group had managed to preserve their own character in Hollywood, in but not of the American film community. Hollywood had little effect on them, and they probably even less on it. Success or failure, their time in America was little more than a strange interlude. For the directors on the whole it was success, for the émigré actors—Jean Gabin and Michèle Morgan chief among them—it was failure or marking time; certainly none managed to become so thoroughly part of the Hollywood scene as Charles Boyer, who was of an earlier generation of transatlantic adventurers. (Again, maybe it was partly because Boyer was there from choice, Gabin more from necessity.) Few of other nationalities were so fortunate in their ability to come when they had to, stay as long as was necessary, and return home afterwards with a minimum of emotional and professional upheaval. In any case, one is inclined to count the principal exception, Max Ophuls, as French even though he was in fact born a German in the Saar. He was bilingual from childhood and when the choice was offered on the occasion of the Saar plebiscite in 1934, he opted for French nationality; he became naturalized in 1938. But more important anyway than the rather complicated defences of his essential Frenchness mounted by chauvinistic French critics, is his nature as a film-maker: for, like Clair, he is *sui generis*, one who carries round his private world with him wherever he may be.

Before coming to America in 1940 Ophuls had made films in Germany, where he began, then after 1933, in France, Italy and Holland. And all of them carry the marks of his own peculiar elegance and style, his passion for elaborate decor and long moving-camera shots, which prompted James Mason, one of his stars in Hollywood, to observe:

> A shot that does not call for tracks
> Is agony for poor dear Max
> Who separated from his dolly
> Is wrapped in deepest melancholy.
> Once, when they took away his crane,
> I thought he'd never smile again...

At the beginning of the war Ophuls was in Paris, but left with Jouvet and his company for Switzerland with the intention of filming one of their productions there, *L'Ecole des Femmes*. But the money ran out, the film was never finished and Ophuls, resisting the temptation to stay in Switzerland for the duration of the war, returned to France, planning to go from there to America. Following much the same route as the rest of the French émigrés he finally arrived towards the end of 1941, unknown and without prospects. But he did know a few people, including Paul Kohner, who arranged for a screening of his best early film, *Liebelei*, to draw attention to him.

In Hollywood he also inevitably found himself drawn into the circle of Preston Sturges, and as Sturges had been instrumental in getting Clair's Hollywood career off on the right foot, so he tried to do the same for Ophuls. But Sturges was more personally involved in this project, and the results were disastrous. He had been hired by Howard Hughes as an all-purpose wonder-boy, and his first idea was a version of Mérimée's *Colomba* as a vehicle to launch Hughes's new discovery (in the wake of Jane Russell), Faith Domergue. Hughes consequently was very concerned with getting it all right, and leant heavily on Sturges, who in his turn, as producer and scenarist of this venture, leant heavily on Ophuls. The result was that after a year of preparation and a few days of shooting, Sturges ignominiously fired Ophuls and took over direction himself, to be replaced in his turn by a succession of other writers and directors until the film finally emerged in 1950 as *Vendetta*, a hopeless hodgepodge and classic case of too many cooks....

Another friendship, with Robert Siodmak, proved more fruitful for Ophuls. Siodmak recommended him to Douglas Fairbanks Jr, who was going into independent production with *The Exile* (1947), a fairly conventional swashbuckler about Charles II of England in exile that Ophuls made into a charmingly artificial romantic fantasy shot against a shamelessly studio evocation of seventeenth-century Holland. In some respects it is surprising he did not get a real chance to work in American studios before this—he had been in Los Angeles for six full years with only the abortive experience of *Vendetta* before he started work on *The Exile*.

From all accounts he was a charmer with an immediate grasp of written and spoken English, even though he persisted in speaking a picturesque variety of his own devising. He settled very comfortably—as comfortably as one can on strictly limited means, with the help of a few good friends—to the lifestyle of Hollywood. He even managed to preserve such 'civilized' European habits as a wife and a regular mistress who knew each other well and belonged to the same circle of friends, mostly émigrés and transplanted New Yorkers, while politely never openly referring to their unconventional relationship. He also seems to have been curiously able to inspire confidence, even though he was, on the strength of his pre-war work, perhaps the least known of the émigrés who came from or via France. Howard Koch recalls in his autobiography that after a mere hour's acquaintance with this impish European he knew for sure that he wanted to work on a film with him—and this was back in 1944 when Ophuls had done nothing in Hollywood and seemed to have precious little prospect of doing anything.

The friendship then created also had a happy consequence for Ophuls. Koch was approached in 1947 by John Houseman with a project that he had been asked to produce for Joan Fontaine and her executive husband William Dozier. It was a Stefan Zweig novella called *Letter from an Unknown Woman*, a very romantic tale about a middle-aged woman looking back on her girlhood idealization of a handsome young musician and her later brief affair with him, which she afterwards discovers meant everything to her and nothing to him. Koch did not fancy the story too much, seeing all kinds of inherent dangers in it that could all too easily make it degenerate into a conventional Hollywood weepie. But then he thought of Ophuls, and agreed to script if Ophuls would direct. Houseman happily knew *Liebelei* and agreed Ophuls would be ideal if the Doziers could be sold on the idea. And so it happened that Ophuls was able to make one of the most 'European' of American films in almost total freedom, its Viennese atmosphere so genuine few could believe it had all been made on the sound stages of Universal, and in all as unmistakable a realization of his own private universe as *Liebelei* or *La Ronde* and his subsequent French films of the 1950s.

Letter to an Unknown Woman was no great success when it was released in 1948—the studio, which regarded it as an unmarketable, highbrow 'foreign movie', saw to that—but it was eventually to become a cult film in Europe. By this time Ophuls was anyway quite well established in Hollywood, with a reputation at least for being a meticulous craftsman, who could handle stars and do an economical, workmanlike job—all of which, in America, was far more important than being regarded as an artistic genius.

In Europe Ophuls had known Reinhardt and his family, and so it was not totally by coincidence that his next film, *Caught* (1949), was produced by Reinhardt's son Wolfgang for MGM. The subject is a typical *film noir* story of a shop-girl who marries a rich sadist and then has to try to escape him in favour of an idealistic doctor. Ophuls managed the atmosphere and the American scenes very well, in his own style, and made a lasting friend in one of the stars, James Mason (playing the doctor), who had not long been in Hollywood himself from England and much enjoyed Ophuls's European sensibilities. Mason was also in Ophuls's next, and what was to be his last, Hollywood film, *The Reckless Moment*, along with Joan Bennett, by 1949 something of an expert in émigré directors. Another subject with *film noir* possibilities (a mother tries to save her daughter from blackmail) it was Ophuls's most idiomatically American film, mostly shot on location and extremely acute in its notation of small-town American life. *The Reckless Moment* was produced by Walter Wanger, who was then Joan Bennett's husband.

Ophuls's next project, one much more obviously up his street, was an adaptation of Balzac's *La Duchesse de Langeais*, to be made in Italy, in colour, and bring Garbo back to the screen with, yet again, James Mason. They all went to Italy, and waited and waited. But though Garbo seemed this time to be willing, one problem after another came up and the film was never made. Instead, Ophuls was offered the chance to make a film in France of one of his favourite works, Schnitzler's *Reigen* (or in French, *La Ronde*). He seized the opportunity, and the rest is history. *La Ronde* (1950) was one of the most sensationally successful films of the post-war era in Europe, and from then on, received back into the bosom of the French cinema (where, as French critics insist, he had always belonged), Ophuls went from triumph to triumph, until his death in 1957. He had had a more difficult time getting started in Hollywood than any other major figure among the émigrés, yet once belatedly inducted into the American cinema had fitted in as comfortably as any. His best American film, *Letter from an Unknown Woman*, remained an oddity for its time and place, and the other films he made in Hollywood, excellent as they are, were just the most convenient stages on a route that led, as it now seems, inevitably back to Europe.

Though Preston Sturges is a name that constantly crops up in the lives and careers of foreigners in Hollywood, particularly French, ironically one can see absolutely no trace of foreign influence in his own films, which remain idiomatically and almost defiantly American. In a sense, it says much for the solidity and stability of the American cinema that this is almost universally so. The *film noir* might arguably be a creation of the Germans in Hollywood, but if so it was constantly absorbed into Hollywood's normal range of styles and genres to an extent that leaves one hard put to it to trace any specific foreign influence on any particular established American director working temporarily in this area. In the Forties, foreign film-makers had before them the possibilities of 'going Hollywood' so that they were seldom consciously considered as foreigners (Lang, Preminger), or of trying to continue to make their own personal films (Clair, Renoir), which may be more or less successful, but were anyway products of their own individual gifts in the same way that, say, Orson Welles's films were, and only in a secondary fashion considered as non-American, foreign films. This meant that, during the Forties heyday of the émigré film-maker, Hollywood somehow managed effectively to sweep most awareness of their foreignness out of sight. The exotic delights of foreignness, which had helped to make Marlene Dietrich and Maurice Chevalier, among a host of others, stars of the American cinema in the previous decade, or had recommended a succession of new European genius film-makers in the Twenties, were now largely forgotten, and anyway played down completely. In the Forties, everyone was somehow expected to be, before all else, a good American. Which was undeniably unfortunate when the concept of the un-American came to be a regular topic of conversation, and it was seldom clear where being non-American ended and being un-American began.

Meanwhile, it is remarkable at the end of the day how little a dent all these émigrés made on Hollywood or on Los Angeles. For most Americans thereabouts, if the foreigners did not join the gang they might just as well not be around. And the few exceptions— Americans who appreciated the special qualities of the émigrés— remained just that: exceptions, whose strange devotion to European culture made them almost as much outsiders as if they were European non-joiners themselves.

Albert Lewin is a good example. A graduate of NYU and Harvard, he had been a professor before being lured into movies—a fact that always enormously impressed those around, particularly Irving Thalberg, whose protégé and right-hand man he was and whose last film, *The Good Earth* (1937), he produced. Lewin was always very consciously and obviously an odd-man-out in Hollywood: it was in a sense his gimmick. With his Savile Row suits, his collection of Pre-Columbian artifacts (years before they were fashionable), his disdain (real or apparent) for commerce, his obsession with surrealism and his host of European friends, he was absolutely what then passed in Hollywood—and probably still would—for an intellectual.

How this showed itself in practice was that his films were stuffed to overflowing with culture. In *Saadia* (1954), one of his later and more bizarre works, one establishing shot of its doctor-hero's desk contains, inter alia, a life of Proust, a heavyweight book on Islamic religion, and a text of *Hamlet* elaborately annotated. From the moment that, in 1942, he took to writing, directing and usually producing his own films, he obviously set out to teach Hollywood people a lesson in what, vulgar Americans that they were, they lacked. His first was *The Moon and Sixpence* (1942), based on Somerset Maugham's novel suggested by the life of Gauguin, and makes the identification complete by concluding with a montage of Gauguin's most famous Tahitian paintings in colour (where the rest of the film has been in black-and-white or sepia). But his passion for painting was later to take more spectacular and enterprising forms. In 1944, for his version of *The Picture of Dorian Gray*, he commissioned the Chicago artist Ivan Albright, who had found fame with his problem picture of a rotting door, 'That Which I

Should Have Done I Did Not Do', to paint the portrait in its final, hideously depraved form, specially for the film. But his biggest coup, and one of the most extraordinary episodes in Hollywood's usually distant relations with European art, was the competition he organized in 1946 in connection with his film of Maupassant's *The Private Affairs of Bel Ami*.

In the novel a painting of 'Christ Walking on the Waters' figures prominently. The Production Code insisted that this was out of the question, because the depiction of Christ was not permitted, but accepted as an alternative 'The Temptation of St Anthony'. It seemed like the perfect subject for Lewin's beloved surrealists, and so he devised a limited competition in which twelve international artists would do paintings on the subject, be paid $500 each for doing so and allow the film's producers to retain the work for the duration of a touring show to publicize the film (in the most discreet way, of course), after which it would revert completely to the artist. The winner, to be used in the film itself (again, a single splash of colour in an otherwise black-and-white movie), would be selected by a jury consisting of Marcel Duchamp, Alfred H. Barr, president of the American Federation of Arts, and Sidney Janis, New York gallery-owner; the winner would be paid an additional $2,500. And it would all 'serve the cause of popularizing notable achievements in contemporary painting'.

Of the dozen painters who agreed, only one, Leonor Fini, failed to deliver. Of the rest, four were American-born—Ivan Albright (again), Horace Pippin (the first notable black painter in America), Abraham Rattner and Dorothea Tanning (who, although American, was at this time living with the émigré Max Ernst). The remainder were made up of Europeans either still resident in Europe (Paul Delvaux, Stanley Spencer) or émigrés, such as the Russian Eugene Berman, the English Lenora Carrington (living in Mexico), the Spanish Salvador Dali, the German Max Ernst, and the Italian-Egyptian Louis Gugliemi. All of them, except Horace Pippin, tended towards surrealism, if they were not right in the middle of it, and Pippin was a semi-primitive whose work would be sympathetic to surrealist taste.

After due deliberation the major prize went to Ernst, who was at that time living and working in Arizona—about the nearest a major artist émigré came to Southern California—and who was anyway a close friend of Lewin's and frequent visitor to his Hollywood home. Not that the choice seems anything but fair: even today, when the canvases concerned are starting to surface again in retrospectives of the artists concerned, Ernst's response seems to be the most vivid and the most appropriate for the purposes of the film. Unfortunately the film itself, despite Ernst and despite the score composed for it by Milhaud (his only important Hollywood assignment), proved to be stodgy and lifeless, too literary by half, as was the general tendency with Lewin. The show of the commissioned paintings opened in Washington in 1946 and was trotted around America, though never it seems to Britain and France, as was originally envisaged.

It is doubtful whether the prestige of modern art increased much in America at large as a result, but Hollywood was certainly impressed. This, after all, was culture conspicuously consumed, with a good dash of that showbiz know-how that kept Lewin regularly in work in Hollywood for many years, even in the midst of MGM, for all his superior airs. And he was charming, he was cultivated, he did get on much better with visiting Europeans like Renoir, Ernst and the completely Europeanized Man Ray than with his Hollywood peers; he was genuinely at home in Paris and much more comfortable in New York than in provincial Los Angeles. It was choice as well as necessity that made him seek a European production for his next film, a mythological mishmash called *Pandora and the Flying Dutchman* (1951), which was shot in Spain and is one of the cinema's headier flights into the higher lunacy. Though he was as much as any a Hollywood native, for him the trip to Europe was like an exile's return. In his love of Europe and Europeans, and the degree to which he was affected by Europeans in Hollywood and affected them in turn, he remained one of a kind.

EPILOGUE

12. How to Be Un-American

Though to a certain extent American attitudes had changed during the war, and some had even been changed forever as a result of the war, it would be a mistake to discount the strong currents of hostility to foreigners and foreign involvements that continued to run beneath the surface. Certainly the war discredited American isolationism as such, but it did not put a stop to the state of mind that created isolationism. Ultimately, foreigners were all right provided they wanted whole-heartedly and completely to become American. Nobody cared—people hardly remembered—that virtually all the Hollywood tycoons had been born in remote parts of Eastern Europe with unpronounceable names they soon modified or dropped altogether. After all, no one could doubt the totality of their commitment to America and American ideas: there were few so pushily patriotic. But with a lot of the others, who came over for political reasons (always suspect, whatever they were) when already formed adults, you could not be so sure. Only the very naive suspected every foreigner of being a spy. But that was not necessary: often just being foreign was enough.

Of course, this kind of distrust was not the only motive of the Un-American Activities Committee, but the very name tells all. The House of Representatives Committee on Un-American Activities (to give it its full name) was created in 1938, and though it was at the outset dominated by Democrats (the first chairman, Martin Dies, and his second-in-command, John Rankin, were both Democrats, but Southern Democrats), it represented a strong anti-Roosevelt faction in the government. It was isolationist in tendency, hostile to the British, the Jews and indeed practically anything that was not totally WASP and American for several generations. Hollywood was almost immediately a subject of its investigation—which is to say, attack—and as already noted, things were beginning to get a little difficult for the liberal and anti-neutralist elements in Hollywood when Japan bombed Pearl Harbor and the situation changed overnight.

But memories were long, and though the committee's investigations of, particularly, the membership of communist, crypto-communist and even generally pro-Russian organizations went into abeyance throughout the war, they were all filed away somewhere. Hollywood was, of course, a particularly fertile ground for such proceedings, because it was still, and in the war years more than ever, a focus of public attention and anything connected with it was ensured maximum publicity. Which, naturally, was what minor politicians on the make wanted. In 1947 the committee, still quietly in existence, had passed into Republican control, chaired by J. Parnell Thomas, a New Jersey representative. And the new chill in relations between the one-time allies—the United States and Russia—suggested that this would be a good time, and showbusiness a good place, to start up again.

The committee was not explicitly against foreigners per se. It claimed to be more concerned with finding and rooting out American 'traitors' within the film industries—people who by subscribing to or being active in left-wing, pro-communist organizations had been helping (even if unconsciously) to undermine the American way of life; known communists who had been given the chance to spread their noisome propaganda through films they had written or directed or starred in. Anything, in fact, that the extremely right-wing Motion Picture Alliance for the Preservation of American Ideals (which helped to lure the committee's attention to Hollywood in the first place) did not regard as accordant with these mysterious American Ideals so worthy of Preservation. And once you had erected 'America' itself into an ideal, there was little chance of clearly distinguishing between 'Un-American' and 'non-American' as undesirable elements to be deplored and cast out.

Curiously enough, among all the émigrés who had come to Los Angeles for primarily political reasons, there were very few who had pronounced left-wing views. Most of the anti-Nazis were perforce anti-Nazi, because the Nazis were very much anti-them. Otherwise, many of the Jewish émigrés were quite conservative and well to the right of centre. Schoenberg, for instance, who had returned to Jewish orthodoxy, deplored the socialists almost as much as the Nazis, and was a sore trial to Brecht in his political obscurantism should they happen to meet in the supermarket; or Werfel, who had

242

a long-running flirtation with Roman Catholicism. Others were at most liberals along Roosevelt New Deal lines. No one ever seriously accused Thomas Mann of being a communist (Heinrich was a different case), and when Fritz Lang found himself on some sort of unofficial black list that prevented him from working for a few months around 1952, he was able easily to brush the charges aside as the workings of personal malice, they were so obviously incredible as anything else.

But all the same, it was difficult for anyone who had lived in Europe at all during the 1930s, or had, as an émigré in the early 1940s, evinced any understandable eagerness to help the Allied cause in whatever way possible in still-neutral America, to have avoided contact entirely with the Left, either through working with known communists or belonging to some committee or fund that had at least a covert connection with Russia. Many had as young men gone through at least a period of communism, even if they were later disillusioned, or drifted away. People like Buñuel, with his brief attempt at combining surrealism and communism, or Renoir, with his two films for the Popular Front, would hardly count in any sane mind as dangerous communist subversives ten years later, but the idea of guilt by association remained strong.

What it tended to amount to was a feeling that those foreigners were a shifty and unreliable lot. You never knew quite what they had been or who they had known before they ran to the protecting arms of America. Consequently, once the mood of the country started to change after the war, it became increasingly uncomfortable for foreigners. Even if they were not directly charged with anything, they came in for more than their fair share of suspicion—however talented, they were, after all, 'not one of us'. It was this kind of generalized discomfort that encouraged Buñuel to move on to Mexico, or Thomas Mann to return to Europe in 1952 to live out his last three years in Switzerland. It was something of the same kind that kept Renoir away for a few years—combined with a joyful acceptance of the new opportunities that Europe offered to make films in freedom.

In many émigrés who returned to Europe it is difficult to disentangle their motivations. No doubt they would have been hard put to do so even at the time. A natural desire to return to their native lands once they could—though not unmixed with some fear and trepidation as to what they would find—must have played a large part. So must the chance of working within their own cultures, both to those who, like Clair or Siodmak, had done very well in Hollywood during their enforced stopover, and more especially, to those like Alfred Doeblin, Jean Gabin or Darius Milhaud, who had found it difficult to work at all.

In this gradual drift back to Europe few of the important figures were exempt. Feuchtwanger and Stravinsky were always very self-sufficient, and anyway had no reason to fear any committee's investigation of their political backgrounds (Stravinsky's non-committal, Feuchtwanger's openly left-wing), since short of deportation there was nothing a committee could do to them. Lang and Hitchcock were professionally so completely integrated into the American cinema, and so consistently successful, that there was no reason on earth that they should look back to Europe, except to make the odd movie there if it seemed like a good idea. Other writers and composers—Huxley, Schoenberg—just stayed on until their deaths because they liked the climate and were generally comfortable.

In fact, the Un-American Activities Committee made direct difference to only a tiny handful of émigrés in America, though of course it created a considerable number of émigrés from America, film people who could find work only in Europe and then for the most part only under assumed names. The three notable émigrés that it did, one way or another, send packing were Bertolt Brecht, Hanns Eisler and of all people, Charles Chaplin. Chaplin was a strange case. His liberal sympathies with the underdog were well known, as was his popularity with communists and left-wingers generally (though, heaven knows, not only with them). He frequently denied that he was or ever had been a communist, and the general opinion of his friends and associates was that he was always too much the egotist to have anything much to do with any other -ism.

Chaplin was summoned to appear before the committee in 1947, but his hearing was delayed a couple of times and then cancelled on his sending a written statement that he had never been a communist. However, he was getting increasingly into trouble with the Hearst and other right-wing press, his film *Monsieur Verdoux* (1947) was badly received, the criticism being heavy with political overtones, and he began to have other troubles with the tax authorities, which seemed to have a suspicious air of victimization. Finally, in 1953, after completing *Limelight*, he planned an extended trip to Europe, and applied in the routine manner for a re-entry visa. He was, exceptionally, grilled for three hours by representatives of the immigration service about his political affiliations, his moral character and—most incriminating of all—why, though he had been resident in America for forty years, he had never become an American citizen. All the same, the permit was granted, and he set sail from New York, only to be cabled, once outside United States waters, that it had been rescinded and that if he tried to re-enter he would be subject to an Immigration Board of Inquiry to answer charges concerned with his politics and morals. He never lived in America or made a film in America again.

Chaplin explained the hostility he aroused in America during the late 1940s and early 1950s as the result of his non-conformism, his unwillingness to make sweeping denunciations of communism just to please the Un-American Activities Committee—at a time when at least a little formal truckling was a condition of survival in the industry—and of course his remaining, throughout his years in America, a British citizen. All of which are no doubt true, though they do not entirely explain why he should have been the object of such peculiar vehemence. But in the days when to persist, perversely, in being non-American was a clear indication of being un-American, one can hardly be surprised.

It was obviously with more reason that Brecht and Eisler suffered the attentions of the committee. For though it was not then and never has been actually illegal in the United States to be a communist, communism had unmistakably come to be regarded as an Un-American Activity, and as leading, declared Marxists in Hollywood (though neither was ever a member of the Communist Party) they were bound to come under some suspicion and questioning at least. Eisler was summoned to Washington on 24–6 September 1947, where he was harangued about his political beliefs (the chief interrogator described him as the 'Karl Marx of Communism in the musical field') and was not allowed to read his prepared statement, though it was placed on record. In it he describes his activities in Hollywood and elsewhere in America, denies that he was ever engaged in any political activity, and suggests that the main reason for his being before the Committee is guilt by association, he being the brother of Gerhart Eisler, who was a well-known communist. All to no avail; he judged it advisable to leave by the next possible boat and resettle in Germany, where he might well have made his way anyhow, though no doubt not quite so soon.

Brecht had been receiving rather vague overtures from Germany to return to the now reviving post-war German theatre, and had been making some (even vaguer) plans of his own to do theatre in Berlin, perhaps in some loose collaboration with Piscator. But at last good things seemed to be happening to him in the American theatre. Elisabeth Bergner had finally put on his adaptation of *The Duchess of Malfi* in New York and, more important, *Galileo* had reached the stage in Los Angeles in the summer of 1947 and was due to open in New York in December. But on 30 October Brecht, too, was required to testify in Washington before the Committee. In broken English and through a battery of interpreters he answered questions about his non-membership of the Communist Party and minimal political activity in America, discussed his relations with others who were undeniably communists, and tried to explain some of his writings, known to the Committee only in sometimes misleading translations. He too was not allowed to read his prepared statement, but at the end of the day no charges were brought against him.

Still, Brecht had too much practice in exile not to see the writing on the wall. The next day he made arrangements to leave America, and flew to Paris after saying goodbye to Charles Laughton, without even risking a stay long enough to see *Galileo* open in New York. For the next two years he was to live mostly in Zurich, then in 1949 he went to East Berlin to start work with his own company, the Berliner Ensemble. Before his death in 1956 he had established himself as one of the most powerful forces in world theatre, and the Berliner Ensemble had become one of the most famous and influential companies in the world. And the irony is that without the Un-American Activities Committee barking at his heels, that might never have happened. He might have spent another nine years hatching abortive schemes in Santa Monica, and beating in vain on the doors of Broadway producers, and be—hard though it is to imagine—virtually forgotten today.

Nobody likes being forced into exile; nobody likes being forced out of it; nobody likes being forced to do anything at all. But the results are always unpredictable, and none more so than those of the many and varied arrivals in and departures from Los Angeles between 1933 and 1950. It used to be too readily assumed in Europe that working in America could do a European artist nothing but harm, and it took years before Europeans could manage to accept that the Hollywood films of Lang and Hitchcock, Clair and Renoir, were at least on a level with their finest achievements on home ground, or that Thomas Mann and Stravinsky and Max Ernst and Christopher Isherwood were not destroyed for ever, or even noticeably diminished, by their proximity to and occasional participation in the activities of Hollywood. Similarly, it is still held by too many Americans that the worst thing that could happen to anybody is to be compelled to leave the land of the free and return to Europe. Between these two extremes, quite a number of the exiles themselves felt qualms about their relationship with American surroundings and the English language, their relationship, if any, with the country and the language they left behind.

All has not been for the best in this best of all possible worlds. Some of the strangers in paradise remained strangers till the day they died; some discovered that to see Southern California as paradise was a dangerous illusion; some found that they were strangers wherever they went, and paradise was anywhere or nowhere, it came to much the same thing in the end. Sometimes it seems that the effect of America on the newcomers was minimal, and their effect on it was even less. Either they vanished into the melting-pot so completely that their origins and national characteristics meant little more than a trick question in a movie quiz—did you know that Bob Hope was English; George Sanders, Russian; Edward G. Robinson Rumanian?—or they remained such resolutely special cases that their successes could always be written off as one-off oddities, not to be seriously taken note of. But through the whole tangle of political and professional conflicts, public complacency and private anguish (or vice versa), some good has come, and not so much bad as has generally been supposed.

Even the Un-American Activities Committee died a natural death in time; Charlie (by then Sir Charles) Chaplin was received ecstatically back into the bosom of the Academy of Motion Picture Arts and Sciences; and as more political upheavals occurred in Europe, new generations of exiles-by-force from Hungary or Czechoslovakia joined the new generations of exiles-by-choice from Italy, France or Britain, in search of the golden opportunities Hollywood had always offered and continued to offer into the era of television and disco records and smog. The last of the old-timers— Lang, Renoir, Feuchtwanger—continued to live in their mansions and look down indulgently on the world below. Los Angeles had not radically changed things for them, or been radically changed by them. But it had changed, and they had changed, and they had been, for at least a brief moment, an important part of one another. It was less than might have been hoped, more than could have been expected. Anyway, it had happened, and the fact is back there, islanded in time and unarguable, even if judgement goes on for ever.

Bibliography

Antheil, George, *Bad Boy of Music* (London, 1945)

Aranda, Francesco, *Luis Buñuel: A Critical Biography* (London, 1975)

Arliss, George, *George Arliss, by Himself* (London, 1940)

Atwill, Lee, *G. W. Pabst* (Boston, 1977)

Bachy, Victor, *Jacques Feyder, Artisan du cinéma* (Louvain, 1968)

Balakian, Anna, *André Breton: Magus of Surrealism* (New York, 1971)

Balcon, Michael, *A Lifetime of Films* (London, 1969)

Banham, Reyner, *Los Angeles: The Architecture of Four Ecologies* (London, 1971)

Barker, Christine, and Last, R. W., *Erich Maria Remarque* (London, 1979)

Barker, Felix, *The Oliviers* (London, 1953)

Baum, Vicki, *I Know What I'm Worth* (London, 1964)

Baxter, John, *The Hollywood Exiles* (London, 1976)

Bedford, Sybille, *Aldous Huxley: A Biography*, 2 vols. (London, 1973)

Behrman, S. N., *Tribulations and Laughter* (London, 1972); published in the USA under the title *People in a Diary* (Boston, 1972)

Bessie, Alvah, *Inquisition in Eden* (Berlin, 1967)

Bogdanovich, Peter, *Fritz Lang in America* (London, 1967)

Borgelt, Hans, *Das Süsseste Mädel der Welt: Die Lilian-Harvey-Story* (Beyreuth, 1974)

Brecht, Bertolt, *Arbeits Journal*, 2 vols. (Frankfurt, 1966)

Caldwell, Helen, *Michio Ito: The Dancer and His Dances* (Los Angeles, 1977)

Carringer, Robert, and Sabath, Barry, *Ernst Lubitsch: A Guide to References and Resources* (Boston, 1978)

Ceplar, Larry, and England, Steven, *The Inquisition in Hollywood: Politics in the Film Community, 1930–1960* (New York, 1980)

Chaplin, Charles, *My Autobiography* (London, 1964)

Charensol, Georges, and Régent, Roger, *50 Ans de cinéma avec René Clair* (Paris, 1979)

Chirat, Raymond, *Julien Duvivier* (Paris, 1968)

Colman, Juliet Benita, *Ronald Colman* (London, 1975)

Conrad, Peter, *Imagining America* (London, 1980)

Dodds, John W., *The Several Lives of Paul Fejos: A Hungarian-American Odyssey* (New York, 1973)

Donaldson, Frances, *Freddy Lonsdale* (London, 1957)

Eisner, Lotte H., *Fritz Lang* (London, 1977)

Ewen, Frederick, *Bertolt Brecht: His Life, His Art and His Times* (London, 1970)

Fermi, Laura, *Illustrious Immigrants* (Chicago, 1968)

Feuchtwanger, Lion, *The Devil in France* (London, 1941)

Finney, Brian, *Christopher Isherwood: A Critical Biography* (London, 1979)

Foltin, Lore B. (ed.), *Franz Werfel, 1890–1945* (Pittsburgh, 1961)

Ford, Charles, *La Vie quotidienne à Hollywood 1915–35* (Paris, 1972)

Frank, Leonhard, *Heart on the Left* (London, 1954)

French, Philip, *The Movie Moghuls* (London, 1969)

Fuhrich-Leisler, Edda, and Prossnitz, Gisela (eds.), *Max Reinhardt in Amerika* (Saltzburg, 1976)

Gebhard, David, *Schindler* (London, 1971)

Gebhard, David and von Breton, Harriette, *Kem Weber: The Moderne in Southern California* (Santa Barbara, 1969)

Grabs, Manfred (ed.), *Hanns Eisler: A Rebel in Music* (Berlin, 1978)

Graham, Sheilah, *The Garden of Allah* (New York, 1970)

Grunfeld, Frederick V., *Prophets without Honour: A Background to Freud, Kafka, Einstein and Their World* (London, 1979)

Gubern, Roman, *El Cine Español en el Exilio 1936–39* (Barcelona, 1976)

Halliday, Jon, *Sirk on Sirk* (London, 1971)

Hamilton, Nigel, *The Brothers Mann* (London, 1978)

Hardwicke, Cedric, *A Victorian in Orbit* (London, 1961)

Hart-Davies, Rupert, *Hugh Walpole: A Biography* (London, 1962)

Hecht, Ben, *A Child of the Century* (New York, 1954)

Higham, Charles, *Charles Laughton: An Intimate Biography* (New York, 1976); *Marlene: The Life of Marlene Dietrich* (London, 1978)

Houseman, John, *Run-Through* (New York, 1972)

Howard, Leslie Ruth, *A Quite Remarkable Father* (London, 1960)

Huvos, Kornel, *Cinq mirages américains: Les Etats-Unis dans l'oeuvre de Georges Duhamel, Jules Romains, André Maurois, Jacques Maritain et Simone de Beauvoir* (Paris, 1972)

Huxley, Julian (ed.), *Aldous Huxley: A Memorial Volume* (London, 1966)

Jay, Martin, *The Dialectical Imagination: A History of the Frankfurt School and the Institute of Social Research 1923–1950* (New York, 1973)

Keats, John, *You Might as Well Live: The Life and Times of Dorothy Parker* (London, 1971)

Koch, Howard, *As Time Goes By* (London, 1979)

Korda, Michael, *Charmed Lives: A Family Romance* (New York, 1979)

Kulik, Karol, *Alexander Korda: The Man Who Could Work Miracles* (London, 1975)

Lambert, Gavin, *On Cukor* (New York, 1972)

Loder, John, *Hollywood Hussar* (London, 1977)

Loos, Anita, *Kiss Hollywood Goodbye* (London, 1974)

Luft, Herbert G., *E. A. Dupont* (Paris, 1970)

Lyon, James K., *Bertolt Brecht in America* (Princeton, 1980)

McCabe, Cynthia Jaffee, *The Golden Door: Artist-Immigrants of America, 1876–1976* (Washington, 1976)

Mahler-Werfel, Alma, *And the Bridge is Love* (London, 1959)

Mann, Thomas, *The Genesis of a Novel* (London, 1961)

Minney, R. J., *Hollywood by Starlight* (London, 1935)

Montagu, Ivor, *With Eisenstein in Hollywood* (Berlin, 1968)

Moure, Nancy Dustin Wall, *Painting and Sculpture in Los Angeles, 1900–1945* (Los Angeles, 1980)

Navasky, Victor S., *Naming Names* (New York, 1980)

Neagle, Anna, *There's Always Tomorrow* (London, 1974)

Ophuls, Max, *Max Ophuls* (Paris, 1963)

Parmalee, Patty Lee, *Brecht's America* (Miami/Ohio, 1981)

Pasternak, Joe, *Easy the Hard Way* (London, 1956)

Pratley, Gerald, *The Cinema of Otto Preminger* (London, 1971)

Preminger, Otto, *Preminger: An Autobiography* (New York, 1977)

Reinhardt, Gottfried, *Der Liebhaber: Max Reinhardt* (Munich, 1973); *The Genius: A Memoir of Max Reinhardt* (New York, 1979)

Renoir, Jean, *My Life and My Films* (London, 1974)

Roud, Richard, *Max Ophuls: An Index* (London, 1958)

Schebera, Jürgen, *Hanns Eisler in USA-Exil 1938–1948* (Meisenheim am Glan, 1978)

Schwartz, Nancy Lynn, *The Hollywood Writers' Wars* (New York, 1981)

Seidman, Steve, *The Film Career of Billy Wilder* (Boston, 1977)

Spalek, John H. (ed.), *Lion Feuchtwanger: The Man, His Ideas, His Work* (Los Angeles, 1972)

Spalek, John H. and Strelka, Joseph (eds.), *Deutsche Exilliteratur seit 1933. I. Kalifornien*, 2 vols. (Berne, 1976)

Stein, Erwin (ed.), *Arnold Schoenberg: Letters* (London, 1964)

Stewart, Donald Ogden, *By a Stroke of Luck!* (London, 1975)

Strelka, Donald P., Bell, Robert F. and Dobson, Eugene (eds.), *Protest-Form-Tradition: Essays in Exile German Literature* (Alabama, 1979)

Stuckenschmidt, H. H., *Arnold Schoenberg: His Life, World and Work* (London, 1977)

Tabori, Paul, *Alexander Korda* (London, 1959)

Taylor, John Russell, *Hitch: The Life and Times of Alfred Hitchcock* (London, 1978)

Tiomkin, Dimitri, and Buranelli, Prosper, *Please Don't Hate Me* (New York, 1959)

Viertel, Berthold, *Dichtungen und Dokumente* (Munich, 1956)

Viertel, Salka, *The Kindness of Strangers* (New York, 1969)

Völker, Klaus, *Brecht Chronicle* (New York, 1975)

Wallace, Edgar, *My Hollywood Diary* (London, 1932)

Weinberg, Herman, *The Lubitsch Touch* (New York, 1968)

Whittemore, Don, and Cecchettini, Philip Alan (eds.), *Passport to Hollywood: Film Immigrants Anthology* (New York, 1976)

Wilcox, Herbert, *Twenty-five Thousand Sunsets* (London, 1967)

Willett, John, *The Theatre of Bertolt Brecht* (London, 1959)

Winston, R. and C. (ed./trans.), *The Letters of Thomas Mann 1889–1955*, 2 vols. (London, 1970)

Witt, Hubert (ed.), *Brecht as They Knew Him* (New York, 1974)

Wood, Tom, *The Bright Side of Billy Wilder, Primarily* (New York, 1970)

Workers of the Writers' Program of the WPA in Southern California, *Los Angeles* (New York, 1941)

Writers' Congress. The Proceedings of the Congress Held in October 1943 . . . (Los Angeles, 1944)

Zolotov, Maurice, *Billy Wilder in Hollywood* (London, 1977)

Zuckmayer, Carl, *A Part of Myself* (New York, 1970)

Index